T0356089

SHIPWRECK RESCUES
of the
OUTER BANKS

SENSATIONAL WRECKS AND HEROIC RESCUES BY THE UNITED STATES LIFE-SAVING SERVICE

JAMES D. CHARLET

Globe
Pequot

Essex, Connecticut

Globe
Pequot

An imprint of The Globe Pequot Publishing Group, Inc.
64 South Main Street
Essex, CT 06426
www.globepequot.com

Distributed by NATIONAL BOOK NETWORK

British Library Cataloguing in Publication Information available

Library of Congress Cataloging-in-Publication Data

Names: Charlet, James D., 1946- author.
Title: Shipwreck rescues of the Outer Banks: sensational wrecks and heroic
    rescues by the United States Life-saving Service / James D. Charlet.
Other titles: Shipwrecks of the Outer Banks: Dramatic rescues and fantastic wrecks
    in the Graveyard of the Atlantic
Description: Essex, Connecticut : Globe Pequot, 2025. | Series: [Shipwrecks
    of the Outer Banks] ; volume 2 | Includes index.
Identifiers: LCCN 2024038649 (print) | LCCN 2024038650 (ebook) | ISBN
    9781493087709 (cloth) | ISBN 9781493087716 (epub)
Subjects: LCSH: Shipwrecks—North Carolina—Outer Banks—History. | United
    States. Life-Saving Service—History. | Shipwrecks—Atlantic Coast
    (N.C.)—History. | Rescue work—North Carolina—Outer Banks—History. |
    Outer Banks (N.C.)—History.
Classification: LCC G525.5.N6 C43 2025 (print) | LCC G525.5.N6 (ebook) |
    DDC 910/.9163/48—dc23/eng/20241129
LC record available at https://lccn.loc.gov/2024038649
LC ebook record available at https://lccn.loc.gov/2024038650

To Linda I. Molloy: my wife, my in-house editor,
my business manager, cheerleader, and more!

One day, people will hear the iconic name Cape Hatteras Island,
and they will say, "Yeah, that is the place with all those heroic
US Life-Saving Service stations and that one really famous lighthouse."

A hero is an ordinary individual who finds the strength to persevere and endure in spite of overwhelming obstacles.

—Christopher Reeve

Hero: a person who is admired or idealized for courage, outstanding achievements, or noble qualities.

—*Oxford Languages*

CONTENTS

Foreword, by Dr. James P. Delgado   **viii**

Preface   **x**

I. The Big Picture

Chapter 1: The United States Life-Saving Service:
The National Picture   **2**

Chapter 2: The "Graveyard of the Atlantic"   **20**

II. Who Did the Saving and from What Base of Operations?

Chapter 3: To Be a Keeper   **30**

Chapter 4: To Be a Surfman   **38**

Chapter 5: Base of Operations: The Station   **46**

III. The Dramatic and Inspirational

Chapter 6: Schooner *John Maxwell*, the Most Serious Casualty
of 1912   **52**

Chapter 7: Barge *Saxon*, October 12, 1907   **61**

Chapter 8: British Steamer *Cragside* Saga: Ocracoke,
February 20, 1891   **69**

IV. The Routine

Chapter 9: US Life-Saving Station 12, Kitty Hawk:
1878 to 1915   **80**

Chapter 10: Barkentine *Angela*, March 5, 1883   **102**

V. Heartbreaking Failures

Chapter 11: Steamer *Ariosto*: The "Entirely Needless" Tragedy   **108**

Chapter 12: The Unfathomable Tragedy and Mystery of the Schooner
Robert H. Stevenson Wreck   **116**

VI. The Mysterious and Strange

Chapter 13: Schooner *Ada F. Whitney*, September 22, 1885:
A Poyners Hill US Life-Saving Station Rescue   **128**

Chapter 14: The Wreck of Brig *Vera Cruz VII*, May 8, 1903:
Portsmouth LSS Station   **136**

Chapter 15: Schooner *Hester A. Seward*, January 6, 1895:
Happy New Year?   **146**

Chapter 16: Steamship *Brewster*: The Ironic Wreck and Rescue,
with Thanks   **151**

VII. Some for the Record Books

Chapter 17: The Single Most Important Shipwreck in
American History—Cue Sumner Kimball   **162**

Chapter 18: The Improbable Rescue of the Wrecked Schooner
Charles S. Hirsch, October 29, 1908   **171**

Chapter 19: Tracking Down the Famous USLSS Quote About What
the Book Says About Going Out   **179**

VIII. Against All Odds

Chapter 20: Schooner *Thomas J. Martin*, January 9, 1883   **192**

Chapter 21: Storm-Tossed Schooner *Ario Pardee*   **198**

Chapter 22: Schooner *Leonora*: Yet Another Tragic
Lesson Unlearned   **206**

Chapter 23: Schooner *Nathaniel Lank*, 1891: Hatteras Island   **213**

Chapter 24: Wreck of the Schooner *Henry P. Simmons*,
the First in a Trilogy of the October 1889 Storm:
"A Peculiarly Harrowing One"   **221**

Chapter 25: Schooner *Francis E. Waters*, Part II:
The Storm of October 23, 1889   **230**

Chapter 26: Schooner *Lizzie S. Haynes*: The "Strike Three" Shipwreck in the Great October Storm of 1889 **237**

IX. Conclusion

Chapter 27: The Wreck and Rescue of the Schooner *A. B. Goodman*: The US Life-Saving Service Going Above and Beyond, "Against All Odds" **246**

Acknowledgments **258**

Appendix A: Glossary of Helpful Nautical Terms **259**

Appendix B: Locations of the Twenty-Nine North Carolina United States Life-Saving Service Stations **262**

Endnotes **271**

Index **288**

About the Author **291**

FOREWORD

The power of the sea, when you are confronted by it, is a frightening thing. I've seen it more than once, both at sea and ashore. There were a few times, in the decades I have spent in my lifelong interaction with the ocean, when it seemed that the moment had come. It's both terrifying and also numbing. You realize, even when gripped with fear, that there is nothing that you can do but hold on. Gordon Lightfoot's famous line in "The Wreck of the Edmund Fitzgerald" about wondering where the love of God goes when waves turn minutes into hours is a perfect line that I did not understand until I went to sea. Time stands still and yet seems endless when you are caught up in an event like that. Your ship—your home, your seemingly safe haven, and the nexus of your existence—is nothing more than a dust speck on God's eyeball.

I will always remember those moments, one in particular in the middle of the vast, open Pacific. However, I will always be thankful that I never encountered the fury of the sea on the shores of the Graveyard of the Atlantic. In the pages that follow, as you read *Shipwreck Rescues of the Outer Banks*, you will be transported to those same beaches more than a century ago, to vicariously be there as the violence of storms and the heroism of the United States Life-Saving Service's crews are matched in very real human dramas and occasional tragedies.

Standing on the beach of Pea Island, years ago on an archaeological survey for shipwrecks, I watched as wind-whipped foam and frothy water struck the dunes and the water rushed up to their base and devoured the sand. As the dunes fell, so too did the highway. It happened very fast, and fortunately, no one died on that beach that day. I will always remember it, though, as sitting in a ranger patrol vehicle, with a working radio and behind the barricades we'd erected, I was handed a lesson in not only the power of the sea but also in the circumstances faced by the mariners whose lost ships I was seeking, which lay buried on that beach by storms of decades and centuries past.

Those shipwrecks and the stories around them are profound human stories with meaning. They are also stories that can be forgotten—and often are in the fast pace of an evolving world with its own events and tragedies, as well as moments of exceptional human responses to those events. It is thanks to historians like James D. Charlet that these stories live on, introduced to modern audiences with fresh perspectives and additional research that substantively builds on earlier works. I will always be a fan of David Stick, whose landmark books on the Outer Banks remain on my shelves, but right next to them I will be placing *Shipwreck Rescues of the Outer Banks* as another go-to resource. Sit back, now, and explore what defined heroism of the best sort of the rugged and dangerous shores of the Graveyard of the Atlantic.

James P. Delgado
Washington, DC
September 2024

PREFACE

The US Life-Saving Service is one of the least known, yet most fascinating and inspirational aspects in all of America's storied history. Author Ralph Shanks says, "They were the greatest heroes of the American coast, routinely risking their lives in the grand maritime rescues . . . yet somehow, America forgot these peaceful heroes." Most Americans have never heard of this valiant predecessor of today's United States Coast Guard.

The brave souls known as surfmen had one mission: saving lives in peril on the sea, "so others may live." During their forty-four-year history, using no more than small, open, wooden boats and cork life belts, often in violent and dangerous storms, they responded to more than 178,000 lives in peril from shipwrecks nationwide—of which they saved *more than* 177,000. Additionally, their own loss of life in these immensely dangerous circumstances was extraordinarily low, at less than 1 percent. How could we forget that?

Why did I write this book as a sequel to my *Shipwrecks of the Outer Banks: Dramatic Rescues and Fantastic Wrecks in the Graveyard of the Atlantic* (2020)? Because America had forgotten these genuine heroes. We have thousands of documented, true accounts of dramatic rescues. Of these accounts, I have picked twenty-seven for this volume. I am working on volumes 3, 4, and 5—and this is just the North Carolina Outer Banks! There are thousands more on the East Coast and the Great Lakes.

So, why the Outer Banks? I have lived for thirty-plus years, full time, on the famous Cape Hatteras Island, the centerpiece of the iconic North Carolina Outer Banks. I have traveled every inch of the land and sea from Oak Island to Corolla. I have experienced much of what the surfmen did years ago, enduring a dozen hurricanes, many more nor'easters, lightning storms, frozen Sound waters, and more. I can *empathize.*

A note about both book covers: I designed the first one and then commissioned artist Gary Gowans to create the original art. The art says the title of the book. Happily, Gary agreed to do this one of his own original design, still visually repeating the title. I am thankful for this talented artist. Both the artist and I live on the North Carolina coast, both book covers are original art, and both are copyrighted.

I.

THE BIG PICTURE

CHAPTER 1

THE UNITED STATES LIFE-SAVING SERVICE

THE NATIONAL PICTURE

From 1871 to 1915, almost three hundred United States Life-Saving Service (USLSS) Stations dotted America's coastlines. Twenty-nine eventually operated on the Outer Banks. The surfmen of these stations had one mission: saving lives in peril on the sea. During their forty-four-year history nationwide, these brave souls responded to over 178,000 such lives in peril, of which they saved more than 177,000. Yet somehow, America forgot these peaceful heroes.

The Predecessors

The United States was one of the last major countries to establish a governmental system of saving the lives of coastal shipwreck victims; but to be fair, the United States was also one of the last major countries to be established.

Instances of coastal shipwreck rescues can be found as far back as Roman records. The first system that formed the basis of modern life-saving was by the Chinese in 1708, who awarded volunteer rescues.

The United States Life-Saving Service logo.
Public domain.

In 1774, the Royal Humane Society was formed in Great Britain. With an approach to treat the survivors rather than attempt preventative rescues, this model was followed in 1776 by the Amsterdam Rescue Society and many others leading up to America's Massachusetts Humane Society.

> In 1785, a group of Boston citizens met several times at the "Bunch of Grapes" tavern to consider the formation of an organization modeled on the British Royal Humane Society. They were concerned about the needless deaths resulting from shipwrecks and drownings and wanted to find ways to save lives.
> Formally established in 1786 . . . The Humane Society of the Commonwealth of Massachusetts . . . from the outset, focused on recognizing selfless lifesaving rescues and preventing

such tragedies. . . . The Humane Society's role in saving lives along the Massachusetts coast is a unique and compelling story. Its work served as a model for the US Life-Saving Service and ultimately the US Coast Guard.[1]

America's beginnings were considerably different than other countries. The *very* first lifesavers on America's isolate shores were the original European settlers. They were severely isolated and lived an extremely difficult, hardscrabble life. As a result, their very existence was dependent upon helping each other, so it was only natural that when a shipwreck occurred within their sight, they would go to help. However, no records were kept of these activities, so we have no hard data.

Lighthouses

For the better part of its first 150 years, American consensus was that lights would help to prevent shipwrecks. Our first lighthouse was built in Boston in 1716. All thirteen original colonies, located on the Atlantic Coast, followed suit with lighthouses and lightships. There were several problems with this approach, however. A lighthouse was a static presence, limited to a fixed, specific spot. It could take no proactive measures; it simply flashed. Second, it was primarily designed to only provide help at night, and mostly during good weather. As a daymark it helped some, but only in good weather. A lighthouse could do nothing to help victims once the inevitable shipwrecks occurred, usually resulting from weather or darkness. A modern analogy would be that traffic lights alone will prevent accidents and that emergency medical services are not needed.

For a definitive volume on the subject nationally, see *American Lighthouses: A Comprehensive Guide to Exploring Our National Coastal Treasures,* by Bruce Roberts and Cheryl Shelton-Roberts.[2]

Actual US Lifesaving Attempts Begin Poorly

As shipwreck deaths, destruction, and cargo losses mounted steadily, a better system was needed. America looked across the Atlantic to our forebearer-parents who had already created the answer: the Royal National Lifeboat Institute (RNLI). It was a strictly volunteer organization, supported entirely by donations. As an island nation with generally populated coastlines, all British citizens were affected and concerned by shipwrecks, and thus had a deep, personal connection and motivation to support the cause. America, however, had one coast at the time and vast inland mainlands, with enormous stretches of isolated, unpopulated coasts.

The Massachusetts Humane Society had made admirable success, starting with mere "houses of refuge" and then establishing lifeboat stations similar to the British volunteer model. They even invented a primitive line-throwing mortar that would eventually become the legendary Lyle gun. They admirably conducted many daring rescues, but these advancements were limited to primarily serving one port: New York.

"By 1700, New York was the breadbasket of the Atlantic, shipping wheat to Europe, the West Indies and down the Atlantic coast."[3] It grew rapidly: "By about 1840, more passengers and a greater tonnage of cargo came through the port of New York than all other major harbors in the country combined."[4] New Jersey was a concerned and affected neighbor; in 1848, New Jersey congressman and physician William A. Newell passionately pushed a bill to establish RNLI-type lifeboat stations. In only one year, sixty-three lifeboat stations were established, mostly in New Jersey and New York. However, there were copious inadequacies with these stations. First, they were also to be run by volunteers, which in our case not only didn't work but was also a disaster. There was no training and no practice, causing most volunteers to have no idea what to do or how to do it. Additionally, stations were neglected, and boats and supplies were taken for private use. Things were stolen. Stations were often unmanned. There were no regulations, no records maintained, and no supervision; technically placed under the US Revenue Cutter Service (born Revenue Marine) the "service" had become a free-for-all political plum.

Drastic federal reforms came as a result of public outcry from the highly publicized fatal shipwrecks in the Great Lakes and Atlantic Coast in the winter of 1870/1871. Personnel were hired and trained as professionals. Stations were repaired and newer ones added. A national supervisor was added: Sumner I. Kimball assumed the role but was restricted by remaining as a subsection of the Revenue Cutter Service. Kimball was an honest, competent visionary who was intent on creating a world-class organization, but there was an enormous disadvantage over which he had no control. The Service was entrenched with cronyism. Government jobs were handed out as favors to family, friends, neighbors, or even potential voters. Training and practice existed on paper but was virtually invisible at the stations. Still, government property was stolen or abused. Often the stations remained understaffed or abandoned. Many keepers felt a royal sense of privilege. The new US Life-Saving Service was no more effective than the earlier Lighthouse Service.

The late 1877 and early 1878 North Carolina shipwrecks of the *Huron* and the *Metropolis*, only twenty miles and two months apart, were the final straw.[5]

A new, independent federal organization was formed in 1878 following a massive national public outcry: the United States Life-Saving Service. While holding the same name as before, its ultimate function was to become vastly different and improved—starting with the new superintendent.

It was obvious who the only clear choice was—his middle name was not only a clue but also prophetic. Everyone wanted Sumner Increase Kimball to be the first superintendent of the new US Life-Saving Service. They also knew that the government would have to take off his straitjacket. Chapter 17 tells the whole story.

This is why you will find three different dates for the beginning of the US Life-Saving Service. Some use the 1848 date, when the name first appeared, but it was restricted to New Jersey and New York. Many use the 1871 date, as it was becoming more national and had the right abstract but not the execution. Others use the newest 1878 date for the "Phoenix rising from the ashes," as it officially became its own federal department.

The United States Life-Saving Service

Eventually the United States Life-Saving Service existed nationally on all of America's coasts: starting on America's primary coast, the Atlantic, then expanding to the Great Lakes, and a few on the sparsely settled Pacific Coast. Ten "Houses of Refuge" were constructed on the Gulf Coast over the next ten years but were definitely *not* Life-Saving stations. The United States Life-Saving Service existed from 1871 to 1915, when it merged with the US Revenue Cutter Service to become the US Coast Guard.

The Personnel

Superintendent Kimball was the epitome of organization and efficiency and it shone brightly in his new Service. To say that his reorganization was extremely, exceedingly, exceptionally, extraordinarily, and remarkably organized and detailed is an enormous understatement. There were standards, specific regulations, and detailed forms for any situation.

Kimball first organized the Service into national districts, eventually being thirteen. The chain of command was (with sections of *Regulations from 1884* for each in parentheses): general superintendent;[6] super-intendents of construction;[7] inspector;[8] assistant inspectors;[9] district superintendents;[10] keepers,[11] and, finally, the surfmen.[12]

The Stations

Originally, three types of stations were used: Life-Saving Stations, Life-boat Stations, and Houses of Refuge.

The Life-Saving Station was the only one with a crew of paid surfmen. Originally all were built on the Atlantic Coast, and all equipped with the specialized rescue vessel called the "surfboat." These would soon be the dominant type of station, and the ones from which most of the dramatic rescue accounts would emerge. These were the only ones with eight, rather than six, surfmen.

The Houses of Refuge consisted of only ten buildings built across Florida's multiple coasts. Following the original Massachusetts Humane Society concept of having a place for shipwreck victims to find shelter, food, and medicine once they saved themselves, the upgraded buildings each had one full-time keeper to live there. There was no staff or rescue equipment.

The construction of Lifeboat Stations was a direct copy of the volunteer RNLI concept. Originally built on the less-trafficked (at the time) US coasts of the Great Lakes, the Pacific, and some remote Delaware and Virginia locations, they soon gave way to full-time Life-Saving stations.

The Rescue Equipment

Each station was furnished with one or more rescue boats, surfboat or lifeboat (a few had both), two beach carts with all components, and later, a life car.[13]

The Drills and Duties

Drills

From the *Revised Regulations of 1884*, section "Drill and Exercise," Regulation No. 168:

> The following weekly routine of drill &c will be observed during the first month of the active season at all regularly manned stations in the Service.
>
> *Monday*—Practice with beach apparatus—overhaul and examine all apparatus and gear.

Tuesday—Practice with surf and life boat [*sic*].

Wednesday—Practice with signals. (flags)

Thursday—Practice with beach apparatus.*

Friday—Practice resuscitation.

Saturday—Clean house.[14]

The original "Regulations" of 1873 had only five directives for "Drill and Exercise." Each station was required to perform a beach apparatus and surfboat drill three times a year—once for the annual inspector's visit, and twice a season for the district superintendent's visits. Regulation No. 102 required launching the surfboat "at least once every month" (for a three-month season) and, in the extremely frugal manner of the Service, Regulation No. 103 for the beach apparatus drill states explicitly, "No expenditure of powder, shot or rockets will be permitted for exercise."[15] They were expected to throw the shot!

Duties

The details of the two basic duties—standing watch and beach patrol—are covered in volume 1.[16] However, it did not address a question that may easily come to the reader. One may ask, "If all these wrecks were discovered by seeing them from the shore, either from the watch tower or the beach patrol, if these ships were close enough to see the shore, why did they still wreck?"

The answer is one word: control. If a ship was under control and got too close to shore (as it happened often), the USLSS beach patrol would warn them off with flares. It is entirely possible that the Life-Saving Service saved more ships that way than the Lighthouse Service.

However, if a ship was *not* in control, it would wreck on or near shore. It could lose control in any number of ways: violent storms, broken or stuck rudder, broken steering linkages, torn sails, broken rigging, masts

---

*After the first month, Monday practices with beach apparatus could be omitted.

snapped, captain injured, asleep, or—heaven forbid—drunk, zero visibility due to rain, fog, etcetera, even aged wooden vessels often became waterlogged and unmanageable. Once the vessel was out of control, the wind and waves would drive it helplessly toward shore. That is how *all* USLSS discoveries and rescues were made. Any wreck that was out of sight the lifesavers never knew about! Most, however, were like this.

Beach Apparatus Drill

Describing the use of the beach apparatus may seem complicated and confusing to the reader. However, to fully understand what happened, as detailed in many of the following chapters, a basic understanding is required. An occasional return here for review may be needed.

This drill was conducted weekly at every station on Thursdays. This was a practice completed at the station on the beach, done almost always in good weather and in the daytime. Things to know: the beach cart was kept in the boat room of the station; the wreck pole (or drill pole) represented a mast of the stricken ship; the pole was the keeper's target when firing the Lyle gun. The arrow drawn in the surf on official illustrations indicates the direction of the wind, which itself dictates placements and procedures. The side the wind is coming from is called the "weather side"; the opposite is the "lee side."

The logistics of the drill are not as complicated as they appear. We will walk through it using text and graphics. During the entire process, which can appear to be a three-ring circus act, the keeper only gives eight short commands:[17]

WORDS OF COMMAND:
Open boat-room doors—man the beach-wagon.
Forward.
Halt.
Action.
Man weather whip.
Haul out.
Man lee whip.

Haul ashore.

1. The station boat room doors are opened, and the beach cart is manned by the crew of eight, each in a specific position.
2. The cart is hauled to a spot on the drill field (or abreast of the actual wreck in reality).
3. When the keeper says stop, he has picked the spot to set up. He then marks the place to dig the sand anchor and the place the Lyle gun.

Man Weather Whip—Haul Ashore, *from* Regulations for the Government of the Life-Saving Service of the United States, *1899, p. 105. Author's photo.*

4. The "Action" command is when all action simultaneously occurs, with each surfman having a specific function and duty.[18] By this point, each surfman has already completed other preliminary functions. Previously, surfmen 1 and 2 have aimed the Lyle gun and setting elevation, per keeper's commands. Surfmen 3 and 4 have taken the whip lines from the reels on the cart and have stretched them out on the beach at opposite sides, now awaiting their next duty to man the lines once it is set up. Surfmen 5 and 6 have dug a four-foot deep "X-shaped" hole to bury the sand anchor. Surfman 7 has already unloaded the shovels and pick and assisted in burying the sand anchor. Surfman 8 is standing by to ascend the wreck pole to take the place of a crew member on the

ship. In the actual rescue, all surfmen remain on the beach, relying on a sailor onboard the wreck to retrieve the shot line. Watching all this activity, the keeper determines when it is safe to fire and alerts his crew with the cautionary word "ready" (and "the ship," in actual rescue) to hold while he fires.

To get to this last command, here is the order of what occurred: the Lyle gun (C) shoots the projectile, or "shot" *over* the wreck pole (A) with its thin shot line attached, which comes from the dumped faking box (D). The shot continues downrange and lands on the beach or the ocean. The shot line drifts down to the platform of the wreck pole (which would be the rigging of the actual shipwreck) where surfman 8 catches it and begins to pull it toward himself. Attached to the end of the shot line is the whip line and block (pulley). When 8 gets the block, he unties the shot line and discards it. Then he ties the block to the pole (mast) about shoulder height.

5. Then the next command is given, "Man weather whip" (B on right, or weather side). Now, the stoutest line, the hawser (F), is tied to the lee whip (B on left side, all one line running through a pulley attached to pole).

6. When the keeper commands, "Haul out," the surfmen (2 through 7) holding the weather whip run inshore, or *away* from the ocean. This pulls the lee whip *toward* the pole, bringing the hawser to the wreck pole. Surfman 8 ties this on the pole (or the ship's mast) *above* the whip line block.

A lot happens before the final command: the shore end of the hawser is tied to the ocean end of the fall line (G)—two large pulleys with lines between them. The beach end of the fall line is attached to the already buried sand anchor (E) that has a line attached to it remaining on the surface. The hawser is stretched as tight as possible by hand, then made extremely taut by tightening the fall line. To further increase the tension and the height of the hawser (to keep victims above the rough surf), the crotch pole (H) is inserted. Now a pulley is placed on the hawser and the breeches buoy is attached to it.

7. The penultimate command, "Man lee whip," brings the breeches buoy out to the wreck pole, in the same but opposite manner as sending the hawser out. One survivor—or in this case—surfman 8, is loaded into the breeches buoy.

8. Now see the figure on p. 11 again. When the final command is given, "Haul ashore," surfmen 2 through 7 are hauling in the breeches buoy and survivor via the weather whip.

(Repeat as necessary in an actual rescue!)

Daily Life

There is little documentation of the daily life of the surfmen, since these things were considered ordinary, mundane, and common knowledge at the time—much like how we do not document our everyday, normal occurrences (until social media, that is!). But we, as normal human beings, *are* interested in what their daily life was like. So, with a lot of digging in a lot of mundane places, presented here is a common picture of the average day of the lifesavers, mostly the ordinary surfman.

Meals

One of the most powerful forces that brings humans together is food. The early LSS stations had a single area called the "Day Room," which had a table, chairs, a stove, and closets. This was the break room, the reading room, the playroom (for cards, checkers, dominoes, and back-gammon) and, most importantly, the kitchen. All meals were taken here. The heat from the stove was welcomed in the early years of the Service during the winter, but as the lifesavers' season extended into the summer, it became nearly unbearable. Eventually cookhouses were built separate from the main station and other outbuildings, in order to alleviate this discomfort and in case of fire.

Fortunately, a well-preserved and stocked cookhouse from 1911 remains, from which we have learned what the Outer Banks surfmen ate.

The 1911 Chicamacomico Cookhouse display recreation by author as site manager.
Author's photo.

The obvious food source for the Outer Banks stations was right in front of them—the ocean and the sounds. The Atlantic Ocean offered the surfman copious amounts of seafood daily, with the huge varieties of saltwater fish easily caught from the surf; the Pamlico Sound with varieties of freshwater fish, plus crabs, shrimp, oysters, and clams, as well as otters, mink, beaver, and muskrat. However, this was just a portion of their well-rounded diet. The air was full of waterfowl and shorebirds: herons, geese, ducks, and many more. The islands were covered with vast tracks of maritime forests with deer, bear, squirrels, rabbits, wolves, and especially wild boars. Blackberries and prickly pears were abundant. Figs grew naturally there. Additionally, every Outer Banks family kept chickens, cows, horses, and grew gardens in spring and fall. Fresh food was obviously quite plentiful! There were variations with resources between each geographical region in the country, but in this similar way, the men made do with what was available locally.

The Service did not supply food to the stations. So, in addition to what they could find and catch, the surfmen could purchase items such as canned goods, coffee, and sugar from local markets at their own expense.

REGULATIONS SPEAKING TO MEALS

It is very interesting, indeed, seeing how utterly detailed the *Regulations* were, that a thorough search for the words food, groceries, meals, eating, cook, mess, and kitchen in the entire documents of 1873, 1884, and 1899 produced *no* results!

The surfmen either volunteered turns to cook or would hire one (again, at their own expense).

Every Day

From the 1884 *Regulations*, No. 208 states, "Great care must be taken to keep the houses [meaning "stations"] in clean and neat condition. The floors of the living rooms must be swept every morning, all utensils cleaned, and the buildings frequently aired. Dirt and rubbish must not be permitted to accumulate in the boat room."[19] Combined with the daily care, maintenance, and repair of all the equipment, this probably filled the majority of activity every day.

One of the popular period newspaper-magazines (such as *Harper's Weekly*) interviewed a surfman and asked the question, "What is your daily life like?" His answer, while not an exact quote, was synonymous with: "Well, it is hours and days and months of routine and dreadful boredom occasionally interrupted by a few moments of sheer terror!"

One of the more boring everyday tasks for each surfman was walking the miles between stations to check the telegraph lines, making sure that none were down, obstructed, or in need of repair.

On the lighter side, 1884 *Regulation* No. 88 states, "Keepers may permit their men in pleasant weather between Sunrise and sunset only to hunt or fish provided they do not trespass on private or club gunning grounds nor violate the game laws. On Such occasions, the men must not go beyond signal distance or where they cannot be easily recalled. In fine weather the keeper may permit in his discretion one surfman at a time to be absent between Sunrise and sunset for the purpose of visiting his home."[20]

Social Life

Surfmen lived with each other for long periods of time, which helped them get to know one another well. Many also had families and all lived in the village off-duty, which sparked conversation. The beach patrol made daily contact with neighboring stations, so each got to know the other and probably their families. The seven stations that were near the Outer Banks lighthouses likely visited each other. See another definitive work on this subject by Cheryl Shelton-Roberts and Bruce Roberts in their *North Carolina Lighthouses: The Stories behind the Beacons from Cape Fear to Currituck Beach.*[21]

Finances

Initially, the surfmen were hired annually for only a three-month period and paid $40 per month with a $3 bonus per shipwreck response. They had no benefits. Surfmen had to pay for their own meals while on duty (as we have seen), provide their own housing, and were even required to buy their own uniforms.

UNIFORMS

There were no standard United States Life-Saving Service uniforms until 1889, a full eighteen years after the Service started. Until then, the surfmen just wore what they could provide. This is one of the more amusing accounts in Ralph Shanks's classic book:

During the early years of the Service the arrival of surfmen at a wreck could actually frighten survivors since surfmen did not get uniforms until 1889. A number of foreign ships, upon seeing a band of rugged, roughly dressed men rowing rapidly toward their disabled ship thought the surfmen must be pirates. It didn't help when the roughly dressed men were seen to possess a small cannon. When surfmen used their Lyle gun to fire a life line toward a stranded vessel, one crew promptly offered to surrender.[22]

Changes in Becoming the United States Coast Guard

In their time, the US Life-Saving Service had the singular mission of land-based ocean rescue. The US Revenue Cutter Service (1790–1915) had the singular mission of ocean-based law enforcement. When they merged to become the US Coast Guard, those two missions became their primary activity, with nine additional missions being added over time. The now eleven are: port and waterway security, drug interdiction, aids to navigation, search and rescue, living marine resources, marine safety, defense readiness, migrant interdiction, marine environmental protection, ice operations, and law enforcement. All this is achieved with a worldwide number of personnel (41,000 active duty) *less* than one US Army base at former Fort Bragg (now Liberty) (52,000; total Army personnel, 1,300,000).

NAME TERMINOLOGY: THE COAST GUARD AND THE LIFE-SAVING SERVICE

The reader may see this term as United States Coast Guard, US Coast Guard, USCG, or simply Coast Guard. The Life-Saving Service can be United States Life-Saving (always hyphenated) Service, the USLSS, the LSS, or simply the Service. Also, notice in the period quotes how the Service routinely refers to the stations as "houses."

Organizational Evolution

1915—The Revenue Cutter Service merges with the US Life-Saving Service, and is officially renamed the Coast Guard, making it the only maritime service dedicated to saving life at sea and enforcing the nation's maritime laws.

1939—President Franklin Roosevelt orders the transfer of the Light-house Service to the Coast Guard, putting it in charge of maritime navigation.

1946—Congress permanently transfers the Commerce Department's Bureau of Marine Inspection and Navigation to the Coast Guard, putting merchant marine licensing and merchant vessel safety in its control.

1967—The Coast Guard is transferred to the Department of Transportation.

2003—The Coast Guard is transferred again, this time to the Department of Homeland Security, where it currently serves.

Nomenclature

The Revenue Cutter Service had used Navy terms such as captain, commander, bosun, seaman, and so on. This terminology was also used in the new Coast Guard organization, which was developed to be more ocean based than land based. However, habit is a strong force, so for many years after the merger, former Life-Saving stations and personnel continued to use the terms "keeper" and "surfman." What used to be surfman 1 was now officially bosun's mate first class, or BM1. However, for several years the old terms persisted. Interestingly, the designation of "surfman" was recently reintroduced by the Coast Guard. It is the highest designation in the Coast Guard for small boat operations. Highly coveted, these new surfmen are stationed at just over 10 percent of the United States Coast Guard's 188 boat stations.

Conclusion

Although starting poorly, the United States Life-Saving Service grew into what was arguably the single most heroic national service. A concise and precise summary is the opening paragraph of Ralph Shank's book:

> They were the greatest heroes of the American coast, routinely risking their lives in the grand maritime rescues. Their work was respected and honored by America's most prestigious leaders, celebrated in the most popular publications of their time and of deep interest to medical, educational, religious and political

leaders. The Wright Brothers [*sic*] knew them well, poet Walt Whitman wrote of them, and the artist Winslow Homer painted them. But somehow America forgot these peaceful heroes. Yet anyone reading of their bravery today will always remember them. The Life-Saving Service answered that most basic of human questions, "Who will help in our hour of greatest need?"[23]

Being a surfman of the US Life-Saving Service was a gruelingly difficult but extremely rewarding life. These were the peaceful heroes that America somehow forgot.

CHAPTER 2

THE "GRAVEYARD OF THE ATLANTIC"

The small strip of Atlantic Ocean off the North Carolina coast is infamously nicknamed "Graveyard of the Atlantic" since it has claimed around six thousand ships.* The common and obvious question, "Why there were so many shipwrecks there?" is a valid one. The answer, however, is complicated. Explained here are some of the largest contributing factors.

Genesis

David Stick, the North Carolina Outer Banks premier historian, meticulous researcher, and author, lists the first recorded shipwreck here as an unnamed brigantine that wrecked at Cape Fear in June of 1526, *almost five hundred years ago!* The first Outer Banks shipwreck that we have great details about was the Sir Walter Raleigh–sponsored expedition's flagship the *Tiger*. It wrecked at Ocracoke Inlet, June 29, 1585, with consequences that would alter the entire history of what would become the United States of America two hundred years later.[1]

For five *centuries* that we know of, North Carolina's Graveyard of the Atlantic has been one of the most feared and dreaded of all coasts to

---

*By 2008, the North Carolina Underwater Archaeology Branch had maintained a database of approximately five thousand ships lost in North Carolina waters.

navigate. There are numerous factors accounting for its notorious reputation; some are natural, and some are not. "Combined, these natural elements form a navigational nightmare that is feared as much as any in the world. Pirates, the American Civil War, and German U-boat assaults have added to the heavy toll nature has exacted."[2]

Cape Hatteras's geography is the main reason the surrounding waters were given the famous nickname. It has been an area to be avoided by mariners ever since the 1500s, but the exact origin of the phrase is unclear.

Name Origin

The nickname is most often attributed to Alexander Hamilton in a letter to a friend in which he describes his harrowing voyage and seeing so many skeletons of wrecked ships in the "Graveyard of the Atlantic." There is no authoritative documentation for this popular claim. This appears to have first been in print in the 1958 book *The Hatterasman* by Ben Dixon MacNeill. However, MacNeill was well known for his exaggeration and historical fabrication. His very first words are "This is not history. I am not a historian."[3] At the beginning of the second paragraph, he reemphasizes, "I am not a historian, and this is not a history. There is historical matter in it, and there might well have been much more."[4]

The fifth paragraph is even more explicit: "if an event of recorded history left any imprint on the life of these islands, it has been explored to the last detail, both in the folklore of the islands, and in the books and documents."[5] What MacNeill wants to do, therefore, is explore the more colorful anecdotes and fascinating yarns that may or may not be accurate, and to add some amusement. MacNeill was aware of what David Stick had published six years earlier. Stick would be *the* recognized, eminent authority on the history of the Outer Banks. In the opening paragraph of Stick's classic book *Graveyard of the Atlantic: Shipwrecks of the North Carolina Coast*, he writes: "You can stand on Cape Point at Hatteras on a stormy day and watch two oceans come

together in an awesome display of savage fury; for there at the Point . . .
is formed the dreaded Diamond Shoals, its fang-like shifting sand bars
pushing seaward to snare the unwary mariner. Seafaring men call it the
Graveyard of the Atlantic."[6]

The Reputation

Thousands of naval documents, journals, magazine and newspaper
articles, and personal letters by mariners over the centuries are filled
with references to the dread and fear of vessels approaching North
Carolina. Of those extremely numerous references, here are presented
only several direct first-person quotes from a veteran "coasting captain"
of the time—Captain Leonard S. Tawes—in his career of sailing the
US Atlantic coast from 1868 to 1922.[7]

> Had a good run to Cape Hatteras. Here our fair northwest
> wind quit. The weather looked terrible bad. My mate wanted
> me to run back to Hampton Roads.[8] . . . Then we had usual
> fair weather until north of Cape Hatteras about 60 miles when
> we had an awful gale of wind from the northeast again.[9] . . .
> I then shaped my course for Cape Hatteras. Heavy westerly
> gales came upon me and I could not hold my course. And
> when I passed the latitude of Cape Hatteras, I was 300 miles
> offshore.[10] . . . I do not remember when we passed out of Cape
> Henry but I well remember the storm I was caught in just
> south of Cape Hatteras.[11] . . . As there was a dreadful hurry-
> cane striking in on the coast.[12]

The most stunning of all images the captain recorded next.

> We followed the Gulf Stream up and when nearly in the
> latitude of Cape Hatteras we experienced a heavy northwest
> wind which kept us in the Gulf Stream. It was so cold that the

vapor would rise off this warm Stream water and form many remarkable scenes. Sometime you would see a great forest rise up with all the shape of large trees. Then in a few minutes this forestry would disappear and a great city would appear. Then this scene would disappear and in its place a thousand water spouts would appear. About this time your heart got to pulsating to its highest. These water spouts would disappear and in their place large, staunch full-rigged ships would appear to be running head on for us. These imaginary scenes would appear and disappear as long as we would be in the Gulf Stream and these strong northwest gales would blow. All it was vapor or steam rising from this warm water.[13]

In 1970, *National Geographic* magazine produced a map titled "Ghost Fleet of the Outer Banks." The coastline was black with silhouettes of wrecked ships, their names and date of demise printed. When the visitor discovered that most experts at that time agreed on the number around six thousand, the second reaction was to ask the most logical thing one could: "Why so many shipwrecks here? What makes it the 'Graveyard of the Atlantic'?"

Why *So* Treacherous?

Several factors, some of which are unique to Cape Hatteras, are the complicated answer to that simple question. Below is a summary from volume 1 with new factors added.

Currents

It is a place where two major ocean currents converge. One current consists of the cold waters from the north called the Labrador Current. It hugs the north Atlantic shores from Baffin Bay in Canada, skirts around Newfoundland, and flow(s) down the US states' coastlines until reaching North Carolina. There it clashes with the other mighty current

Waves, by Daniel Pullen.
Daniel Pullen Photography, Outer Banks artist.

flowing north: the Gulf Stream. These two mighty currents don't just meet at Cape Hatteras; they explode there.

Opposing Waves

As David Stick tells us in his opening paragraph, if a person stands at "Cape Point" on a clear winter day, they will be treated to an unbelievable sight. Miles offshore, the observer will see waves running parallel to the shore and in opposite directions, violently butting into each other.

These wave explosions do more than provide a spectacular show. Besides tons of water and energy, each wave carries more tons of loose sand. As the waves explode, sand "shrapnel" is randomly dispersed over a large area in all directions. This is gradually building and reshaping constantly changing shoals— the dreaded and "unchartable" Diamond Shoals, so named because of their overall shape.

Diamond Shoals

Due to the massive, unrelenting amount of energy, the Diamond Shoals off Cape Hatteras extend as far as twenty miles of shallow water and may be several miles wide, which is why the Cape Hatteras Lighthouse light is over a mile wide and reaches twenty miles.

Conflicting Winds and Currents

Sailing ships of old used both the wind and the currents for propulsion. The Cape Hatteras area, as we have seen, has two conflicting currents. It also has two conflicting prevailing winds. In summer, the prevailing and mostly constant winds are southwest. In winter, they are northeast. Every time a captain left port along the Atlantic coast, depending on if he was going south or north, and whether it was summer or winter, there would be a massive conflict of wind and current at some point.

A Treacherous Choice

There was a seemingly simple choice each captain would have to make at the beginning of each voyage. The cold Labrador Current was close to shore and the warm Gulf Stream was considerably farther out. Consequently, the choice became: either stay close to shore riding the Labrador Current, but risk shoals and running aground, or go out around and ride the Gulf Stream. The second choice was certainly safer, but much longer, therefore taking more time. Safer or quicker?

The Risk of Rushing

Cape Hatteras is three hundred miles *east* of Jacksonville, Florida! Then, for ships' captains wanting to navigate around it, add another twenty miles. Too many captains tried to cut it too close by choosing the shorter route.

No Safe Harbor

There is only one major safe port along the entire three hundred miles of North Carolina coast: Wilmington. If any problem develops in that long passage, it likely will lead to disaster.

Unreliable Navigation

Many ships' captains of the time did not trust the simple and few navigation instruments available. As a result, their method was to always stay within sight of the shore. That worked well along many coasts, but not North Carolina's.

Another Reason for "Coast Hugging"

Using the two currents to the navigator's advantage was not the only reason mariners would hug the coast.

> As the population of the Americas expanded, more and more merchandise was shipped between the Caribbean, South American, and US ports. The fastest and most direct route was—and still is—hugging the shoreline. And at a time when navigational tools were still in their infancy, being able to identify landmarks enabled navigators to mark their passage.[14]

Underwater Obstructions

Many of those shipwrecks that went down in shallow water, yet being completely submerged, constituted what today's Coast Guard calls "hazards to navigation." Ironically, some ships wrecked on submerged shipwrecks.

Ordinary Weather

Heavy rain can easily become blinding and cause navigational mishaps. The addition of lightning and thunder can be disorienting. Fog itself has been the direct cause of numerous shipwrecks here, where it can be "as thick as Pea Island soup!" Windstorms of only forty miles per hour can cause waves and surf strong enough to wreck a ship. And while "rogue waves" are not part of ordinary weather, they have often been known to wreck ships.

Major Storms

Cape Hatteras is famous for several things, but at the top of the list are storms. Hurricanes and nor'easters sent most ships to the Graveyard. Remember, although there were some instruments on board, the chief weather forecasting method that wooden sailing ships' captains used was scanning the horizon—three to five miles away. A deadly storm could be twenty miles away only to be discovered too late.

Shipwrecking Machines: German U-Boats

By World War I, the U-boat was *the* ultimate stealth weapon: it could not be seen or detected, so there was no defense for it, and Germany relentlessly attacked America from underwater between 1917 and 1918. Although Germany lost nearly half of its almost four hundred submarines, they nevertheless destroyed an astounding 2,600 Allied ships and thousands of lives.

You would have thought that we had learned something by World War II, but we had not. Once again, America was totally unprepared for the vicious German onslaught hidden beneath the waves. In the first six months of WWII in 1942, more than four hundred Allied ships were sunk and eighty-seven of those were along the North Carolina coast.

Lighthouses

Ironically, lighthouses themselves were the indirect cause of some shipwrecks. Indirect because it was the ship captains' mistaken interpretations.

> Captain F. Hinz of the *Brewster* took his bearings from the Cape Hatteras Lighthouse thinking it was the Diamond Shoals Lightship and set a course that would take him up the coast some five miles east of the light. But that landed the German right in the middle of the most rugged part of Diamond Shoals.
> Captain Hinz was not the first mariner to make this mistake, nor the last; for the log books of the ships lost in the Graveyard of the Atlantic and the official reports of the lifesavers show wreck after wreck caused by the same error."[15]

Frequency of Vessel Traffic

For most of its years as a nation, the Atlantic Coast was the "I-95" of its day for commercial shipping. As David Stick again describes,

During the heyday of the coasting trade in the nineteenth century, southbound sailing vessels often were unable to round Cape Hatteras for weeks because of the combined forces of the steady northbound Gulf Stream flow and the prevailing winds from the southwest. Old-timers at Kinnakeet, north of the cape, have recounted seeing as many as 150 sailing ships, tacking back and forth, waiting for the wind to change.[16]

Modern Legacies

There were some unexpected results from this massive collection of shipwrecks in one locale. Most, if not all, of the early houses were not only built with recovered ship timbers but were also largely furnished with furniture, utensils, tools, and accessories from the wrecks. Many of those houses still exist on Hatteras and Ocracoke. Some of the unintended original settlers were shipwreck survivors who simply stayed.

The wrecks make reefs, which attract fish, which attract fishermen, a major tourism factor for today's Outer Banks. Similar, but less so, is the wreck diving industry there. Many tourists are initially attracted to the Outer Banks because of pirates, the Lost Colony, and shipwrecks!

The modern Graveyard of the Atlantic unfortunately still exists. US Coast Guard units from Motor Lifeboat Stations (MLB) Hatteras Inlet and MLB Station Oregon Inlet, Station Ocracoke (Small), MLB Station Hobuken, and Aids to Navigation (ANT) Wanchese are busy and active every day. A frequent sight over the skies of the Outer Banks are the H-60 Jayhawk helicopters and the C-130 fixed-wing airplanes from nearby Air Station Elizabeth City, as they patrol the beaches and surf, just like their forerunners.

As site manager of a local maritime museum, I was often asked by tourists, "When was the last Outer Banks shipwreck?" Truthfully, I would respond, "Don't know. Haven't read today's paper online yet."

II.

WHO DID THE SAVING AND FROM WHAT BASE OF OPERATIONS?

CHAPTER 3
TO BE A KEEPER

Becoming a station keeper in the United States Life-Saving Service during the late 1800s was one of the most coveted of any jobs almost anywhere, but most especially in the remote areas where the stations were necessarily located.

Odds are, if you asked people today if they knew who or what a "keeper" was, that 99 percent would say, "The person in charge of a lighthouse." Right?

Usually, there was only one person (a few had assistants) who worked in each lighthouse: the keeper. Adding to the popular misconceptions, keepers were universally romanticized. "The tedious workload and isolation could take its toll. Depression and alcoholism were common among [lighthouse station] keepers," states the National Park Service's Cape Lookout National Seashore website.[1]

The United States Life-Saving Service Personnel Hierarchy

Like any business or organization, there was a "chain of command," especially for the military-oriented United States Life-Saving Service. This order changed over the years. The following is from the 1899 *Regulations for the Government of the Life-Saving Service of the United States and the Laws Upon Which They Are Based.*

The order was: general superintendent, assistant general superintendent, the Board on Life-Saving Appliances (seven members), superintendent of construction (two in the 1899 *Regulations*), assistants to the superintendents of construction, inspector, assistant inspector, superintendent of telephone lines and telephone linemen, district superintendents (twelve at this time), assistant district superintendents, keepers, and surfmen.

As it is with any federal government branch, all but the last two positions were office jobs as bureaucrats, a necessary evil. Only the last two positions, keeper and surfman, were where the actual lifesaving took place. These were literally the first and only "boots on the ground."

Although the *Regulations* changed over the years, we will start with one of the very earliest, the *1873 Regulations*, to see how it originated.

Keeper

The "book" listed all duties in the order listed above and each paragraph was numbered. Those for the keeper were numbers 26 through 51. Each was a specific duty.

"26. Keepers will be held in strict accountability for the proper care, preservation, and good order of the apparatus, boats, buildings and their appurtenances, and for the economical use of all supplies of every kind placed in their charge."[2] It goes on to make the points of responsibility and competence and ends by warning that "articles not satisfactorily accounted for will be deducted from their pay." Notice the priorities here: the equipment and expenditures. No mention yet of the crew.

Paragraphs 27 through 29 continue with the theme above. By number 30, it starts talking about his reporting duties, and those were highly detailed and extensive. By 34, his attention is directed to the crew (finally), to make sure the beach patrol is strictly kept.

The keeper was the instrumental and critical position in the saving of 177,236 lives saved nationally from 1871 until 1915 by the United States Life-Saving Service. The keeper was very much like the captain of a ship—he had *absolute* authority—whatever he said or decided was exactly what happened. This is probably why the surfmen at all the stations unofficially referred to the keeper as "captain."

About All Those Reports

A great deal was asked of a station keeper for the United States Life-Saving Service. Although his critical role was to flawlessly execute lifesaving rescues, mostly in dangerously violent storms, he was also accountable as a bureaucrat. It starts with a seemingly simple statement in paragraph 28—"Keepers will enter upon the journals, daily, all the transactions occurring, according to Form 1." Below is Form 1 verbatim:

Instructions for keeping Journal for United States Life-saving Stations

The journal must embrace all occurrences relating to the service. In the following order:

1. Day of week, date and names of month and the year.
2. State of the weather; direction and force of the wind, whether gale, fresh or moderate breeze, or calm. (These to be noted at sunrise, noon, sunset and midnight.)
3. Number of persons belonging to the station present, and number absent, with name of absentee and cause of absence.
4. Number and kind of vessels passing the station, in either direction, during the day.
5. If a wreck occurs, a full description of the same, according to Form 3, must be entered, stating all the circumstances and the proceedings of the crew of the station.
6. Nature of the surf for the day.
7. Expenditure of supplies.
8. Damage to boats or other apparatus.

9. Whether house* has been opened for ventilation.

10. Names and complete description of all deceased persons and circumstances under which found.

11. Whether the patrol was kept previous night, and names of patrolmen for the night.

12. All transactions or occurrences relating to house† or service.

The journal will be written up every day and signed by the keeper.

FORMS.

FORM 1.
UNITED STATES LIFE-SAVING SERVICE.

Instructions for keeping Journal for United States Life-Saving Stations.

A book 9 inches wide, 12 inches long, 200 pages, with the following printed on 1st page:

The journal must embrace all occurrences relating to the service, in the following order:

1. Day of the week, date and name of month, and the year.

2. State of the weather; direction and force of the wind, whether gale, fresh or moderate breeze, or calm. (These to be noted at sunrise, noon, sunset, and midnight.)

3. Number of persons belonging to station present, and number absent, with name of absentee and cause of absence.

4. Number and kind of vessels passing the station, in either direction, during the day.

5. If a wreck occurs, a full description of the same, according to Form 3, must be entered, stating all the circumstances and the proceedings of the crew of the station.

6. Nature of the surf for the day.

7. Expenditures of supplies.

8. Damage done to boats or other apparatus.

9. Whether house has been opened for ventilation.

10. Names and complete description of all deceased persons and circumstances under which found.

11. Whether the patrol was kept previous night, and names of the patrolmen for the night.

12. All transactions or occurrences relating to house or service.

The journal will be written up every day and signed by the keeper.

"Forms" page from the 1873 Regulations.
Author's photo.

---

*Meaning the Life-Saving Service station.
†Meaning the Life-Saving Service station.

Now my take: Take a few minutes and review those instructions again. From the *Regulations*, the section for "Duties of Officers," which then lists "Keepers," the sections are from number 26 to 51, pages 9 to 13. That is a total of twenty-six (26) duties listed. We just looked at *one* of them.

Filling out Form 1 every day required quite a bit of time and effort, all done, remember, by longhand. That is a lot of detail. And that is just Form 1, of twenty-six separate duties.

That was done by *every* keeper of *every* United States Life-Saving Service station. That was done by nearly three hundred stations on all of America's coasts. So, it is extremely important to see why so much detail and information is recorded every day.

Why? To be ready. To be "Always Ready." And the Life-Savers *were* always ready—long before it became a motto it was standard operating procedure, a way of life. It would become "Semper Paratus."

Fortunately for historians and researchers, this vast wealth of daily detail covering nearly half a century is still available to the public through the wonderful existence of our National Archives.

So Others May Live

When a shipwreck occurred during the late nineteenth century, there was one, single, solitary person who would be the critical key to success or failure: the United States Life-Saving Service station keeper. Once a wreck was spotted and reported, *he* alone was in total command.

His first call was to neighboring stations. The keeper of each station was told of the location and condition of the wreck. Discussion quickly focused on what equipment would be needed. Often, "just to be sure," the lead keeper would suggest that duplicates of equipment show up. That would mean one or more beach apparatus carts with the Lyle gun, breeches buoy, and remaining equipment needed to fire the life line. That also meant one or more surfboats would be hauled out by surfman power on the bulky carts. All of this, usually, required slogging over the wet sand, heavy over wash, and fierce rain and winds in a storm—day or night, summer or winter.

Usually, the keeper whose station was closest to the wreck was in charge. Then, the other keepers would take instructions and perform the tasks that the other surfmen did. The exception was when one of the other keepers was more experienced; then he was in charge.

Within minutes, the commanding keeper would determine where to stop the beach cart and or the surfboat. If employing the breaches buoy rescue method, he then literally began to bark out well-rehearsed orders practiced as drill twice a week:

1. "Action."
2. "Man weather whip."
3. "Haul out."
4. "Man lee whip."
5. "Haul ashore."

In the weekly drills, if the time between "Action" and "Haul ashore" exceeded five minutes, that crew was not subject to discipline—they were subject to dismissal! The Life-Saving Service could not afford "do-overs."

If launching the surfboat, a drill practiced once a week, all surfmen would take place on the oars and the keeper was the coxswain, steering the surfboat with a rudder and an elongated steering oar. The keeper made all decisions during the rescue, with most requiring split-second choices as many were life-and-death decisions.

Finally returning to the station—usually exhausted—the lifesaving crew's work was not over. The surfmen were required to clean and stow all the equipment. The shipwreck survivors were taken to the station, given new dry clothing, first aid if needed, food and drink, and a place to stay until relocation. The Service referred to this entire process as "succoring." It was all free, and there was more. The surfmen would stand watch over the wreck to prevent thefts. Later, they would assist in unloading salvageable cargo and reloading in arriving company vessels. They even buried the non-survivors.

More Forms and Reports

Meanwhile, the keeper had paperwork. Most critical was the *Wreck Report*, Form 3:

LIFE-SAVING STATION, DISTRICT No. __.

Date of disaster: _____, 18__.

1. Name of vessel.
2. Rig and tonnage.
3. Hailing-port and nationality.
4. Age.
5. Official number.
6. Name of master.
7. Names of owners.

. . .

17. Supposed cause of wreck (specifying particularly).
18. Nature of disaster, whether stranded, sunk, Collision, &c.
19. Distance of vessel from shore at time of accident.
20. Time of day or night.
21. State of wind and weather.
22. State of tide and sea.
23. Time of discovery of wreck.
24. By whom discovered.

. . .

61. Amount of insurance on vessel.
62. Amount of insurance on cargo.
63. Number of persons sheltered at station, and how long.
64. Number and names of persons resuscitated from apparent death by drowning or exposure to cold.
65. Number of persons found after death and cared for.
66. Remarks. (All particulars not included in the above list will be here stated, giving specially the nature of the assistance rendered by the Life-Saving Service; and if the wreck occurred at a time when the crew was not employed at the

station, give the names of those persons who rendered assistance, using additional sheets of paper if necessary.)

. . .

Date of report: _____, 18__.
_____, Keeper.

NOTE. Two copies of the above to be filled up, as directed in paragraph 72 of the Revised Regulations, and sent to the Superintendent, who will forward one to the inspector. Copy to be entered upon the journal.

Then there were the rest of the forms:

Form 4. Quarterly Report from Station No.__, District No.__, for the quarter ending _____, 18__.
Form 5. For Requisitions.
Form 6. Quarterly Estimate for Funds for the Life-Saving Service, Coast of_____.
   The following sums are required by _____, Superintendent of Life-saving Stations in District No. __, to defray the expenses of the Life-saving Service in said District, for the Quarter ending _____, 187__, viz:
Form 7. For payroll.
Form 8. Voucher.
Form 9. Inventory of Public Property at Station No. __, District No. __.

These are the forms just for 1873. Over the years, this list of forms grew considerably. The keeper of a United States Life-Saving Service station was very important and, indeed, he was very busy. It could become overwhelming; his pay was low compared to the risks and hardships he endured and there was no retirement.

But it was a highly coveted position. And he was a national hero everywhere he went. He had the most noble of all professions—*saving lives*. That is why every surfman's goal was to eventually be a keeper.

CHAPTER 4

TO BE A SURFMAN

Becoming a surfman in the United States Life-Saving Service during the late 1800s was filled with obstacles and had serious disadvantages. But the rewards were so great that these men risked it all and joined against all odds.

The stations of the United States Life-Saving Service across America from 1871 until 1915 were staffed by six to eight lifesavers (eight for stations with excessive surf routinely) called "surfmen" and one officer in charge called the "keeper." The surfmen were ranked 1 through 6, with 1 being the highest and 6 where new staff would start. To become a surfman in the United States Life-Saving Service early on meant a number of things. First, you would have to pass a civil service test. That required literacy. Then, you would need to read, understand, agree to all terms, and sign the "Articles of Engagement for Surfmen."

For the modern reader to fully appreciate the moment, this is the original 1873 document in full:[1]

Articles of Engagement for Surfmen

We, the subscribers, do, and each of us doth, hereby agree to and with _____, keeper of Life-saving station No. ___, on the coast of _____ , and in the Life-saving Service of the United States, in manner and form following, that is to say:

In the first place, we do hereby agree, in consideration of the monthly wages against each of our names hereunto set, payable at such times and in such proportions as are or may be prescribed by the Secretary of the Treasury of the United States, to enter into the Life-saving Service of the United States, for the term of one year unless sooner discharged by the order of the Secretary of the Treasury, and to repair to station No.___, on the coast of _____, by the first of December, 18__, and remain there for four months, that is to say, during the months of December, 18__, and January, February, and March, the first day of April, 18__, and during that time, unless sooner discharged by proper authority, to the utmost of our power and ability, respectively, to discharge our several duties, and in everything to be conformable and obedient to the lawful commands of the officers who may, from time to time, be placed over us.

Secondly. we do, also, oblige and subject ourselves, and for that purpose do hereby covenant and agree to serve during the term aforesaid, and to comply with and be subject to such rules and disciplines as are or may be established for the government of the Life-saving Service of the United States.

Thirdly. The said _____, for and in behalf of the United States, doth hereby covenant and agree to and with the parties who have hereunto severally signed their names, and each of them, respectively, that the said parties shall be paid in consideration of their services, the amount per month which, in the column hereunto annexed, is set opposite to each of their names, respectively, at such times and in such proportions as are or may be allowed by the General Instructions for the government of the Life-saving Service.

Names	Date of entry	Term	In what capacity	Pay per month	Remarks

Notice these critical details:

- Payment is monthly, but at an unspecified time.
- Your contract is for one year only with no guarantee for renewal.
- You are only on duty (for pay) for four months; the other eight months you are own your own.
- You can be discharged at any time purely on the discretion of the keeper; it was certain for drunkenness and even probable for laziness or even swearing.
- You must follow all orders by those superior—which includes the station keeper, the assistant inspectors, the general inspector, the district superintendent, the assistant general superintendent, and the general superintendent (and, technically, the US president on down).
- You agree to follow all rules and perform all duties and drills.

Now for the *bad* news!

- You will work at your assigned station for __ hours, six days a week, but you cannot live there—you must supply your own housing.
- You can be transferred at any time to another station far from your home.
- You will have to pay for and supply your own work clothes. At this time, there is no standard uniform.
- You will pay for all of the food you eat at the station while on duty.
- You have no sick or vacation leave.
- You will live in a very remote place that may or may not have any stores or businesses.
- One of your weekly duties is "beach patrol." This means at night, walking miles of beach next to the surf, during the winter and storms, and carrying a lantern and flares to warn or signal passing ships.
- You will have no retirement compensation; hang in as long as you can! (Which is why we see keepers in their seventies.)

The 1882 Cape Hatteras Life-Saving Station. Formal photographs were taken of all the stations with uniformed crews lined up in numerical order with keeper first (the only one with a double-breasted jacket), then surfmen 1 through 8. Usually, it started with keeper on the far left. This image may have been reversed.
National Park Service, Cape Hatteras National Seashore.

So, what *is* the good news?

- You have the most coveted job anywhere in your village or surrounding area.
- You are a national hero.
- You are saving lives—the most noble of all human activities.
- You may be the star in local parades.
- Some of you will be the main attraction in US World Fairs.
- You have been the subject of hundreds of magazine and newspaper articles for years throughout this period. Here are a few actual examples:

  From *Frank Leslie's Popular Monthly* (1878)

  > The life of a coastguardsman and the patrol along the treacherous coast, unrecognizable in the uncouth paraphernalia of his calling, is regarded as a superlative hero.

The public make his acquaintance only upon the saddest occasions, for his bravery is heralded by the press and from the pulpit in the same moment that disasters, involving the loss of life and property, are announced. For all the humanity he has displayed, for all the risks of life and health he has sustained, the people are apt to thank him heartily one day and forget him utterly the next, so rapidly do events crowd upon the mind in these busy days.[2]

From *Scientific American*:

Nor should we fail to count the stalwart arm and brave heart of the surfman, ready to risk all to save human beings from undertow and breaker.

Without the surfman, all inventions fail. It is to his ready hand, sagacious eye, and equipoised head that we mainly owe the triumphs of the service. He acts under strict discipline, as well in his "beat" upon the shore as in his venture through the surf.

The patrol system is directed by rigid rules. At night, and in fog, the surfman, at great peril, patrols the beach from two to four miles on each side of his station. His eye is on the sea.

He bears a lantern for his guide, and a Costen light with which to warn, by its red flaring flame, the endangered vessel, or to signal those already stranded. At the station, where his five companions and keeper live, are the large life-boat and the small surf-boat. These, at his summons, are hauled by hand (why not by horse?), through blinding storm and wet sand, to the point where needed. If the boat cannot be used by reason of the overwhelming surf, then the gun and shot-line, block and hawser.[3]

From *Scribner's Monthly*:

THE UNITED STATES LIFE-SAVING SERVICE OFF TO A WRECK.

In the principal newspapers of commercial cities there may be seen, under the caption of "Marine Intelligence," or some such title, a column made up of items, set in nonpareil type, like the following, cut from a recent journal:

Bark Halcyon (of Bath) Dickinson, from Boston for Perth Amboy, in ballast, went ashore on Long Beach, LI, AM of Sept 4. All hands were taken off by the crew of Life-Saving Station No. 32.

Has the reader any idea of the stirring drama a dry paragraph like this may conceal? Let us endeavor to make it apparent.

No portion of the ten thousand and more miles of the sea and lake coast-line of the United States, extending through every variety of climate and containing every feature of coast danger to the mariner, can exhibit a more terrible record of shipwreck than the long stretch of sandy beaches lying between Cape Cod and Cape Hatteras. Of this region the New Jersey coast is notoriously the worst. It has been said that if all the skeletons of vessels lying upon or imbedded in the sand between Sandy Hook and Barnegat could be ranged in line, the ghastly array would reach from one point to the other. Here, in 1848, the government placed a few rude huts that formed the nucleus from which the United States Life-Saving Service has been developed. These were intended to afford shelter to distressed mariners and to contain boats and such other life-saving appliances as were then known, volunteers from among the fishermen being relied upon to use them on occasions of shipwreck. And right gallantly, in many instances, did the brave beachmen respond, though their undertakings and deeds remain mostly unwritten, existing chiefly in the legends of the coast.[4]

From James Otis's *The Life Savers*:

At sunset two men start from each station, one going to the right and the other to the left. They are equipped with lanterns and Coston signals, and each pursues his solitary and perilous way through the soft sand, in spite of flooding tides, bewildering snowfalls, overwhelming winds, and bitter cold.[5]

And here is another taken from the *Scientific American*:

The Life-Saving Service is more than is indicated by the title. It is also a property-saving service. It has, too, its houses of refuge for the castaways who may survive disaster. More than this: by its signal-lights and vigilance, upon the shore, it has saved and is saving vessels and life, by warning them of fatal nearness to the breakers; whie [*sic*] in various other ways—as in bestowing medals for daring in life-saving, in saving properly from fire, and rescuing icebound vessels—it has a larger round of humane employment than is generally supposed.

Even upon the remote shores of our lakes (where, in one hundred and thirty-six disasters during the past year, only one single life was lost), these agencies challenge admiration and astound belief. . . . If it be that the highest refinement of civil polity is the pursuit and attainment of human happiness, what object of society can be named in comparison with this paragon of institutions! Humanity, more beautiful than art, and more profound than science, has bent over the sad seas, with their wild waves and wintry storms, her ethereal bow, unfolding its prism of promise.[6]

So, How Has It Changed?

Today's United States Coast Guard, excerpts from their website:

THIS IS COAST GUARD

When you join the US Coast Guard, you'll work with passionate individuals who share your drive to save lives, serve others and your country, and shield our nation from threats. If you have a sincere desire to make the world a better place while setting yourself up for a bright future, Coast Guard service is for you.

There's no such thing as an average day in the Coast Guard.

Every day, you'll work on exciting missions. You'll gain in-demand career skills and have life-changing experiences, all while making lifelong friends. Just ask our servicemembers. They'll tell you that adventure is part of their job—and making a difference is their priority.[7]

CHAPTER 5

BASE OF OPERATIONS
THE STATION

Today's first responders—fire, police, emergency medical services (EMS)—owe much of their design and format to the first first responders: the United States Life-Saving Service.

The third component that was critical for actually saving lives was the Life-Saving Station. This contained the keeper, the surfmen, and the lifesaving equipment. The latter are detailed in volume 1[1] and summarized in this volume's chapter 1.

Much like today's first responders, the United States Life-Saving Service had a self-contained base of operations supplied by a larger, outside force. We are going to skip the very earliest attempts since they were minimal, crude, and ineffective. The more sophisticated ones started in 1871. Nationally, there were dozens of different architectural designs, and, at some point, it became almost an artistic competition. North Carolina only had a handful of different designs, but of the total twenty-nine, seventeen were either 1874 or 1878.

Contents

Regardless of design, all 1874 stations measured nineteen feet wide, forty-three feet long, and a story and a half high. North Carolina stations had elaborately decorative architecture: US Life-Saving Service architectural historian Wick York says, "Most exterior finishes combined Stick Style diagonal boarding at all four corners applied over a continuous run of beaded vertical siding on the first-floor level."[2] These original stations had to contain the following: watch tower, keeper's room, crew quarters, day room, survivors' quarters, and boat room. The later kitchen (or "mess") and the bathroom were separate outside structures. Many changes and improvements occurred in the design over the years.

From the beginning, and continuing for a long time, the watch tower was on top of the station itself. Most had interior access. This design remains a widespread architectural aspect of many coastal cities and towns in homes, businesses, and buildings. Today's visitor would probably be confused by entering the watch tower—it was totally bare of furniture. The reason? The surfman on duty was literally *standing* watch!

Interior of typical 1874 LSS station. Interesting detail in this rare illustration. On the left is a beach cart with breeches buoys hanging overhead. On the right is the surfboat, marked USLSS. Below the boat is the opened shot box and additional equipment. The rear wall shows miscellaneous equipment. What looks like cannonballs are the front of the projectile shots. In the background is the "Day Room" with cookstove.
Harper's Weekly, 1886; public domain.

Originally, the station keeper was the only one who could live at the station. So, one room was his private bedroom, and many stations also included a separate office for the keeper. The crews' quarters were for the surfmen on duty at the time; they had to provide their own housing. All had storage areas and closets of some kind. The rest of the rooms were of standard appearance. However, one room was completely different—it was very special, and critically important:

The Boat Room

The boat room contained all the rescue equipment. Although that meant two specific objects—the surfboats and the beach cart—they were each composed of many individual pieces. Let's take a closer look.

The Surfboat

The surfboat is commonly referred to as a "lifeboat." However, they are quite different. Most Life-Saving stations in the Northeast and the Great Lakes did use lifeboats. Plus, today, everyone knows that cruise ships have lifeboats. But the North Carolina Outer Banks produces the most intense surf on the East Coast. They need a special boat for these special conditions.

The surfboat had two bow ends, meaning it had no flat transom at the stern but was pointed at both ends. Purposely designed so that if turned around in the heavy surf, it was still pointed to go ahead. It was also eventually designed to be both self-righting and self-bailing. Extra buoyancy placed in the bottom would flip it upright if overturned. Ingenious scuppers and valves allowed flooding seas to drain out the bottom. Originally powered by "Armstrong engines" (picture surfmen moving their arms in a rowing motion as they said that), most were later converted to gasoline engines. The surfboats also explain this difference: the *Regulations* for all United States Life-Saving Service stations specified six surfmen for each station. The "surf stations" had eight surfmen for the extra strength needed to oar in heavy surf.

The Beach Cart

The beach cart was considered rather large, heavy, and somewhat cumbersome. It carried all of the components for the beach apparatus drill, often called the "Lyle gun" or the "breeches buoy rescue." The detailed functions of each piece are fully described in volume 1[3] and more is added in chapter 1 of this volume. Instead of repeating that information, let us simply identify each piece of the equipment.

- *cart*—holds all the equipment
- *whip lines*—used to send out and retrieve hawser and breeches buoy
- *Lyle gun*—black powder, small mortar that fires the whip line to eventually form the "zip line"
- *shot* ("faking") *box* and *shot line*—stored to keep line from fouling when fired
- *shot*—the twenty-pound carrier of the shot line fired from the Lyle gun
- *hawser*—the heavy line attached to the mast that will carry the breeches buoy
- *breeches buoy*—the "life-ring and shorts" that forms the seat for victims to ride ashore
- *sand anchor*—buried in the beach to create the tension needed on the hawser
- *fall line*—set of pulleys used to drastically increase hawser line tension
- *crotch pole*—assures height over the surf and beach

The First "First Responders"

The United States Life-Saving Service set the stereotype for effective emergency action: one commanding leader, one well-trained crew, and a station to house them and the equipment needed and to be critically located as close to the need as possible. The United States Life-Saving

Service accomplished this from 1871 until 1915, when it merged with the US Revenue Cutter Service to form today's United States Coast Guard, who honorably continue this tradition. Of their current eleven missions, remaining as number one is "So Others May Live."

Semper Paratus.

III.

THE DRAMATIC
AND
INSPIRATIONAL

CHAPTER 6

SCHOONER *JOHN MAXWELL*, THE MOST SERIOUS CASUALTY OF 1912

A classic mariner's mistake cost lives; but the classic persistence of lifesavers,
even after six failed efforts, with the incredible endurance and providence/
luck of a lone survivor all produced a dramatic and inspirational classic saga.

An Official Tribute

The first paragraph of the *Annual Report of the Operations of the United States Life-Saving Service for the Fiscal Year Ending June 30, 1913,* on this wreck is a huge testament to the incredible successes and efficiency of the surfmen of the United States Life-Saving Service: "The wreck of the schooner John Maxwell in the early morning of November 2, 1912, three-fourths of a mile southeast of the New Inlet Life-Saving Station, coast of North Carolina, furnished the most serious casualty of any that occurred upon our eastern seaboard during the year within the scope of operations of the service."[1] What is so stunning about this statement is that the total loss of lives in the wreck was six. Yet, the *Annual Report* says that was "the most serious casualty of any" that occurred in the entire year on the American coastline, which, historically, had the most shipwrecks and loss of lives. Even more remarkable is that the *Annual Report's* language laments that loss, giving further recognition to the excellence of the Service.

The Ship

Little information is available about this vessel other than she was a large schooner of 532 tons and had a crew of seven. She was owned by A. H. Bull & Co. (New York, 1902, later renamed Baltimore Insular Line Inc.) and valued at $10,000, more than $260,000 in today's dollars. On the fateful voyage of November 2, 1912, she was carrying a cargo of coal from Norfolk, Virginia, to Savannah, Georgia. Her master was Captain Fred Godfrey. Adding to possible confusion about this vessel's identity is the fact that there were numerous sailing vessels named *John Maxwell*.

Unfortunate Circumstances

The only explanations and testimony regarding the wreck and its causes came from the sole survivor, Captain Godfrey. What was particularly unfortunate was he laid blame on the crew, who all perished. "Asked as to the cause of the disaster, he declared it to have been the fault of the mate in not obeying his orders to get a cast of the lead."[2]

Godfrey further testified that almost immediately after grounding, the mate and remaining four crew (except the cook) mutinied by hurriedly leaving the schooner in the ship's boat. The captain elaborated: "with all hands assisting, the line that was finally laid across the schooner from the beach could have been hauled out and the breeches buoy apparatus set up, thereby making possible the rescue of the entire company."[3] In this, he was correct. In all the years of the Service assisting shipwreck victims, the number one cause of fatalities was victims leaving the ship on their own. The Service addressed this

SOUNDINGS

Measuring the depth of the water. Traditionally done by "swinging the lead." Soundings of this type were usually taken using leads that had a wad of tallow in a concavity at the bottom of the plummet. The heavy lead was to have it sink fast. The tallow or wax on the end was to retrieve the bottom makeup: rocky, sandy, silty, muddy, and so on. These measurements had to be taken often in shallow waters to prevent running aground. It is one probable reason the shallow bodies of North Carolina's waterways between the Outer Banks and the Mainland are called "sounds."

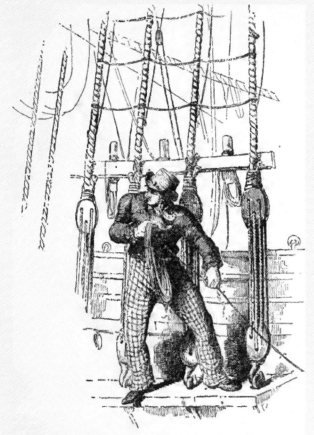

MAN IN THE CHAINS HEAVING THE LEAD ON AN
OLD WOODEN SAILING SHIP.

Period illustration of "taking the soundings" by swinging and dropping the lead.
E. K. Chatterton, Ships and Ways of Other Days, *1913. WikiCommons.*

numerous times, most emphatically in their publication *Instructions to Mariners in Case of Shipwreck*:

> If the vessel is not discovered by the patrol immediately after striking, rockets or flare-up lights should be burned, or if the weather be foggy guns should be fired to attract attention, as the patrolman may be some distance away on the other end of his beat.
>
> *Masters are particularly cautioned, if they should he driven ashore anywhere in the neighborhood of the stations, especially on any of the sandy coasts where there is not much danger of vessels breaking up immediately, to remain on board until assistance arrives, and under no circumstances should they attempt to land through the surf in their own boats until the last hope of assistance from the shore has vanished* (original emphasis). Often when comparatively smooth at sea a dangerous surf is running which is not perceptible four hundred yards off shore, and the surf when viewed from a vessel never appears as dangerous as it is. Many lives have unnecessarily been lost by the crews of stranded vessels being thus deceived and attempting to land in the ships' boats.[4]

Heroes Here We Have Seen Before

The remaining personnel, Captain Godfrey and Alexander Tillman, the cook, had only one option: climb into the rigging, wait, and pray for help. This was a wise choice, for by 1912, the United States Life-Saving Service had a stellar reputation for expedient successes, and Captain Godfrey was well aware of that. Sure enough, almost in minutes, the "angels in oilskins"[5] appeared. Surfman P. L. O'Neal from the New Inlet Life-Saving Station was making the south patrol at 3:10 a.m. when he discovered the wreck. Within thirty minutes, Keeper Patrick H. Etheridge had his crew from the New Inlet Station abreast of the wreck with the beach apparatus ready to go. The neighboring stations to the south were also Johnny-on-the-spot. Coming from the farthest was our old friend and hero of volume 1;[6] John Allen Midgett Jr., then keeper of Gull Shoal station (was keeper of Chicamacomico for the SS *Mirlo* rescue in 1918) is at the wreck site with his crew and surfboat. Keeper Bannister L. Midgett of the adjacent Chicamacomico station also appeared with a crew and surfboat. With this much experience, training, available personnel, and rescue equipment so quickly on site, Captain Godfrey's assessment was clearly sound, had the crew remained onboard.

The Rescue

In spite of the experience, leadership, and abundant crew and equipment, these surfmen were to be cruelly tested. The *Maxwell* lay approximately 350 yards offshore in the breakers—certainly, within range of the Lyle gun, but it would literally be a long shot. This was compounded by the strong winds, becoming a full gale by dawn.

Keeper Etheridge's crew immediately set up the beach apparatus. Etheridge's first shot fired a projectile with a number 7 shot line, which immediately parted but would have been on target. Etheridge tried a number 9 shot line next. Although it successfully landed in the best location, the lifesavers felt no tension from the schooner's survivors and helplessly hauled the line back ashore. A third identical shot produced the same lack of success. The lifesavers' frustration of not having the cooperation of the persons on the wreck meant the surfboat was the only next option.

To fully understand what was happening here, a basic review/summary of how the beach apparatus works is necessary. The Lyle gun fired a

SHOT LINES

Three sizes of shot line were available for use. The smallest was $4/32$-inches diameter rope and would be used when firing the greatest distance. The other sizes were $7/32$-inch and $9/32$-inch lines. So, for brevity, the Service referred to the $4/32$-inch diameter line as a number 4 and so on for the rest.

twenty-pound steel projectile called the "shot." Attached to this was one of the thin shot lines. This allowed the shot its greatest range. But that line was too thin and weak to use in hauling in survivors. So, the shot line was tied to a much stouter line, called the "whip line." To get the whip line to the ship, personnel onboard the ship were required to haul in the shot line to the ship so the whip line could be attached to the vessel. Only then could the rest of the equipment be assembled so that the breeches buoy could save them.

The three keepers then conferenced and agreed that the next best step would be to wait until daylight and hope conditions would improve enough to launch the surfboats. Using the surfboats, however, would have an additional set of problems. The bad news: conditions had gotten seriously worse. The wind was now blowing between seventy and eighty miles per hour. The tide had also risen. The *Annual Report* describes the scene: "Giant waves were leaping clear over the schooner, while between her and the shore the water was a turmoil of furiously racing whitecaps."[7] The good news, however, was that for the first time the lifesavers could see that two survivors had climbed into the mizzenmast

The standard crew of six, wearing their storm oilskins, manually hauling the multi-thousand-pound surfboat. Start of the Lifeboat, 1900, Cape Cod, same as Outer Banks. **Courtesy of the US Coast Guard; public domain.**

rigging, at the stern of the schooner. Now, a shot line could be fired to be placed within their easy grasp. Indeed, it was, but the men were too weak to "overcome the united force of sea and current tugging at the line between the schooner and the shore," the *Report* continues. So too did the frustration of the lifesavers continue.

These resolute surfmen, like all their kin, knew that if one thing did not work, to keep trying other techniques. Their next choice was not "by the book," but it was reasonable. Seeing that the two onboard had no cork lifebelts, the lifesavers tied two of theirs to the shot line they retrieved and signaled to the victims to haul that in to them. "But the current again defeated their efforts—they could not drag even the belts through the water."[8]

Running out of options, the "Lifesaving Committee" decided to use one surfboat and eight hand-picked strongest and most experienced crew from the three stations. Keepers Etheridge and Midgett would be the coxswain (pronounced cock-sun) steering the Beebe-McLellan surfboat. The surf was still so violent that all twenty-four lifesavers from the three stations as well as a number of civilian volunteers were needed to launch the surfboat.

Unbelievably, this resulted in yet another failure. With monumental forces working against them, "the seasoned men at the oars might as well have been exerted against a stone wall. Referring to the efforts of the boat's crew to proceed, keeper Etheridge testifies that in all his experience as a life saver, covering a period of 26 years, he never saw the tide running stronger."[9] They had to return to the beach but refused to give up.

Etheridge launched another perfect shot to the wreck. This time, the survivors were able to secure the shot line to the mast. Apparently not understanding the correct procedures, the cook, Tillman, desperately tried to dangle from the line and walk himself hand-over-hand to shore. The outcome was predictable: he fell and was swept away. The lifesavers' frustration became heartbreak.

One would imagine that things could not have gotten worse—but they did. The already dangerously high gale force winds grew even higher. The cauldron of violently churning surf increased. The schooner's inevitable fate began as it started to break up. It is impossible for us to empathize with the lifesavers as they had run out of options and "could do nothing but look helplessly on in momentary expectation of seeing the single remaining survivor go down with the swaying mast."[10] Training daily to save lives and willing to risk all, their greatest fear was exactly this: impotently standing by and powerlessly watching.

And Then, the Miracle

As the schooner was violently and literally broken to pieces, spars flying, rigging collapsing in heaps of spaghetti, and seams parting, Captain Godfrey found himself on a piece of the stern large enough to support him. "The part of the broken hull that supported him was providentially borne by the swift tidal current in toward the land."[11] Finally, at last, the lifesavers can save a life. One waded into the pounding surf far enough to throw him a line and instruct the captain to tie it around himself. Then the crews hauled him in.

Standard Operating Procedures for Saving Lives

A *New York Times* article of the day of the wreck (November 2, 1912) published quickly but before the rescue was completed, stated, "The lone survivor who, through glasses, appeared to be an aged man, was making a brave fight for life, but it is feared that he is doomed."[12] "Old" Captain Fred Godfrey not only survived but was carried back to Patrick Etheridge's New Inlet Station to receive the standard operating procedures (SOP) care from the lifesavers of dry clothes, food and drink, first aid, rest, and comfort. It was said that the young men of the station were amazed and remarked about how quickly the elderly captain recovered from such a grueling and lengthy experience.

NEW INLET LIFE-SAVING STATION, N.C.,
November 4, 1912

MY DEAR SIR: I wish to express my appreciation of the
efforts of the crews of the New Inlet, Chicamacomico and Gull
Shoal Life-Saving Stations in saving me from the wreck of
the schooner *John Maxwell* on the 2d instant. If my crew had
not deserted me in the yawl boat, I think we would all have
been saved. I got the line the life-savers shot out to me, but on
account of the strong current I could not haul it off alone. I wish
also to express my thanks for the kind treatment I received from
the captain of the New Inlet Station during the time I remained.
Captain Fred Godfrey.[13]

Retrospect

In this modern day and age, it is exceedingly difficult to imagine ordinary people—like us—to be willing and able to persist in efforts in the
face of so many obstacles, difficulties, and failures. But the iconic men
of the United States Life-Saving Service—also ordinary persons of
their era—time and time again, were able to accomplish *extra*ordinary
feats, coming from different values and a different time—now gone
with the winds. More than dramatic—profoundly inspirational.

CHAPTER 7

BARGE *SAXON*, OCTOBER 12, 1907

The story of a wrecked barge, at first glance, may not seem too exciting. This story, however, is not only engagingly interesting but also a complicated saga. On the negative side, it is maritime lessons still unlearned. On the positive side, it demonstrates, once again, the amazing tenacity of the United States Life-Saving Service as well as how multiple stations worked together, setting the precedents the US Coast Guard uses today. As a bonus, it takes place in a period of US history with which many Americans are not familiar.

Prologue

A steamship *Katahdin* was towing the large barge *Saxon*, from Georgetown, South Carolina, bound for Philadelphia, Pennsylvania. The barge had a cargo of lumber and "She carried a crew of four—the master Frank Pilong; mate, Fred Lund; one seaman (a negro); and a cook. The names of the seaman and cook could not be ascertained."[1] On the afternoon of October 12 (1907), when the two vessels were off the dreaded shoals of Cape Hatteras, they ran into rough weather. For several hours they wrestled with the turbulent ocean, but finally the *Katahdin* "parted their towline, the barge going ashore" says the *Annual Report,* two and a half miles south of the Gull Shoal station and about four miles north of the Little Kinnakeet station on the coast of North Carolina. A third station also responded. The barge and cargo were a total loss and three of the crew were tragically—because it was unnecessary—lost. The lone survivor tells the story.

The Ship and Its Epoch

The *Saxon* was a 1,193-ton steamer built in Philadelphia in 1862. This was during the second year of the American Civil War and actually had much more to do with the causes of that conflagration than with the commonly held belief that it was *only* about slavery, which indeed was one factor.

America was extremely divided by 1860 into the industrial Northeast, the agricultural South, the Midwest and the Wild West. None had anything in common with the other. For the bitterly contested presidential election of 1860, *four* political parties offered candidates. That had never happened before. Each party had a platform strongly favoring only their section of the country. The Republicans stood for improvements only in the industrial Northeast.

So, improving transportation in the Northeast, which included more shipbuilding, was the Republicans' most important priority. They won the election. Lincoln was the candidate.

Portents of *Saxon's* Association with Trouble

In her very first year of operations in 1862, the *Saxon* became involved in shipwrecks. The damaged vessel *Vermont* was under tow by the federal gunboat *Aroostook* on March 7 of that year. The following day, both vessels ran into such a fierce gale that the towboat was so seriously damaged she had to withdraw for repairs and withdrew from *Vermont* on March 15. Enter the *Saxon*. At 10:00 a.m., the *Saxon* reported seeing the two vessels struggling and began to render assistance. "On coming up with the *Vermont*, the *Saxon* supplied her with sails, a rudder and two ship-carpenters. The rudder was lost in hanging it. The *Saxon* took a hawser from the ship, and commenced towing, but at 6½ P.M. [*sic*] the hawser parted, and a heavy southwest gale coming on, lost sight of her."[2]

Only two years later, the *Saxon* was involved in a similar incident, but with a more positive result. The clerk of the steamer *Saxon*, Mr. George W. Snow, reported to the *New York Times* that his ship "fell in with the ship *C. Grinnell*,"[3] which was stranded on the Five Fathom Bank of the Nantucket Shoals. She was a passenger ship having departed Liverpool, England, and bound for New York with 150 passengers, who were most unhappy at this turn of events. Again, the *Saxon* happened to be in the right place at the right time and, again, offered assistance. The plan was to tow the *C. Grinnell* into port, so a hawser was fitted. After several attempts were thwarted by broken towlines, the *Saxon* then acted as pilot to guide the liner as she worked her way off the bank.

Fade to Black

Forty-one years after being built, in that same iconic 1903 year that the Wright brothers (often misspelled) made their famous flights, the huge, old, tired *Saxon* was unceremoniously cut down and repurposed as a highly utilitarian 555-ton barge.

The Fabric of America at the Time

This is now the *Saxon* of our story. The time was nearly a half-century later. By the early 1900s, America was still strictly divided geographically, politically, economically, and socially. Now America had an amazing 193,000 miles of railroad tracks, its first oil wells were operating, and Andrew Carnegie had built the world's largest steel mill.

The South was still trying to recuperate from the devastation of the war and the West was still wild. In the year 1903 alone, in addition to Wilbur and Orville's fame, the first World Series game was played, Butch Cassidy left the States to live in South America, the "Buffalo Bill Wild West" show* was touring mostly in the East, Geronimo was

---

*The title of the program is commonly, but mistakenly, called "Buffalo Bill Wild West Show," but the word "show" was never in the program title.

Poster for the "Buffalo Bill's Wild West," 1899. Commonly, but mistakenly, the word "show" is added. WikiMediaCommons.

on a warpath, the wreck of the Old 97 inspired an iconic ballad, John Dillinger was born, and Theodore "Teddy" Roosevelt was president of the United States.

In all sections of America, transportation was still primarily by horse, carriage, railroads, boats, and ships.

The *Saxon* was simply in the midst of all that. "Towboats have been employed moving barges on all navigable waters and have been an important component of the American transportation system since the 1850s. . . . Towboats became a distinct type by 1860. . . . Barges of all kinds were carrying more than 19 million tons of freight per year by 1889. . . . Towboats were designed as floating engines to propel barges. Only the barge need be detained while loading or unloading cargo, and not the expensive towboat."[4]

Saxon's Last Voyage

Facts gathered from the United States Life-Saving Service *Annual Report* of the year 1908 tell us that "About 9 o'clock on the night of the disaster, when Surf man [*sic*] W. B. Miller, of the Little Kinnakeet

Vol. XCVIII. No. 2535   New York, April 7, 1904   Price 10 Cents

LATEST PHOTOGRAPH OF THE PRESIDENT.
IT IS CONCEDED TO BE THE BEST LIKENESS OF MR. ROOSEVELT EVER TAKEN.

Front cover of Leslie's Weekly *98, no. 2535, New York, 1904.*
WikiMediaCommons.

lifesaving station, was covering the north patrol, he saw a white light seaward which he took to be the masthead light of a steamer standing in toward the beach,"[5] but he determined there was no danger and dismissed the sighting.

However, from the same report it is learned that "Surfman A. V. Midgett, of the Little Kinnakeet station, who covered the north patrol from midnight to 3 a.m., also saw the masthead light of the steamer offshore." Midgett did not dismiss the sighting; instead, he continued his patrol on horseback in the direction of the lights. "Continuing, he discovered her [the wrecked *Saxon*] in the breakers some 250 yards from the beach. This was about 12:30 a.m. As he stood watching the vessel, he saw a rocket go up in the direction of Gull Shoal and knew that the crew of the station at that place had also discovered the wreck."[6]

Now, it got a little complicated. Gull Shoal Station was the northern neighbor to Midgett's Little Kinnakeet Station, so he continued in that direction to assist. On his way, Midgett ran into three surfmen from Gull Shoal who informed him that keeper Captain Zera G. Burrus of Gull Shoal had telephoned Chicamacomico, the next station farther north, to bring their beach apparatus cart. Here the *Report* itself becomes confusing and unclear. It says, at this point, "Midgett therefore turned back with the surf men [presumably coming back from Chicamacomico, so heading back south toward Gull Shoal and the *Saxon* wreck]."[7] Upon arriving at the wreck, yet another surprise: Keeper Captain Edward O. Hooper of Midgett's own Little Kinnakeet Station had deployed at the wreck with the entire crew and had set up and begun rescue procedures.

"At this time," says Captain Hooper in his testimony, "The stranded vessel could be seen about 200 yards offshore on the outer bar heading southward, the seas breaking over her, lumber washing overboard, sails lowered, and two side lights burning. A light could also be seen through the cabin window, but there were no signs of life on board."[8]

The Chicamacomico crew arrived with the beach apparatus. Two Lyle gunshots were fired and the second was spot on, but there was no response from the wreck. "While the perplexed lifesavers were grouped on the beach awaiting the coming of the surf boat, Mate Lund put in his appearance and soon cleared up the mysterious features of the night's tragic event."[9]

The Sole Survivor's Account

When the towline broke, the *Saxon* was dangerously on her own. The *Katahdin* told the *Saxon* to try to make it alone to Hatteras but it was simply uncontrollable. Next, the *Katahdin* tried to reconnect a towline, but two attempts were unsuccessful due to the storm conditions. First Mate Fred Lund recorded in the *Annual Report*, "The *Katahdin* then signaled us to anchor. I sounded and found a little over 3-½ fathoms of water. We let go our anchor, running out about 45 fathoms of chain, but it would not hold in the sea and current, and the *Saxon* dragged into the breakers and stranded."[10]

Mate Lund describes the resulting turmoil: nearly in a panic, the barge crew began to furiously offload the deck cargo, "but the seas were breaking over the barge and she was pounding so hard that the captain ordered the boat launched."[11] This was not only a classic mistake; it was a fatal one.

An Avoidable Tragedy

From the earliest days of the Service, the lifesavers well knew that the number one cause of injury and death from shipwreck victims was their leaving the ship in a panic. The lifesavers routinely conveyed this message in many ways. To expedite having the shipwreck crew successfully set up the breeches buoy, the United States Life-Saving Service had a booklet of instructions with text and diagrams printed and should have been aboard all sailing vessels. It was *Instructions To* [*sic*] *Mariners In Case Of Shipwreck*, detailed in chapter 6.

The booklet goes on to say, "The difficulties of rescue by operations from the shore [meaning the breeches buoy apparatus and/or launching the surfboat] are greatly increased in cases where the anchors are let go *after entering the breakers* as is frequently done, in the chances of saving life correspondingly lessen."[12]

This is precisely what led to the avoidable *Saxon* loss of life. Lund continues with the launch of the small ship's boat, "We had scarcely got away from the side of the vessel, however, when a sea came along and capsized us. I got clear and swam ashore; I do not know what became of the rest."[13] Drowning is what became all three. Miraculously, after being washed back several times before reaching shore, Lund found himself abreast of a surfman's halfway house where he took refuge. Exhausted, he spent the night and was discovered the next morning by the surfmen and taken to the station.

As per standard operating procedures, an investigating officer of the Life-Saving Service asked Keeper Burrus whether or not the *Saxon* crew could have been saved had they stayed aboard the wreck; he sternly replied, "Yes, we would have saved them, every one, without any trouble. The second shot put the line across the deck abaft* the main-mast, and the gear could have been rigged in a few minutes."[14]

Epilogue

The *Katahdin* survived. Four days after the wreck, and twelve miles away, the body of the cook was found by the Cape Hatteras Station crew. The body of the seaman was picked up by the Big Kinnakeet crew on the 18th, even farther away. The captain was never found. The *Annual Report* concludes, "a considerable portion of the lumber she carried was saved."[15]

---

*Archaic nautical term meaning: at or toward the stern (aft, after part or rear of ship).

CHAPTER 8

BRITISH STEAMER
CRAGSIDE SAGA

OCRACOKE, FEBRUARY 20, 1891

The expression holds true: "You can lead a horse to water, but you can't make it drink." The sound judgement of the Life-Saving Service prevails over the lesser judgement of this ship master. Entirely needless drama; entirely expected rescue inspiration.

A Too-Oft-Repeated Theme

In the opening paragraph of his classic book on the US Life-Saving Service, Ralph Shanks makes this powerful statement that cannot be matched by any other organization in the history of America.[1]

It is worth exploring the wider and deeper meanings. In particular, the part about their work was "of deep interest to medical, educational, *religious* and political leaders."[2] This saga is a vivid example of how and why the Life-Savers' work was of deep interest to religious leaders, which will become crystal clear by the end of this chapter.

The Saga Begins

The *Cragside* was a British schooner-rigged steamer of considerable size— 1,278 tons and requiring a crew of twenty-three mariners. In February of

Cragside is a Victorian country house near the town of Rothbury in Northumberland, England. It was the home of William Armstrong, First Baron Armstrong, founder of the Armstrong Whitworth armaments firm. The vessel was possibly named after the baron. **WikiMediaCommons.**

1891, with Master W. L. Sinclair in command, she had departed from her homeport of Liverpool, England, crossing the Atlantic Ocean bound for Galveston, Texas, to deliver a cargo of cotton and cotton oil, or cottonseed, cake. So, why was she stranded on Ocracoke, North Carolina?

COTTONSEED OIL CAKE

Cottonseed cake or cottonseed meal is a by-product obtained by extracting oil from cotton seeds. It may come in the form of meal, cake, flakes, or pellets. Good quality oil cake is greenish-yellow in color. Cottonseed oil cake is the second most valuable product of cottonseed, accounting for over one-third of total product value of cottonseed.

Cottonseed oil cake is a major source of livestock feed. It is also used as fertilizer, either alone or in mixtures with other ingredients. It is an excellent organic source of nitrogen, phosphorus, potash, and many minor plant foods.[3]

The *Cragside* had burned most of her coal crossing the Atlantic and would not have been able to reach Texas directly. Therefore, she stopped at the largest coal-supplying port on America's East Coast—Norfolk, Virginia.

English settlers discovered coal in Eastern North America in 1673, but commercial coal mining did not begin until the 1740s. It remained a small industry until the early 1800s, as American settlers preferred to use the plentiful supplies of wood. Vast coal fields in the eastern US run from just south of the Virginia line's mountains, to West Virginia and Pennsylvania. The largest natural harbor on the East Coast, Chesapeake Bay, gave prominence to Norfolk as the dominant coal-supplying port.

Only a month after the wreck of the *Nathaniel Lank* (chapter 23), "On February 20, 1891, at 7 o'clock in the evening, the British steamer *Cragside* stranded about one mile south of the Ocracoke Station (Sixth District), near Hatteras Inlet, coast of North Carolina," the *Annual Report* tells us.[4] The Ocracoke Station keeper was James W. Howard. The steamer had run hard aground due to the typically dense Outer

The original Ocracoke Life-Saving Service Station. Howard and family, 1894, Lorena on left. Ocracoke Island Journal, 1891, 40–44, Courtesy of Philip Howard.

Banks fog. (Some say it is thick as Pea Island Soup.) Similar to the episode of the *Lank*, the *Cragside* presented harassing obstacles, as well as the saving of all aboard except one. Unlike the *Lank*, these obstacles were unnecessarily man-made.

A Disastrous String of Decisions Ignoring Life-Saving Service Advice

Against the imploring advice of the United States Life-Saving Service time and time again,[5] *Cragside*'s captain made the number one mistake by immediately sending out one of his ship's boats. One of its crew, seaman Andrew Last, drowned when the boat capsized.

What the captain did correctly was to blow the vessel's steam whistle as a distress signal. Naturally, that was quickly picked up by the nearby surfman on beach patrol who, by standard operating procedure (SOP), immediately returned to his station with the news to prepare for rescue. Arriving on scene, however, they found the fog was so thick that the vessel could not be seen. Efforts to locate the position were by continued steam whistle soundings. To let the *Cragside* know that rescue was at hand, the lifesavers fired the standard Coston flares.[6]

"At about 11 o'clock the fog settled a little so that the mastheads could be seen, and the crew went off alongside and offered their

DISTINGUISHING BOAT TERMS

Ship's boat—these are small boats carried on the larger vessel used in calm to go ashore or used in distress to escape ship sinking. Often referred to by the public as "lifeboats." However, see next.

Lifeboat—a specific design vessel used by the United States Life-Saving Service. These were larger and heavier craft used by stations with calmer waters. Not like the "lifeboats" on the *Titanic*, and so forth.

Surfboat—a completely different specific design vessel used by the United States Life-Saving Service. Used only at stations with high, rough surf. These were smaller and lighter with a bow shape at both ends.

services," the *Annual Report* tells us.[7] Then, the second tragic captain's decision, again, against the advice of the Life-Saving Service. Sinclair declined the assistance offered by the lifesavers. To cover his bet, however, he did ask them to standby, which they did remaining onboard the ship itself until 5:00 a.m. the next morning, when they returned ashore to their station. The captain and the keeper had prior agreed on a signal if the situation changed to require the surfmen's assistance. To add to the false sense of security, the report says, "It should be noted that at the time the vessel grounded, and during the night, the sea was comparatively smooth, and there was consequently no immediate danger to the people on board."[8]

True to the meaning of the later US Coast Guard motto, *Semper Paratus*,[9] the Ocracoke lifesavers remained "Always Ready" by keeping a close watch on the steamer even after they had returned to their station. They knew that conditions could suddenly get worse; and they did. The surf had risen and was becoming dangerously violent. Captain Sinclair now made the next move by hoisting the prearranged signal. The lifesavers launched their trusty surfboat and struggled mightily to reach the steamer. Keeper Howard "again endeavored to persuade the captain to let him land all hands by the boat before the surf became too rough,"[10] but, unwisely, Captain Sinclair again refused. Instead, he asked Keeper Howard to deliver a telegram to Norfolk, via transmission from the Hatteras Village "telegraph station" (probably the Hatteras Village Weather Station), requesting wrecking tugs to come to his assistance. Sinclair seemed determined to accomplish a "do-it-yourself" rescue. Another bad decision.

The string continues: before Keeper Howard left the steamer, "the captain asked the keeper to be on hand to assist him in landing in case he decided to use his own boats. The keeper promised all the aid in his power but urged the captain not to attempt such a course, as the ship's boats would be unsafe."[11] By 2:00 that afternoon, the surf had become so dangerous and violent that it was completely engulfing the steamer *Cragside*. Worse yet, this now put the lifesavers in danger as Sinclair then panicked and raised the signal again for the "angels in oilskins" to come to his rescue. The rescue surfboat struggled valiantly, but almost in a "cliff-hanger" Hollywood movie scene, "when almost alongside the boat was checked by the insurmountable waves and ultimately driven back upon the beach."[12]

Being used to using a variety of techniques and properly trained in other resources, without hesitation the lifesavers knew what to do next—set up the beach apparatus. Unbelievably, things got worse before they got back. Earlier, the *Cragside* had stabilized herself by having anchor lines set at either end. Suddenly, one cable parted, which swung the ship broadside to the beach. Then the string of bad decisions continued. "To the consternation of [Keeper] Howard, who had reached the shore in advance of his crew, the [*Cragside*] sailors were observed hoisting out a boat. Howard instantly signaled to them not to make such a foolhardy attempt," but again it was dismissed. The ship's boat, not designed for rough surf, foundered with its crew of eight. The disastrous became ridiculous: "According to the keeper's testimony, a most singular feature of the proceeding was that all the men were laboring at the oars, and nobody appeared to be steering the boat." The outcome was predictable, and exactly what the lifesavers had consistently been giving advice *not* to do. A heavy breaker capsized the boat, throwing all eight into the ferocious waters.[13]

Semper Paratus once more—neighboring station Hatteras Inlet had their crew on scene. The Ocracoke crew had yet to return with the beach apparatus, and now *Cragside* had put Keeper Howard, his number 1 surfman, and some of the Hatteras Inlet crew in peril as they had little choice but to relaunch the surfboat and attempt to save those eight in the worst possible circumstances. All of which would have been avoided by initially following all of the lifesavers' advice.

Of course, the *Cragside* capsized crew inadvertently made things even more difficult for the lifesavers; instead of being in one close group, presenting one rescue target, they had separated into three groups: five huddled near the overturned boat, two apparently swimming successfully toward the shore, and one alone in a life-preserver, motionless. As in another Hollywood hero scene, the Ocracoke surfboat scooped up the group of five, looked to the two swimmers next but saw they had reached shore and were being taken care of, then proceeded to the motionless one. When the lifesavers reached sailor Andrew Last, he appeared to be dead. But the Life-Saving Service is about life saving, so an "attempt was made as soon as he could be landed to revive him by the method in vogue in the Service for the resuscitation of apparently drowned persons."[14] It was in vain, as he had apparently deceased from shock earlier.

Finally, Standard Procedures Successfully Prevail

The beach apparatus having been expeditiously established in place, a single Lyle gunshot started the productive "three-ring circus" of activity resulting in the rapid breeches buoy rescue of all fifteen crew remaining on the steamer *Cragside*. The standard procedures continued—survivors were brought to the station, given dry clothes and succor as needed, and given comfort, rest, and a place to stay—all at no cost to them.

The wrecking tugs finally arrived and set to work "heaving" the ship off the grounding. Yet another standard procedure often unnoticed "behind the scenes": the Ocracoke Station, as most of them at the time, did not have enough space to house the entire crew of survivors, so, some "were billeted for a few days at the Durant's Station, at the north side of Hatteras Inlet, until the salvage company had the vessel in such a position that they could safely return on board. The steamer floated off and proceeded to Norfolk on March 21 in a damaged condition and with the loss of part of her cargo."[15]

Captain Sinclair sent a lengthy letter of explanation and thanks to Keeper Howard.[16]

Wreck and Rescue of the Cragside by the Numbers
- a ship large enough to have 182.5 tons per crew member
- thirty-one days between the wreck of *Nathaniel Lank* and *Cragside*, less than sixty miles apart
- five ignored sound pieces of advice from years of experience, with disastrous consequences

- two trips of the surfboat
- fifteen trips of the breeches buoy
- twenty-two lives saved
- one life lost

Coming Full Circle

It is now easy to see—and appreciate—why the US Life-Savers' work was of deep interest to religious leaders. It was a straightforward analogy for preachers and ministers in sermons and writings to compare how the men of the United States Life-Saving Service saved one soul at a time as the men of the cloth were doing the same thing. In each case, the rescuers offered salvation whether or not the victim wanted or requested it. In each case, the victims were led to water.

In all cases, the survivors were born again into a new life.

Post-Script

OCRACOKE, NORTH CAROLINA, February 26, 1891.

Lieutenant W. A. FAILING,
Assistant Inspector Life-Saving Stations,
Elizabeth City, North Carolina

 I, W. L. Sinclair, master of the British steamer Cragside, do hereby certify that on the evening of the 20th of February 1891, my vessel, during a dense fog, stranded on Ocracoke beach, one mile from Hatteras Inlet. Half an hour after stranding the crew of the Ocracoke Life-Saving Station came alongside and told me if I wished to leave the ship they would take all the crew on shore. I replied that I would endeavor to get the steamer off, with the understanding that I was to make a signal if the sea made, and I wanted to be taken off by the beach-apparatus gear. On the afternoon of the 21st the wind increased and the sea made very rough, so that the vessel parted one of her cables and commenced to drag the other one home. As the ship drove broadside on the beach, and the sea was breaking all over her, I hoisted signal to be taken off. My chief officer thought he could reach the beach in one of our own boats, and in making the attempt the boat was swamped in the breakers. One A. B., named Albert Last, was lost, and I am of the opinion that he died through the shock, and was not drowned, as he was suffering with heart trouble, and had a life preserver on. I also beg to state that great praise is due to Captain Howard and his crew, for they did all that it was possible for men to do, and the Life-Saving Service should not be held responsible for the loss of life that occurred. I may also mention that the appliances used by the United States Life-Saving Service are all that could be desired.

Respecting our treatment after being landed in the breeches buoy I can say we received the greatest kindness at the station, and that the lost seaman received proper burial at the hands of the crew.

W. L. SINCLAIR,
Master Steamship Cragside.[17]

IV.

THE ROUTINE

CHAPTER 9

US LIFE-SAVING STATION 12, KITTY HAWK

1878 TO 1915

The surfmen of the United States Life-Saving Service were not just national idols as the "storm warriors" and the "rescue heroes" of America's coasts; they were also the ultimate community providers and all-around "good guys." They did it all.

It is only natural to think of the men of the United States Life-Saving Service in dramatic, daring, successful shipwreck rescues; they did that a lot, more than 177,000 times! Everything they did was by teamwork. When a wreck occurred in the district monitored by one station, the keeper would immediately notify his neighboring stations by telegraph, then telephone, then radio, to come or standby to assist. In the majority of shipwreck rescues, there were two or three stations involved, with the original taking the lead. Most of the time, the other stations did physically assist; other times, they were on standby if needed.

Their other major function regarding shipwrecks was to help prevent them! On their nighttime beach patrols, the surfmen carried lanterns and flares. When they spotted a ship perilously close to shore, they would warn them by waving lantern signals. So, in addition to everything else they did, the Life-Saving Service also duplicated the single function of

An excellent period painting of multiple stations responding to an incident. There are two ship-wrecks and five different life-saving station crews. One, on the far left, is launching a rescue boat into the surf. Above them, on the beach, another station arrives with its beach cart. The lower left crew has set up the breeches buoy and is already retrieving a survivor. To their right is another crew who just fired off the Lyle gun to set up the breeches buoy rescue. Finally, on the far right, the fifth crew is launching their surfboat.
WikiMediaCommons.

the Lighthouse Service. Amazingly, they also made a few similar warnings during daytime watches. These incidents were all recorded. Every station was required to also record the passing of every ship, in both directions, and its type, done every day during daylight hours.

But the whole truth is, the men of the United States Life-Saving Service did *far* more than all that! That is the purpose of this chapter. One station that had very few major rescues in its thirty-seven years as a US Life-Saving station—the Kitty Hawk Station—was chosen on purpose to graphically illustrate this point. The Service issued highly detailed, voluminous *Annual Reports* during its existence. Each and every time that Kitty Hawk was recorded, it is noted below.

Refences in regular type are all direct quotes from the *Annual Reports* for that year. Some spelling, punctuation, and grammar have been changed. Note this possible source of confusion: each *Annual Report* was done for the fiscal year ending June 30 of that year. So, events after June 30 that year will appear in next year's annual report. *Comments in italics are author's editorials.*

Next is a copy of the table of contents for the 1912 *Annual Report*. The sections remained much the same for each issue from 1878 until 1914, save for a few special reports, such as the notable one in the 1878 issue, "Report Of Lieut. D. A. Lyle, Ordinance Dept., USA, Upon Life-Saving Ordinance."

ANNUAL REPORT OF THE

United States Life-Saving Service

FOR THE FISCAL YEAR ENDED JUNE 30

1912

TABLE OF CONTENTS.

Page

ORGANIZATION--. 5

STATEMENT OF OPERATIONS DURING YEAR. 11

RESTORATION OF THE APPARENTLY DROWNED. . . . . - - - - -.27

AWARDS OF LIFE-SAVING MEDALS-- . 37

DISASTERS TO VESSELS INVOLVING LOSS OF LIFE. 47

ILLUSTRATIVE INSTANCES OF RESCUE AND SALVAGE WORK-----. 61

LETTERS ACKNOWLEDGING SERVICES OF LIFE-SAVING CREWS. 91

PERIODS OF EMPLOYMENT OF SURFMEN. 107

APPROPRIATIONS AND EXPENDITURES... 111

BLUE ANCHOR SOCIETY, ETC- 119

TABULAR STATEMENT OF CASUALTIES To VESSELS WITHIN THE FIELD OF OPER

ATIONS OF THE LIFE-SAVING SERVICE. --- 121

TABULAR STATEMENT OF CASUALTIES To VESSELS IN UNITED STATES WATERS,

AND TO AMERICAN VESSELS AT SEA, ETC. 167

SUPPLEMENTAL STATISTICS FOR YEAR 1911. 207

PLACES WHERE VESSELS HAVE STRANDED DURING LAST TEN YEARS. 213

Beginning of Annual Reports from 1879 to 1914 Extracts

1878/1879

Not long after the telephone was invented in the mid-1870s, it became a vital aid to the life-saving stations. It became standard operating procedure that when one station spotted a wreck, the keeper of that station would immediately telephone to keepers of his neighboring stations to his north and south to standby ready to assist. It was so important that most stations' daily log began with "telephone test made."

The telephones referred to in the last annual report as placed by the Chief Signal-Officer of the Army at the several stations between Cape Henry and Kitty Hawk, in connection with the telegraph line of the Signal Service upon that coast, have proved, as was anticipated, of great advantage to this service, and their usefulness as an appliance completely demonstrated. The Chief Signal-Officer has recently established a telegraph-line along the coast from Cape Henlopen to Cape Charles, in the Fifth District, for the uses of his office, and it is gratifying to state that he contemplates extending the benefits of the telephone to the several life-saving stations upon that coast. (60)

1880: No events recorded.

1881: No events recorded.

1883: No events recorded.

1884: *Typical straightforward successful rescue and assist by brother station. Use of surfboat and beach apparatus.*

October 3. The schooner *Luola Murchison*, of and from New York, bound to Savannah, Georgia, laden with phosphate, and having a crew of eight men, stranded at a quarter past 4 in the morning nearly abreast of the Kitty Hawk Station (Sixth

District), coast of North Carolina, and was soon afterwards discovered by the patrol. The wind was blowing a fresh gale from the northeast and the surf was rough. The boat was launched and proceeded to the vessel, the life-saving crew arriving on board at half past 5. They immediately assisted in running an anchor off shore to keep the vessel from working farther onto the beach. By the time this was done the crew of the Kill Devil Hills Station arrived, and at the master's request the two crews landed all the personal effects, although the sailors remained on board. After the baggage was safe the Kill Devil Hills crew returned to their station and the Kitty Hawk crew kept watch on the vessel, ready to go off at a moment's notice, word having been sent to Norfolk for the assistance of wreckers. On the afternoon of the 4th the schooner fell over on her starboard side and the sea made a complete breach over her, compelling the master to make signal of his wish to abandon her. The state of the sea prevented the surf boat from getting alongside; the beach apparatus was brought into use and the entire crew were safely landed and conducted to the station. (108)

On the 5th the wrecking-steamer *V. J. Peed* arrived from Norfolk, and the master and crew of the *Murchison* were again carried on board to assist in the operations for saving their vessel. The wrecking company made strenuous exertions to get her off, working upon her until November 20, when she bilged, and all further efforts had to be abandoned. The hull and cargo became a complete loss, the only property saved being the sails, rigging, and outfit. The life-saving crew did all in their power to aid in getting the schooner afloat and afforded shelter to both sailors and wreckers whenever by stress of weather they were compelled to suspend operations and seek refuge on shore. (108–9)

It never seemed to be easy.

[September 21] At sunrise of this date the schooner *C. W. Lewis*, of Thomaston, Maine, from Brunswick, Georgia, bound to Boston, Massachusetts, with a cargo of lumber, was discovered at sea, six miles south east of the Kitty Hawk Station (Sixth District), coast of North Carolina, dismasted and having a signal of distress displayed on a pole over the stern. The surf-boat of the station was launched through a heavy line of breakers, and after a pull of two and a half hours arrived alongside the hulk. Two men only were on board, and from them it was learned that the *Lewis* was found dismasted and abandoned by the schooner *Mary Bradford*, to which vessel they belonged. The *Lewis* was in tow of the *Bradford* for thirty-six hours, when the tow-line parted. This occurred on the 18th, and the *Bradford* proceeding on, to obtain steam assistance, the men were left to take care of themselves and without any provisions to sustain them. After drifting some hours and finding the vessel getting into shoal water, they let go both anchors and waited for assistance. When the station crew arrived the two men were in a pitiable plight. They were exhausted from their labors at the pumps and were nearly famished. The steam-tug *Battler*, of Baltimore, hove in sight shortly after the surf-boat arrived alongside the hulk, and as soon as it was possible, she was boarded for provisions for the starving men. The *Battler* then, by the aid of the station crew, got a line to the *Lewis*, and, the anchors being slipped, she steamed up the coast with the wreck in tow for Baltimore. (95).

Assisting any way that they can.

[October 13] Shortly before 6 o'clock in the evening the wrecking steamer *Victoria J. Peed*, of Norfolk, anchored abreast of the Cape Henry Station (Sixth District), coast of Virginia, and made signal for a boat. The life-saving crew boarded her and found that she was from a vessel ashore on the Isaac Shoal, and that the captain desired to send a telegram to Norfolk, Virginia, for further instructions. The surfmen took it ashore, and upon receiving a reply, after dark, transmitted it by signal to the steamer, which at once proceeded to the assistance of a vessel ashore down the coast at Kitty Hawk, North Carolina. (The schooner *Luola Murchison*, wrecked on October 3; 108)

1885: *Again, the importance of the telephones:*

The telephonic communication announced in last year's report as having been established between nineteen stations on the New Jersey coast, has more than justified the anticipation of advantages to be derived from it. The utility and practicability of the establishment of the system between the stations upon the coast may safely be considered as settled, and this communication between all contiguous stations and also between many isolated stations and the nearest settlements, where it can be provided without excessive expense, is desirable. Seven additional stations on the New Jersey coast, namely, those between Barnegat Inlet and New Inlet, are being supplied with this accessory, and preparations for its introduction into fourteen stations on the coast of North Carolina, located between Kitty Hawk and Hatteras Inlet, are in progress. When this work is completed all the stations on the New Jersey coast, with the exception of the Little Beach Station, situated upon an island, from Sandy Hook as far south as Atlantic City, and the entire coast from Cape Henry, Virginia, to Hatteras Inlet, North Carolina, will be provided for in this respect. In this connection the thanks of the Service must be expressed to the Chief Signal Officer of the Army, for his generous aid and co-operation. (34)

1886: No events recorded.

1887:

U.S. COMMISSION OF FISH AND FISHERIES

This is what Ralph Shanks meant when he wrote that the lifesavers were "of deep interest to medical, educational, religious and political leaders."

Washington, D.C., January 31, 1888. Hon. S. I. KIMBALL, General Superintendent U.S. Life-Saving Service.

Treasury Department: SIR: I have the honor to present the following report respecting the specimens contributed to the National Museum through the agency of the employees of the Life-Saving Service:

A common dolphin, Delphinus delphis, from Kitty Hawk Station, North Carolina. (James R. Hobbs, keeper.)

Nighttime beach patrol warning a ship in a storm away from shore.
Antique postcard; public domain.

Routinely helping the Lighthouse Service, a common occurrence:

> [November 19] The watchfulness of the south patrol of the Kitty
> Hawk Station, (Sixth District) coast of North Carolina, pre-
> vented a schooner, that was evidently unaware of her proximity to
> the beach, from stranding. While on his beat shortly after mid-
> night he discovered the vessel heading into danger and immedi-
> ately flashed a red Coston light. No sooner was the signal shown
> than she put about and gave the land a wide berth. (169).

*What is interesting about the report below is that it illustrates an important
detail in their communications at the time. Every station was connected by
telegraph to each other station, but only a few were then connected to the
outside world.*

> [January 2, 1887] The lookout of the Nag's Head Station,
> (Sixth District,) coast of North Carolina, in the afternoon of
> this date, sighted a schooner standing in towards the land with
> her ensign at half-mast, union down. At 4 o'clock she anchored
> about a mile offshore, abreast of the station. The weather was
> clear, with a moderate northwesterly wind and a rough sea.
> The life-saving crew immediately launched the surf-boat and
> pulled out to her. She was loaded with lumber, and proved to
> be the *Joseph Baymore,* of Philadelphia, Pennsylvania, bound
> home from Charleston, South Carolina, with eight men on
> board. The captain informed the keeper that the vessel was
> leaking and that the crew refused to work the pumps. The surf-
> men, therefore, promptly turned to and pumped the water out
> of her and offered to assist in any other way that they could,
> but as no further help was apparently desired, they finally
> returned ashore. The captain stated that the craft had been run
> in under the beach for fear she would fill and roll over outside,
> and in order to be near a life-saving station in case of accident.
> Bad weather set in and for a number of days it continued

stormy, the sea being so high that it was impossible to board her, although an attempt was made in the morning of the 5th, the life-saving crew getting as far as the outer bar, where their further progress was completely obstructed by the huge breakers. A strict watch was kept on the vessel, however, day and night, and several dispatches were sent off pursuant to her signals, which were made by prominently displaying a board marked with the message in large letters and which the station men deciphered by the aid of a glass [telescope]. On the morning of the 7th flags of distress were set in the rigging, and the word MUTINY was made out on the board. A surfman was at once sent on horseback to the telegraph office at Kitty Hawk, some nine miles up the coast, to report the condition of affairs, while the rest of the crew, for the second time, exhausted every means in efforts to launch their boat, but the wind and sea were so high that it was utterly impossible to get clear of the beach. Suddenly, at about noon, all the signals on the craft were taken down, sail was made, the chain slipped, and she stood away out of sight to the southward in the direction of Cape Hatteras. (209–10)

An almost identical situation occurred shortly after for a different station, which also needed to send a message to the Kitty Hawk telegraph office. Perhaps most interesting of all, this situation accounts for many in the world thinking the Wright brothers flight took place in Kitty Hawk. The brothers were working near, and getting significant help from, the Kill Devil Hills United States Life-Saving Service Station. When they succeeded on December 17, 1903, they sent a telegram home. But the nearest telegraph to the outside world was four-plus miles to the north: Kitty Hawk.

[January 26, 1887] At about half-past 5 o'clock in the evening a schooner stood in toward the shore and anchored about three miles north of the Kill Devil Hills Station (Sixth District), coast of North Carolina. The weather was stormy and it being evident that something was amiss the surfmen manned their boat and started out to her. After a hard pull they got alongside and ascertained that she was the *Delhi*, of Saco, Maine, on her way from Booth Bay, in the same State, to Jacksonville, Florida, with a cargo of ice and a crew of seven men. . . . The vessel was a mile and a half from the land, and with the wind and sea on shore it required the most skillful maneuvering to take the boat successfully through the surf, which seemed to rise up as if by magic. By excellent management, however, they reached the beach without accident and the next patrol carried the telegram to the Kitty Hawk Signal Station, nearly five miles up the coast, where it was transmitted. (222)

Another example of the many times that the United States Life-Saving Service assisted the United States Lighthouse Establishment.

[February 22, 1887] During rainy weather, at half past 8 o'clock in the first night watch, one of the patrolmen of the Kitty Hawk Station, (Sixth District,) coast of North Carolina, warned off with a Coston light a schooner sailing too near the beach for safety. She at once took heed of the signal and kept away out of danger. (232)

1888: No events recorded.

1889: *Illustrating so well why the term "service" was a vital part of their name.*

[September 9] In the evening the crew of the Kitty Hawk Station, (Sixth District) coast of North Carolina, floated the small sloop *Mary Ann*, of Elizabeth City, in the same State, which having been moored and left with no one on board during the afternoon, had been blown ashore in a sudden storm. She had brought up on the beach at the head of Kitty Hawk Bay, about three-fourths of a mile to the west ward of the station, and as the gale did not abate until after sunset, nothing could be done for the craft until that time. She was found upon her release to have sustained no damage. (107)

1890: *Their words but my emphasis added at end of this brief report.*

[November 6] On this date, in the morning, the lookout at the Pea Island Station (Sixth District) coast of North Carolina, sighted a vessel anchored several miles off shore with a signal of distress flying. She had lost her foremast, flying jib boom, and main topmast. As a steamer and two other vessels were seen to heave to and speak to her and then proceed, it was evident that she needed a tug[boat]; and the surf being too rough after the recent gales to go off to her in the boat the keeper telephoned up the coast to the United States Signal Service Observer at Kitty Hawk, twenty-odd miles to the northward, requesting that a tug be telegraphed for from Norfolk. The message was promptly forwarded, and by half past 6 o'clock in the evening a tug arrived and took the craft in tow for Hampton Roads. *This incident is another striking illustration of the value of the telephone System established by the Service on that desolate coast.* (203; emphasis added)

1891: No events recorded.

1892: *Good Samaritans, from* Annual Report *section "Services of Crew" (miscellaneous).*

[August 1] Shelter and succor Kitty Hawk, North Carolina: Four young men, unable to return to the mainland on account of the weather were given shelter during the night at the station. (94)

1893: *From* Annual Report *section "Services of Crew"—continued.*

[December 23] British Schooner *Chantauguan,* Kitty Hawk, North Carolina: Dismasted and compelled to anchor: out of drinking water. Seeing her boat coming ashore, warned her not to attempt to land through heavy surf; boarded vessel and supplied her with water; then sent telegram for tug, which came and towed schooner into port. (102)

American Tug, *Hercules,* Whales Head, North Carolina: Unable to locate dismasted schooner for which she was looking; had given up search, and was standing back up the coast. Launched surfboat, intercepted tug, and directed her to Kitty Hawk, where she found the vessel and towed her to Norfolk. (102)

1894:

[June 9] Dory; no name . . . Kitty Hawk, North Carolina. Adrift. Towed it ashore and hauled it up on beach clear of surf. (158)

1895: *Standard Beach Patrol:*

[January 20] Barge (Trinidad Sugar Co.) No. 1, Kill Devil Hills, North Carolina. Broke adrift from tug and stranded early in the morning, three-quarters of a mile north of station. As the life-saving crew had gone to the tug Manatee (see next case), stranded south of the station, she was discovered by the patrol from Kitty Hawk Station, to whom— as the vessel was well up on the beach—the two men on board threw a line and were safely landed with his assistance. The men came to Kill Devil Hills Station, where the keeper cared for them. Two days later ran hawser to the tug *Asher J. Hudson*, which floated barge and towed her to Norfolk. Transferred the sailors with their effects to the tug. (146)

They do everything!

1895:

[February 8] Skiff; no name. . . ! Kitty Hawk, North Carolina. Caught in the ice with a young man on board. Three men who attempted his rescue were unable to pull back to the shore against the strong gale. Keeper rescued the entire party with sailboat and towed their skiff ashore. (153)

[February 23] Sloop; no name . . . Kitty Hawk, North Carolina. Washed up on the beach. Stripped her and advertised for owner. (157)

[March 11] Kitty Hawk, North Carolina. Seven fishermen, whom [*sic*] stress of weather had compelled to seek harbor in Kitty Hawk Bay, came to the station thoroughly drenched with water. The keeper provided them with dry clothing from the supply of the Women's National Relief Association while their own apparel was being dried and gave them food and shelter until the following afternoon, when the weather moderated sufficiently for them to proceed to their camp. (222)

THE WOMEN'S NATIONAL RELIEF ASSOCIATION.

The supplies of clothing furnished annually to the stations since 1880 for the use of shipwrecked persons have been liberally continued during the past year by the Women's National Relief Association, and have, as usual, done much to relieve the discomfort and distress incident to marine disasters. Those who have come drenched, half-frozen, bruised, and in many cases unconscious from wrecks, and have experienced the timely relief such stores afford, can most fully appreciate the inestimable benevolence which renders them available.

Within the period covered by this report eighty instances occurred in which articles supplied by the association were furnished to those in need, as follows:

Long national list included Kitty Hawk:

September 19, 1896; the crew of the steamer *Fredk de Barry*, at the Kitty Hawk Station, coast of North Carolina, September 23, 1896; eight men from a capsized boat near the Kitty Hawk Station, coast of North Carolina. (57)

A lengthy, detailed report follows and is summarized thusly: The passenger steamer Fredk de Barry *was beached in a gale several miles from Kitty Hawk. There was no imminent danger to the passengers, but the Kitty Hawk lifesaver crew assisted to remove "portable property" and then returned to their station. Meanwhile, wrecking steamer* William Coley, *named for her master and agent, began attempts to refloat the passenger steamer. It took several days. On the third day, the* William Coley *launches a small boat headed for the beach with seven crew and Captain Thomas. It strikes the bar, is rolled over by a wave, and all eight are in the surf. Mr. Coley sees the disaster, ties a rope around himself, wades into the surf, and retrieves all seven sailors. Captain Thomas had disappeared. The* Annual Report *continues,*

All the witnesses testify, and the circumstances clearly show, that nothing could have been done to save the man even if the life-saving crew had known of the capsize the instant it occurred. The station is two and one-half miles from, the scene, and the man was drowned within ten or fifteen minutes. The whole affair was over, says Captain Nelson, "long before any help could have arrived from the station. "I saw Surfman Hayman," he adds, "in the surf assisting the boat's crew to land, and he behaved with great coolness and courage." "He rendered valuable aid in the work of rescue," testifies Captain William Coley, "and did all that any man could do. No aid was possible from the keeper and crew of the station." (27)

[December 11] Str. *Teaser* . . . Kitty Hawk, North Carolina.
——Missed the channel and grounded lightly. Keeper and surfman answered steam signal and went alongside. She was soon floated, and keeper guided her through the channel into Currituck Sound. Gave the master directions for proceeding to destination. (145)

1898: *Help is always available if needed.*

[October 7] American schooner. *Marvin D. White*, Kitty Hawk, North Carolina. Stranded on a shoal 4 miles westward of station and flying a distress signal. Station boat went to her assistance, but as the tide did not serve for floating her, and as she was in no immediate danger, the surfmen returned to station, promising to go back the next morning. At that time, keeper and two surfmen went out again and found that the high tide had floated the schooner. Keeper piloted her up Currituck Sound to a safe anchorage and telephoned to keeper at Caffeys Inlet to pilot her to her destination, as master was unfamiliar with the channel. (100)

1899: No events reported.

1900:

[October 7] British steamer *Honiton*, Paul Gamiels Hill——Stranded at low water during a fog, 2¼ miles S. of station. Life-saving crews from both Paul Gamiels Hill and Kitty

Hawk stations boarded her, took telegrams ashore for her master, and then assisted to plant two anchors to seaward. At high water she floated without apparent injury and continued her course for Norfolk. (132).

1901:

> [November 9] American schooner, *Ella Creef*, Kill Devil Hills and Kitty Hawk, North Carolina–Dragged anchor during a strong NW wind and stranded in Kitty Hawk Bay. On the 16th surfmen from both Kill Devil Hills and Kitty Hawk stations assisted the master to pry her up and put skids under her bottom, but they were unable to move her into the water. On the 17th surfmen from both stations again went to her and, with the aid of some fishermen, succeeded in launching her without injury. (97)

1902: No events reported.

1903: No events reported. *However, on December 17 of this year, Kitty Hawk's neighboring station—Kill Devil Hills—had a very exciting (but still secret) event. It involved two brothers from Dayton, Ohio, who did the right thing.*
    The only event recorded in the Annual Report *of that day was for Station Mosquito Lagoon, Florida, "The keeper provided the master of a house boat with fresh water, his stock having given out" (111).*

1904: *The US Life-Saving Service really did it all, including . . .*

> Stations Paul Gamiels Hill and Kitty Hawk—Surfmen from these stations took charge of the body of a dead man, found on the beach by a fisherman, and, after removing several articles of value, buried the remains. It was later learned that the body was that of Captain J. M. Cookson, and on the 30th the crew of

Kitty Hawk station disinterred it and delivered to responsible parties. (185; *this entry was in the section titled "Miscellaneous Services of Crew"*)

[January 3] Kitty Hawk, North Carolina. Assistance at fire— Four surfmen assisted in saving the personal property of Mr. Walter W. Best, whose house was totally consumed by fire. (188)

1905: No events reported.

1906: *Typical teamwork success:*

[December 9] Kitty Hawk, North Carolina, America steamer *Aragon* —The patrol, discovering the vessel perilously near the beach, hastened to the station to report her situation to the keeper; but before he could reach the end of his beat she struck the beach about ¾ mile S. of the station. The keeper at Kill Devil Hills station, being notified by telephone, the beach apparatus was taken to the wreck, the Lyle gun set up, and a line fired over the stranded craft. The crew from Kill Devil Hills now arrived upon the scene and aided in the work of rescuing the ship-wrecked people. The hawser was successfully run off and twenty-one persons, with their baggage, were safely landed on shore in the breeches buoy and taken to the station and succored for four days. On the 13th instant the wreckers arrived and began operations to float the vessel; their efforts proving successful, she was towed to port. (112)

A very busy day!

[December 9] Kitty Hawk, North Carolina, Barge, *Thomas A. Goddard.* During a NE gale prevailing on this date a telephone message reached the keeper apprising him of the fact that a steamer had stranded near Kitty Hawk station and that a barge she had been towing had been cast adrift offshore to prevent it going on the beach. At about the same time the N. and S. patrols reported at the station at Nags Head that they had sighted the barge drifting towards the shore, where it appears that she soon brought up. After notifying Kill Devil Hills crew to come down and lend a hand in the work the beach apparatus was quickly transported down the beach by horses and set up abreast of the barge, which having brought up on her anchors was drifting about in the gale and breakers. Owing to the wreck not remaining stationary, it was with the greatest difficulty that a shot was sent over her. On the first two attempts the shot line parted, but at the third the line fell on board and was hauled off by the sailors. The barge now swung completely around, fouling the whip line, her cables parted, and she struck the beach with terrific force, the heavy sea making a clean breech over her. There was no time to be lost. The whip was soon cleared, however, the hawser run off and secured, and the entire crew of 5 men brought safely to shore in the breeches buoy. The destitute men were taken to the station and succored for four days, also dry clothing being furnished them from the stores of the Women's National Relief Association. The master remained at the station until the 18th, hoping to save his vessel, but she continued to break up and soon became a mere hulk. (113)

1907: No events reported.

1908: No events reported.

1909:

Schooner *Charles S. Hirsch* ~ 29 October 1908, involved Stations Paul Gamiels Hill, Kitty Hawk, and Caffeys Inlet. (46–51)

1910: *Here is one reason the Lighthouses are today better known than the Life-Saving stations. The former were built out of bricks and lasted hundreds of years. The latter were built of untreated lumber and would last twenty years or so. Here we find that the 1878 Kitty Hawk Station, now thirty-two years old, has a replacement under construction. Even then, it would not be completed until 1915.*

REBUILDING AND IMPROVEMENT OF STATIONS

It was mentioned in last year's report that a desirable site had been selected for a station at Galveston, ex., to replace the one destroyed in the great Galveston flood of September 8, 1900. The construction of the new station is now well advanced. New stations are also under construction at Kitty Hawk and Chicamacomico, N.C., the old structures at those places, built many years ago, being of antiquated type, and too small to house the modern boats and life-saving appliances of the service. (23)

1911: *This is an excellent example of how the lifesaving stations worked together. At first, it might seem that the Kitty Hawk Station was slow in arriving. However, realize this: they were six miles away, in the darkness, covering wet sand on foot, and it could not have easy manually hauling a two-thousand-ton beach apparatus cart and/or a four-thousand-pound surfboat.*

[December 12] Shortly before daylight the south patrol of the Paul Gamiels Hill Station [NC] discovered the three-masted schooner *Wm. B. Davidson* stranded, 1½ miles south of his station and 150 yards offshore. When the vessel struck her rudder was carried away, as was also the lifeboat and davits. The patrolman burned a Coston signal to inform those on board that assistance was near, then hastened to the station. After telephoning news of the wreck to the Kitty Hawk station, 6 miles to the southward, the Paul Gamiels Hill crew went to the wreck with the breeches-buoy apparatus. A line was fired squarely across the vessel. The breeches-buoy apparatus was quickly rigged up, and the schooner's crew of 6 men were safely landed. The crew of the Kitty Hawk station did not arrive on the scene until after the rescue had been made, but they helped to save the personal property of the sailors, which was brought ashore in the breeches buoy. The schooner was totally lost, and but a small part of her cargo of lumber was saved. (73)

1912: No events reported.

1913: *Routine Teamwork: if at first you don't succeed . . .*

[February 18] The 1,104-ton schooner *Montrose W. Houck*, from Port Tampa, Florida, to Baltimore, Md., with a cargo of phosphate rock, misstayed, dragged her anchors, and went ashore a third of a mile east of the Paul Gamiels Hill [NC] Station. Her crew of nine men were rescued by a boat's crew of surfmen from the Paul Gamiels Hill, Caffeys Inlet, and Kitty Hawk Stations, after a hard battle in a fresh wind, strong current, and high sea. The vessel and her cargo, having a combined value of $70,000, were totally lost.

About 1:30 a.m. the north patrol from the first-named station discovered the schooner near the beach and heading directly on shore. The patrol burned a warning signal and the vessel anchored. On learning of her dangerous proximity to the land, Keeper Harris sent a telephone call for a revenue cutter in the hope of getting assistance in time to prevent her from coming ashore. Sometime during the forenoon an International Code signal was displayed aboard the schooner asking for assistance. Soon after the signal went up the vessel began to drag. She stranded about 11:45 a.m. 500 yards from the beach.

After calling up the two adjacent stations, Keeper Harris hauled his beach apparatus and surfboat abreast of the vessel. An attempt was promptly made by him to put a No. 7 shot line over her, using 6 ounces of powder. The shot fell short. By this time the two other life-saving crews previously mentioned arrived. As the great distance between the schooner and the shore rendered the prospect of effecting a rescue by the medium of line communication extremely uncertain, the life-savers now resorted to a surfboat, and to such good purpose that the shipwrecked sailors were soon safely landed. (108)

1914: No events reported.

1915: *On January 28, 1915, the United States Life-Saving Service merged with the United States Revenue Cutter Service to become the United States Coast Guard. The* Annual Reports *were discontinued in 1932.*
The Rest of Their Official Activities: **Daily**
See details in my volume 1, chapter 1, and more in chapter 1 of this volume.
The Rest of Their Official Activities: **Occasionally**
Same as above.
Off the Record: **Unofficially**
Again.

CHAPTER 10
BARKENTINE *ANGELA*, MARCH 5, 1883

There are hundreds upon hundreds of shipwreck and rescue accounts faithfully documented in great detail in the Annual Report of the Operations of the United States Life-Saving Service *for each year from 1876 to 1914. Most are dramatic; some extremely so, such as the rescues of the* Ephraim Williams, *the* Priscilla, *the* E. S. Newman, *and the* Aaron Reppard. *Some are very sad indeed, such as the* Strathairly, *the double-act of the* Huron *and* Metropolis, *the* Central America, *and the inexplicable* Nuova Ottavia. *A few, but not many, are even humorous. This is one of those stories!*

This will involve an intentional grounding, the response of two neighboring stations, a self-rescue attempt, a temporary disappearance mystery, and, finally, a happy and humorous ending.

The Wreck

The barkentine *Angela* was transitioning from Genoa, Italy, to Baltimore, Maryland, bound with a cargo of iron ore from Cartagena, Spain, had a crew of ten men, and was mastered by Captain Carlo. *Angela* was nearing the American East Coast, then in the vicinity of the North Carolina Outer Banks. The vessel, which had earlier sprung a leak that continued to worsen during the crossing, was beginning to sink and was run aground to save the lives of her crew. She was stranded at midnight three hundred yards from shore, and a quarter of a mile south of the Paul

Typical barkentine of the period. Painting by William Edgar of the American barkentine Thomas P. Emigh.
WikiMediaCommons.

Gamiels Hill Life-Saving Station (Sixth District). At the time the sea was high, the surf raging, and the wind blowing freshly from the north. The wreck was immediately seen by the two patrolmen just starting from the station on their respective beats, one of which was clearly Paul Gamiels Hill and the other was her neighboring stations, either Caffeys Inlet to her north or Kitty Hawk to her south, the *Annual Report* does not say. Whichever it was, one of the patrolling surfmen promptly fired the red Coston light as a signal to those on board and gave the alarm. The keeper of Paul Gamiels Hill Station, William H. O'Neal, at once roused all hands, and they turned out with the surfboat and beach apparatus. As was usually the case, they speedily got abreast of the wreck and from that time until morning were engaged in efforts to communicate with the grounded barkentine via international signal flags.

The steepness of the beach at Paul Gamiels Hill Station would strongly play into the outcome of this story. First, it caused greater than normal surf and breakers. Therefore, use of the surfboat was ruled out in favor of using the beach apparatus with the Lyle gun and breeches buoy.

Two shots fired in succession fell short of the wreck and a third parted the line; this was not an uncommon occurrence. Rarely would the shot line simply break, since they were inspected and maintained routinely, but it did happen occasionally. More common was the exploding black powder when the gun was fired, which would ignite the line and slowly burn it through in flight. Never giving up, a fourth line reached the vessel. Then something strange happened: this process always involves someone onboard the ship retrieving the shot line and starting to haul it into the ship. But nothing was happening, so the lifesaving crew waited, wondering why the sailors did not haul the line onboard. "The solution came at daybreak, when the barkentine's men were discovered out at sea in the ship's boat, beyond the line of breakers, having abandoned the vessel under the conviction that she was going to pieces."[1] They were attempting to rescue themselves! But their lack of knowledge of the circumstances and even the local language would have gotten them in serious, if not fatal, trouble. That is what the United States Life-Saving Service was for.

Looking back toward the beach from their ship's boat out at sea, the Italian crew saw the Paul Gamiels crew of lifesavers on the beach. So, they began rowing back that way to be professionally rescued. "But the lifesavers waved him back, displaying a large red flag as a warning. Soon the Italian tried again, was waved back a second time; he moved up the beach and headed in a third time but was still warned away. What he did not know was that the tide was at its highest and the beach at that particular spot was so steep that it was impossible to successfully guide a boat through the surf."[2] It would have been certain death for the entire Italian crew and probably some of the surfmen trying to save them.

Understandably confused and frustrated, and perhaps annoyed, the *Angela*'s captain, Carlo, at 9:00 a.m., directed his nine sailors to take the small ship's boat farther out to sea, beyond the breakers heading north. Perhaps more friendly people would be found there. "Four miles, five, seven, his crew rowed, until a building came into view and another group of men on the beach opposite."[3] This was the Caffeys Inlet

Caffeys Inlet LSS Station No. 10. Originally, the United States Life-Saving Service used the apostrophe for possessive station names but eventually dropped them.
Courtesy of US Coast Guard; public domain.

Life-Saving Service Station No. 5, with Keeper Austin the officer in charge. Here, the official record in the *Annual Report* becomes confusing, but apparently Keeper O'Neal of Paul Gamiels Hill notified Keeper Austin of Caffeys Inlet via telephone to be on the lookout for the Italian crew, which had been seen heading in that direction.[4]

Caffeys Inlet crew, as per the later Coast Guard motto *Semper Paratus*, were "always ready." They were on the beach with their surfboat ready to launch waiting to spot the *Angela* ship's boat. Soon it was spotted, and the surf had substantially subsided; Caffeys Inlet dutifully launched their surfboat. Still, in the half mile of rowing to get to the Italians, the Caffeys Inlet surfboat "shipped," or took on about a barrel, or more than fifty gallons, of salt water over wash. They returned five of the sailors to the beach and relaunched to retrieve the remaining five. "This time they even saved the captain's chest of books, papers, and instruments, and returned safely to the shore. It was then 11 o'clock in the forenoon."[5] The vessel and cargo were entirely lost.

Thus is the short, true, and somewhat amusing rescue story of the Italian barkentine *Angela* in March of 1883 on the northern shores of Dare County by the heroes of the United States Life-Saving Service Station Caffeys Inlet No. 5.

V.

HEARTBREAKING
FAILURES

CHAPTER 11

STEAMER *ARIOSTO*

THE "ENTIRELY NEEDLESS" TRAGEDY

This was a huge disaster that could have easily been averted. It is a story with negatives and positives. It is a story of a ship captain's confusion, the terror of panic, and the avoidable loss of thirty human lives. Unhappily, it was on Christmas Eve. Ironically, it took place in a year of enormous unavoidable tragedies. It is also the story of the amazing tenacity of American surfmen and lifesavers, and of their teamwork with neighboring stations and volunteering residents. Nevertheless, it is a story of yet another simple lesson still unlearned.

Prologue

The year 1899 on the North Carolina Outer Banks will always be remembered for the worst hurricane ever—with the most shipwrecks, destruction, and loss of lives on Hatteras Island and other Outer Banks locations recorded by that time. It was in August that storms would begin to receive names; but this one would forever be called San Ciriaco. The *Annual Report of the Operations of the United States Life-Saving Services* the year 1900 starts sternly: "The most calamitous, because entirely needless, loss of life during the entire year, or indeed for many recent years in the history of the Service, occurred on December 24, 1899, at the wreck of the British steamship *Ariosto* on the coast of North Carolina about 2 miles to the southward of the Ocracoke Life-Saving Station. Of 30 persons on board the vessel, 21 perished, while there was in the conditions *not the slightest necessity that a single one should have been lost.*"[1]

The Ship

The *Ariosto* was a schooner-rigged steel steam-powered vessel of 2,265 tons and was owned by R. McAndrews & Co. of London. Only seven years old at the time of this voyage, she was laden with very valuable cargo of wheat, cotton, lumber, and cottonseed meal valued at $1.5 million (approximately $45 million today). This large schooner was carrying thirty men, including officers, and commanded by Captain R. R. Baines. When lost, she was bound from Galveston, Texas, to Hamburg, Germany, via Norfolk, Virginia. The object of the call at Norfolk was to refill the coal bunkers. Due to its mid-Atlantic location and the size and ease of accessing its ports, the Hampton Roads area remains a major coal suppler of steamships today.

The Setting

It is not recorded whether or not "visions of sugar plums danced in their heads,"[2] but something similar would have been expected of the schooner's crew since this was late in the evening of December 23. But instead of hearing,

> *He sprang to his sleigh, to his team gave a whistle,*
> *And away they all flew like the down of a thistle.*
> *But I heard him exclaim, 'ere he drove out of sight,*
> *"Happy Christmas to all, and to all a good night!"*

It was not a good night; it would soon be a horrific nightmare.

Later that day, the weather began to worsen. Then, the *Annual Report* tells us, "At midnight the weather was thick all around, and heavy showers of rain passed over from time to time, while the sea was constantly making."[3] Winds were gusting forty to fifty miles per hour. Just before 4:00 a.m., while asleep in his cabin, Captain Baines was awakened by a request from the first mate to join him on deck. To his great surprise, Captain Baines saw that his ship was completely surrounded by "white water," meaning it was in shallow breakers, usually occurring only close to shore. This surprise slowly turned into terror as Baines tried to figure out where he was and what to do about the dangerous situation. He knew that he was somewhere off the North Carolina coast. Since he could not see land, he judged that they were most likely in the midst of the infamous Diamond Shoals, extending twenty miles out to sea from Cape Hatteras. If that were the case, immediate action was required.

Actually, the *Ariosto* was fifteen miles to the southwest, near Ocracoke Island and the Ocracoke US Life-Saving Service Station commanded by Keeper Captain James Howard. The wind and surf pushed the heavily laden cargo schooner farther into the breakers, where she grounded and was "bumping and thumping in such a manner that it seemed probable her masts would come down," comments Captain Baines in the *Annual Report*.[4] All hands scurried to the weather deck and began to fire off distress rockets; so far, the correct procedures.

Ship in violent storm with similar conditions to Ariosto. *Duncan MacFarlane's* The Emigrant Ship, Carnatic, of Boston in a Hurricane *(1847).* ***WikiMediaCommons.***

Then, a red flash of light was seen to the north, hopefully a sign of assistance. Indeed, it was. Standard operating procedures (SOP) for the United States Life-Saving Service were that, after spotting a shipwreck, the beach patrol would fire a red Coston flare. This one came from the Ocracoke Station beach patrol by Surfman Guthrie.

COSTON FLARE

Twenty-six-year-old Benjamin Franklin Coston was a promising inventor for the US Navy. He had been experimenting with color-coded night signals to allow communication between ships, but he died suddenly before completing his work. His twenty-one-year-old wife, Martha, was determined

COSTON'S MARINE SIGNALS
Percussion or Friction

The only signal recognized by the British Board of Trade in their report, and is used exclusively by the United States Government.

Distress Outfits for lifeboats in compliance with the rules and regulations of the Board of Steamboat Inspectors; friction or percussion.

Fog, Pilot and Distress Signals, all different steamship and yacht club distinguishing signals, friction or percussion, also regulation ship rockets and staves.

WATER LIGHTS
For Life Buoy, Embarkation or Deck Flares.

Distinguishing colors arranged and registered.

Send for our pamphlet entitled "Communication at Night on the Road at Sea."

Highest award, Gold Medal and Diploma, Jamestown Exposition, 1907.

Originators and largest manufacturers of marine night signals in the world.

COSTON SIGNAL CO., Inc.
7 Water St.   New York
Entrance on Moore St.   Telephone 3454 Broad

Deliveries made by Steam Lighters Day or Night

Coston signal–period advertisement flyer, 1913.
Courtesy of US Life-Saving Station No. 30, Ocean City, Maryland;
vintage advertisement; public domain.

to finish his work and did so in 1859. She explained the invention this way: "This is a very ingenious and effective semaphore, which commends itself from its simplicity. Three lights of different colors, white, red, and green, are so flashed or burned in combinations representing the numerals 1, 2, 3, 4, 5, 6, 7, 8, 9, 0, and also two letters, A and P (for time of day, a.m. or p.m.)—in all twelve combinations. The light is produced by the combustion of a peculiar pyrotechnic composition for each of the desired colors. A handle or holder is all that is necessary, ordinarily, to hold the selected color."[5]

The rough sea had already destroyed the starboard lifeboats and was now rolling the *Ariosto* so violently to the port side that Captain Baines feared the lifeboats on that side would also soon be lost. He immediately ordered them launched and for the crew to abandon ship. "Here was where the fatal mistake occurred," the *Annual Report* laconically states.[6]

From the earliest days of the Service, the lifesavers knew well that the number one cause of injury and death from shipwreck victims was leaving their ship in a panic. The lifesavers routinely conveyed this message in many ways. As we have seen earlier, to expedite the shipwreck crew's successful setup of the breeches buoy, the United States Life-Saving Service published a booklet of instructions with text and diagrams that was to be aboard all sailing vessels. It was titled "Instructions To [*sic*] Mariners In Case Of Shipwreck: With Information Concerning The Life-saving [*sic*] Stations Upon the Coasts of the United States."[7]

The strongest statements admonished the ship's crew to *not* launch lifeboats but, rather, to wait for the lifesavers.

Launching the ship's own boats *was* the fatal mistake—one that had been made so many times over so many years with the "entirely needless" loss of so many lives.

Confusing Circumstances

In his defense, if Captain Baine's assumption of his location had been correct, he had little other choice but to abandon ship, for he would have been as much as twenty miles from shore in a location infamous for wrecking ships. No US Life-Saving station would be anywhere near or able to assist that far out, or so he thought. But they had seen a flare; surely that meant rescue was imminent. It is hard to judge someone for panicking in such a terrifying situation when things were happening so fast. Panic, indeed, was the determining factor in launching the lifeboats: "It would appear that these entire operations were conducted with such haste that they were completed in less than 30 minutes from the moment the vessel stranded," from investigations by the Service found in the *Annual Report*.[8] Still, the captain's plan was not entirely flawed. His objective was to get the crew off the schooner into the two remaining lifeboats, but to have them lay on the lee side of the large schooner to be protected from the strong winds. Hopefully, they would, therefore, be safe until morning when their position could be more correctly determined. That was the plan. The reality was this: all but four—Captain Baines, Third Officer Reed, Chief Engineer Warren, and Carpenter Peltonen— had gotten away into the lifeboats. For those four, it was a happy accident. Soon afterward, both lifeboats capsized. The drama is described: "Twenty-six persons were now battling for their lives in one of the worst seas with which desperate men have ever contended. And yet one of them, Seaman Elsing, a man of infinite skill in the water and of brave heart and wonderful physical power, actually swam ashore, absolutely unaided even with so much as the slightest piece of wreckage to help bear him up."[9] All but four of them from the ironically named "lifeboats" drowned. Two were retrieved by the schooner, while two more remarkably were pulled from the rough surf by the lifesavers on the beach. It was reported by a *New York Times* article of the same day that "Captain Baines, on the wrecked vessel, as he saw his men perish—this mariner who had sailed the world over for twenty-five years—wept like a child."[10]

Monday Morning Quarterbacking—Hindsight

Captain Baines originally judged that his ship would go to pieces quickly and thus decided to abandon it. In fact, however, the ship remained completely intact for several days. Once the Ocracoke Station lifesaving crew was abreast of the wreck, Keeper Howard gave the signal "remain by your ship" using the international signal code flags. Much travail, obstacles to overcome, and coordination of plans and resources then occurred for the lifesavers to get into position. This is what they did. Routinely.

The Lifesavers Respond

Ocracoke Station's beach patrols, both the north and south, had spotted the wreck around 4:00 a.m. Christmas Eve. Upon returning to his station, Surfman Davie Williams, the north patrolman, found his crew already in motion. Starting out in the dark was not a problem, until the surfmen encountered a deep inlet scoured out by the San Ciriaco hurricane in August. Here they were assisted by five local citizens to get their heavy beach apparatus cart across. They reached the wreck by 5:30 and soon discovered half-conscious seaman Elsing, who had miraculously swum ashore by himself. He debriefed the surfmen to the situation the best he could, and they commenced immediately to set up the breeches buoy apparatus.

Anyone witnessing a modern reenactment of the beach apparatus drill is always amazed at the speed and complexity of the performance. It is a difficult procedure, requiring skill, knowledge, and experience. Yet it is done in the daytime, in the warm seasons, in great weather conditions. What the modern visitor may not realize is that the actual rescues were done under far more trying conditions. The modern reenactor surfmen simply bury the sand anchor quickly and plop down the Lyle gun in preferred locations. Not so for Keeper Howard's crew this dark and stormy night.

The Rescue Begins

Due to the high surf, they had to frequently relocate both the sand anchor and the Lyle gun as the ship was constantly moving. In addition, the schooner was at the very extreme range of the Lyle gun's shot. Then a miracle happened. The first shot expectedly fell short, so it was hauled back in. "And with it came a half-drowned man, who was later found to be Boatswain Andersen. He was unconscious, but was resuscitated by the surfmen, and subsequently told them that the [shot]line fell across him as he was struggling in the surf; that he had sufficient consciousness to hitch it around his arm and was thus drawn ashore—an almost miraculous escape from death."[11]

Inspired by the miracle, the surfmen lunged into the heavy surf, at times up to their necks, searching for more sailors. Several were found, but only Fireman Henroth was alive. Numerous shots continued to be fired but all fell short due to the distance and conditions. Neither the ship nor the lifesavers' equipment remained stationary; the schooner's continued movement and rolling in the surf required constant adjustments of the beach apparatus.

Here, the *Annual Report* compliments the Ocracoke surfmen: "For these reasons the operations were necessarily so extremely difficult that their completion without mishap affords the best of evidence that they were judiciously and skillfully conducted."[12] It was not until 11:00 a.m. that a number 4 shot line, the smallest, was successfully placed over *Ariosto*. But the difficulties remained. Numbers 7 and 9 shot lines were added so the heavy hawser could finally be sent out and all remaining on board could be safely taken ashore by the breeches buoy. It was at this time that Keeper Burrus and his crew—of the Durants Life-Saving Station—arrived to assist. They had left much earlier but, due to poor conditions, had to take a longer route.

Following long-standing nautical tradition, *Ariosto*'s Captain Baines was the last off the ship. When his feet hit the beach at 2:30 p.m., "a loud cheer was sent up by all the people who had by this time assembled."[13]

The *Annual Report* praised the Durants Station for their cooperation as well as complimenting the local citizenry. Interestingly, the *Report* specifically mentioned the resident family names of Stowe, O'Neal, and Austin, names still prominent in Ocracoke today. Still, it was made clear that "under the most unfortunate circumstances following the launching of the boats, and if all had remained patiently on board not one would have been lost." Just as so many had been told so many times before. An "entirely needless" loss of life, indeed.[14]

CHAPTER 12

THE UNFATHOMABLE TRAGEDY AND MYSTERY OF THE SCHOONER *ROBERT H. STEVENSON* WRECK

What follows is an incredible and essentially unknown saga of a lone survivor in Cape Hatteras, January 13, 1906.

The historic records of the schooner *Robert H. Stevenson* have largely been lost. She was only three years old when she disappeared forever on the infamous Diamond Shoals. Very little makes sense about the wreck and the subsequent non-rescue. As we shall see, there is a significant measure of mystery surrounding the entire affair. The degree of mystery ranks right up there with the famous *Carroll A. Deering*, also known as the "Ghost Ship of Diamond Shoals."[1] The unfathomable difference, however, is that while the *Carroll A. Deering* is extremely well known, the story of the schooner *Robert H. Stevenson* is virtually unheard of.

A Summary of the *Deering* Story

Much has been written and told about the ghost ship of Cape Hatteras—half a dozen books, a few documentaries, and hundreds of articles in magazines and newspapers. They all tell us details of the surprising discovery that is followed by the inexplicable scene that was found. Then, the theories emerged. Here is what was found:

> Prepared food was found in the galley, indicating a very sudden departure. The two lifeboats were missing. Also, critically missing were all the documents, charts, navigational instruments, and the chronometer. Whoever took these knew what they were doing, for these items were crucial for navigating anywhere, but especially in the Outer Bank's Graveyard of the Atlantic. It was confirmed that the anchors were indeed missing, as reported earlier at Cape Lookout.
>
> Further details that might have a bearing on the mystery were that red light distress signals had been sent up the mast. Inspection of the captain's cabin revealed a spare bed having recently been slept in and three pairs of boots that were left behind. Finally, Captain Wormell's handwritten log entries on the ship's map was replaced with another hand after January 23.[2]

The theories are intriguing and almost seduce the reader to conjure up their own. Many of the more popular theories are plausible, but not one explains all the details. My book *Shipwrecks of the Outer Banks: Dramatic Rescues and Fantastic Wrecks in the Graveyard of the Atlantic* offers its own teasing explanation in chapter 16. So, dear readers, do you have a theory for the mystery of the Schooner *Robert H. Stevenson*? Let's see what we know about what happened.

Early 1900s

If Hollywood had made a movie of the event of the wreck and the results of the *Robert H. Stevenson* during this time, it would have produced yet another extremely exaggerated story that no one would have believed—and everyone was likely to laugh at. But this was real.

At times, it may not seem so to the reader. There is scant public reference to this dramatic event. The account in the *Annual Report of the Operations of the United States Life-Saving Service for the Fiscal Year ending June 30, 1906*, has but a single word beside the schooner's name: "stranded." There is no article in David Stick's famous classic book, *Graveyard of the Atlantic: Shipwrecks of the North Carolina Coast*. There are only two small newspaper articles: one, a nine-inch column in the *New York Times* dated five days after the event, and the other a four-inch column in the *Boston Daily Globe* dated thirteen days after, albeit on the front page. Yet there were notable names involved in this story—the cities of Boston and Savannah, the country of Germany, a ship named *Europa*, and the most iconic name, the Diamond Shoals of Cape Hatteras, in the Outer Banks of North Carolina. Even stranger, at the risk of being repetitive, there was a significant amount of mystery surrounding the whole affair.

The Ship

Little can be found about this vessel. The *Robert H. Stevenson* was a 1,290-ton, four-masted schooner, built in Bath, Maine, in 1902,

ADRIFT ON GANGPLANK.

Castaway Saved. After. Three Days—
Twelve May Have Perished.

Special to The New York Times.

SAVANNAH, Ga., Jan. 17.—After having been adrift on a gangplank from 9 o'clock Saturday morning until 5 o'clock Monday afternoon, Karl Sumner, a seaman of the schooner Robert H. Stevenson was picked up at sea by the German steamer Europa, Capt. Keller, which arrived this afternoon from Philadelphia. Of the twelve others who were aboard the Stevenson, Sumner believes not one escaped.

He says the schooner was bound from Havana to Philadelphia, when last Saturday morning at 3 o'clock, during a northeaster, she went on Diamond shoals. Capt. Higbee had a lifeboat lowered and First Mate Lewis and two seamen had entered it when it was smashed against the vessel, the three men drowning before the eyes of their shipmates. A smaller boat was successfully launched and the women passengers, being the wife of Capt. Higbee and two of his relatives and a colored servant, were lowered into it The Captain, yielding to the entreaties of his wife, also entered. as did the second mate.

The option of remaining on the vessel was given to four other members of the crew by Capt. Higbee, as it seemed an even chance. They elected to reman and. saw the boat put off. The sea was running high, and to them the overloaded craft seemed to have no chance of remaining afloat.

The four seamen remaining aboard the vessel soon saw that she was going to pieces. Three of them determined to leave as best they could, the other deciding to stay where he was. Two patched up a sort of raft and put off on it. Sumner selected a gangplank three feet wide by fifteen feet long, threw it overboard, and got on. Ship after ship passed, but none within distance to discover him until the Europa approached more closely and saw the coat he waved. He was picked up more dead than alive.

Sumner thinks all the others perished. He drifted past an overcoat belonging to the second mate that had been wrapped about one of the women, and argues from this fact that the boat was swamped.

𝕿𝖍𝖊 𝕹𝖊𝖜 𝖄𝖔𝖗𝖐 𝕿𝖎𝖒𝖊𝖘
Published: January 18, 1906
Copyright © The New York Times

New York Times *article, January 18, 1906. Public domain.*

according to the Steamboat Inspection Service.[3] Her homeport was Boston, Massachusetts. Thus, she was only three years old when she met her demise. Her payload was not specified, but being a large cargo vessel coming from Cuba in 1906, a good guess would be sugar or tobacco. That year, sugarcane was, by far, Cuba's number one export, mostly to the United States. The publication *Sugar*, volumes 11 and 12, reports that in 1907, Cuba exported 1,282,791 tons of sugarcane, primarily from its main port of Havana.[4] Her number two export that year was tobacco for the famous Cuban cigar. In 1906, Cuba exported $13,500,000 of tobacco to the United States alone.

Newspaper Articles

The first report came from the *New York Times*. It had a dateline of Savannah, Georgia, Wednesday, January 17, but was published in New York on January 18. The headlines read: "ADRIFT ON GANG-PLANK. Castaway Saved. After Three Days—Twelve May Have Perished."[5] Details were sketchy at best, all based entirely on the accounts of Karl Sumner, a sailor on the schooner *Robert H. Stevenson*, and the sole survivor of thirteen aboard.

According to Sumner, "the schooner was bound from Havana to Philadelphia, when last Saturday [January 13] morning at 3:00 o'clock, during a nor'easter, when the *Stevenson* went hard aground on the treacherous Diamond Shoals off Cape Hatteras."[6] Sumner then described the "falling dominoes" of the fate of the other twelve persons aboard.

Captain Higbee ordered a lifeboat to be lowered. First Mate Lewis and two seamen entered it when the violent surf smashed the lifeboat into the schooner, exploding it to bits and immediately drowning the three of them as the rest of the ship's personnel witnessed the horror.

A second but smaller ship's boat was successfully lowered and filled with the captain's wife, two of his female relatives, an African American servant, and Captain Higbee himself, who reluctantly agreed to enter. Sumner saw all of this but never saw them again, nor did anyone else. Eight persons were lost so far, leaving five, including Sumner. Three

THE POWER OF WATER

It is easy to question, "How can just water completely smash a huge wooden ship to pieces?" The answer is, because it is not "just water." Perhaps this will help: picture a one-gallon jug of water. Better yet, pick one up. It weighs eight pounds. Imagine (don't actually do this) what would happen if you threw it against your seventy-inch flat screen TV. Imagine someone hit you in the head with it. *That* is merely *one* gallon. Now picture a fifty-five-gallon drum full of water, weighing 440-pounds. If that hit you, it would kill you. Run into it with your car, and it will no longer be able to drive.

Now, imagine one ocean wave that contains *thousands upon thousands* of fifty-five-gallon drum equivalents of 44 -pounds water. And it may be travelling at forty, fifty, sixty, seventy miles an hour—or more. And there is another wave just like that behind it. And another. And another. And another. Wood splinters easily with enough force. This is *far more* than enough force.

of those decided to leave "as best as they could"; two of those quickly assembled a makeshift raft and launched into the boiling surf. The fourth decided to remain on the schooner, which by then was soon going to pieces, as can happen so quickly to a wooden ship bashed with the enormous power of gigantic, rushing waves.[7]

As a last resort, with the vessel coming apart all around him and acting mostly out of desperation and panic, Sumner found a loose gangplank that was about three feet wide and twenty feet long and threw it in the ocean. He jumped overboard, crawled up on the gangplank, and somehow managed to tie himself to it with a stray piece of rope. This is where people in the theater would start walking out, if this were a 1906 Hollywood movie—Sumner was neither MacGyver nor James Bond. But the story gets even more unbelievable.

"Ship after ship passed," the *Times* article continued, "but none within distance to discover him until the *Europa* approached more closely and saw the coat he waved. He was picked up more dead than alive."[8] If you need a visual, this episode feels a lot like the scene with Tom Hanks in the 2000 feature film *Castaway* (with "Wilson," the volleyball) as the gigantic steamer drifted silently by. Picture that.

The *Boston Daily Globe*

Published on Friday, January 26, 1906, thirteen days after the incident, and being in the schooner's homeport, the *Globe* was able to afford greater detail. These were her actual headlines that day: "WAS SOLE SURVIVOR—Karl Sommers Near Death—Rescued From Raft by Steamer—Sch Stevenson's Crew All Lose Lives—Boston Vessel Strikes on Shoals."[9]

We now learn the names of many of the other twelve: Captain Jonas E. Higbee; his wife of Northport, Long Island, Miss Wicks, a neighbor of the captain's family at Northport; "a colored stewardess"; First Mate William Lewis of Everett; Steward Frank Carroll of East Boston; and a sailor named Olaf Olsen. Sommers did not know the other names—the second mate, the engineer, and three of the sailors.

The *Boston Daily Globe* reports that Sommers "was adrift on a 20-foot plank from the morning of Jan 13 until the evening of the 15th, lashed by a piece of rope to prevent his being washed overboard, and during that time he was fighting off sharks which hovered about the plank waiting to devour him."[10]

A Necessary Tangent

"Yellow journalism" is a term during this period for the use of lurid features and sensationalized news in news publications to attract readers and increase circulation. The phrase was coined in the 1890s to describe the tactics employed in the furious competition between two New York City newspapers: the *World*, owned by Joseph Pulitzer; and the *Journal*, owned by Randolph Hearst. Hearst had brought in some of his staff from San Francisco and hired some away from Pulitzer's paper, including Richard F. Outcault, a cartoonist who had drawn an immensely popular comic picture series "The Yellow Kid," for the

Sunday World. After Outcault's defection, the comic was drawn for the *World* by George B. Luks, and the two rival picture series excited so much attention that the competition between the two newspapers came to be described as "yellow journalism."[11]

So, was the description about the sharks accurate? Probably not. Note also the different spelling of "Sommers." It was common at the time to have conflicting "facts" in early newspaper accounts. Here is the classic example; the actual headlines of the *Virginial Pilot* on December 18, 1903, following the Wright brothers' first flight the day before: "Flying machine soars 3 miles in teeth of high wind over sand hills and waves at Kitty Hawk on Carolina Coast." It was actually only twelve seconds and covered 120 feet and never went over the ocean.[12]

Continuing the Newspaper Accounts

Here, the *Globe* report had more details to add to the *Times'* account. In the rescue of Sommers by the German steamship *Europa*, the report said, "His tongue was swollen and protruded from his mouth, and his limbs were so weak that he was unable to stand. He was tenderly lifted into the lifeboat sent from *Europa* and taken on board where he was put between blankets and carefully nursed until the vessel reached Savannah."[13] Sommers remained in the Savannah hospital for another four days, until January 19, when he had recovered enough to return home back north. While he was still in the hospital in Savannah, the *New York Times* was able to interview him for their story.

Scorecard

It can be a little confusing who was going where and when:

- Schooner *Robert A. Stevenson*, homeport of Boston, going from Havana to Philadelphia, wrecked Cape Hatteras January 13, 1906.
- Sailor Karl Sommers (a.k.a. "Karl Sumner" in the *New York Times* article) drifts on gangplank January 13, 14, and 15.
- German steamship *Europa*, leaving Philadelphia bound for Savannah, spots and picks up Sommers, January 15.

- *Europa* takes two more days to reach her destination, arriving in Savannah January 17 with Sommers taken to hospital there. *New York Times* gets an article then.
- Sommers recovers and returns to Boston, January 19. The *Boston Globe* publishes an account on January 26.

The Unknown Tragedy

The initial reaction to hearing the basics of this saga for the first time might be, "Why didn't the US Life-Saving Stations in the area

Wooden sailing ship battered in violent storm. De Windstoot—A Ship in Need in a Raging Storm, *by Willem van de Velde II, circa 1680.*
WikimediaCommons.

respond?" There were at least six in that vicinity: Big Kinnakeet, Cape Hatteras, Creeds Hill, Durants, Hatteras Inlet, and even Ocracoke, all being mere miles apart from each other on the coastline beaches. The most obvious answer to this good question, after examining all of what was known as well as what was *not* known at the time, is—they never knew about it. The stations did not see anything, nor did they hear anything; the event was beyond their visual horizon. To find all this out days after the tragedy would be the saddest of sad situations for these souls dedicated to saving lives from the peril of the seas at their own utmost risk. Why this did *not* happen is a mystery that makes no sense.

The Makings of a Mystery

What is known:
- The schooner *Robert H. Stevenson* wrecked at 3:00 a.m. on January 13. That was in the middle of a stormy, pitch-black, and cold night.
- It wrecked on the infamous and dreaded Diamond Shoals off Cape Hatteras. The farthest reaches of those shoals go out twenty miles.
- The distance to the horizon from a six-foot person at sea level is three miles.
- The distance to the horizon from a six-foot surfman on watch from the thirty-foot-high floor of the station's watch tower is still only 6.7 miles.
- So, if this wreck was seven miles or more off the coast, it would have been impossible for any watchmen to see it, even in daylight on a clear day.
- All US Life-Saving stations in this Sixth District's station logs are kept on file at the National Archives, in Atlanta. A search of the logs from all nearby stations from January 12 to 19 of 1906 reveal no trace of any shipwreck, distress signals, or even shipwreck flotsam—zero. No flares were sighted; no international signal code flags shown; no rockets fired; no wireless messages of distress—no CQD, no SOS.

- We also know this was a very large schooner with cargo that was probably very valuable.
- We know it had come from Havana, Cuba, in 1906. A political/military revolution had just begun there.
- We know that it had an unusual contingent of people on board: not only four women—highly unusual at the time for a huge cargo vessel—but they were a tight-knit social group: captain's wife, his female relatives, neighbors, and even a servant.

The Unknown Whys of the Mystery

- Why did the schooner have no warning of an impending wreck?
- Why was the captain unsure of where he was—a cardinal rule of navigation violated; especially during a storm, at night, and in one of the most notorious shipwreck locations?
- Seaman Sommers reported that after the "schooner struck with a terrific force" it was then "pounded heavily for two hours." *Two hours.*[14]
- This was plenty of time to fire distress flares and/or rockets; why did they not?
- Plenty of time to send *multiple* telegraph distress messages; why did they not?
- Plenty of time to come up with a much better survival plan than they used; why did they not?

We have no answers to these questions.

The surfmen of the United States Life-Saving Service stations around the Diamond Shoals off Cape Hatteras deeply regretted that the distressed ship personnel did not do even one of those things.

In the End, the Real Tragedy

For the lifesavers to learn of a shipwreck's loss of life—*after* the fact—when no help could be offered, was almost more than they could bear. With all of their extensive training, commitment to their duties, and their utmost fidelity and vigilance, the outcome was heartbreaking.

Yet, it was these very circumstances that led to continued improvements and increases in their astounding records of success—so that others may live.

In the End, the Real Mystery

Long before the Outer Banks of North Carolina's most famous maritime mystery, the "Ghost Ship of Diamond Shoals," the schooner *Carroll A. Deering* in 1921, and before the multitude of unanswered questions about the inexplicable loss of the "unsinkable" *Titanic* in 1912, whose fatal telegram was received in Hatteras Village, was a nautical mystery on par with both of these. Yet, while the stories of the *Deering* and the *Titanic* are wildly famous, what happened to the *Robert H. Stevenson* is still virtually unheard of by the public.

So, perhaps the greatest puzzle of this mystery is why this incident is still so unknown to this day.

VI.

THE MYSTERIOUS
AND STRANGE

CHAPTER 13
SCHOONER *ADA F. WHITNEY*, SEPTEMBER 22, 1885
A POYNERS HILL US LIFE-SAVING STATION RESCUE

The wreck of the schooner Ada F. Whitney *was a somewhat weird event during a somewhat unusual time in America.*

The Times

In the year of this wreck, 1885, America had thirty-eight states; yet to be added to the count were Washington, Idaho, Montana, the two Dakotas, Utah, Arizona, New Mexico, Wyoming, and Oklahoma, as well as the obviously missing Alaska and Hawai'i. The population was a bit over fifty million. We had two US presidents that year: when Chester A. Arthur died in office, Vice President Grover Cleveland became president. An economic depression had started in 1882, being a gradual development rather than a sudden crash, and was waning to a conclusion in 1885. Notable events that year included the introduction of two of America's icons: the dedication of the Washington Monument and the arrival of the Statue of Liberty in the New York Harbor from

France. Somewhat less significant, but notable, were the publication of Mark Twain's *The Adventures of Huckleberry Finn* and the patenting of the soft drink "Dr. Pepper."

Commerce was dominated by the US East Coast. Domestically, the coastal Atlantic was then akin to our I-95: almost all traffic north/

Frank Leslie's Illustrated Newspaper, *cover, New York, June 13, 1885.* **Public domain.**

south traveled there. Five of the top US cities were on the Atlantic coast: New York, Philadelphia, Brooklyn (a separate city then), Boston, and Baltimore, our ship-building capital. And almost all of this trade was carried out by a specific type of sailing ship: the schooner. It was the eighteen-wheeler of its day, typically carrying huge amounts of a homogeneous commodity—such as lumber, cement, iron ore, chalk, coal, sugar, molasses, and many other items.

A Brief Lesson on Schooners

A schooner was a sailing ship rigged with fore-and-aft sails on its two or more masts. To the foremast there may also be rigged one or more square topsails or, more commonly, one or more jib sails or Bermuda sails (triangular sails extending forward to the bowsprit or jibboom). Though it probably was based on a Dutch design of the 17th century, the first genuine schooner was developed in the British North American colonies, probably at Gloucester, Massachusetts, in 1713, by a shipbuilder named Andrew Robinson.

Although ships with square-rigged sails are excellent for long voyages before trade winds, they are poor for coastal sailing, where all varieties of winds must be dealt with. Fore-and-afters, or schooners, handle better in coastal winds, have shallower drafts for shallow waters, and require a smaller crew in proportion to their size. By the end of the 18th century the schooner had become the most important North American ship, used for the coastal trade and for fishing, as on the Grand Banks, off Newfoundland; and soon after 1800 the schooner caught the attention of European shipwrights, who built versions of their own. The fore-and-after became popular all over the world. In the United States, where speed became a premium in the China trade and the California gold trade in the mid-19th century, the schooner design was married to that of the old full-rigged, three-masted merchantman, resulting in the famous clipper ships.[1]

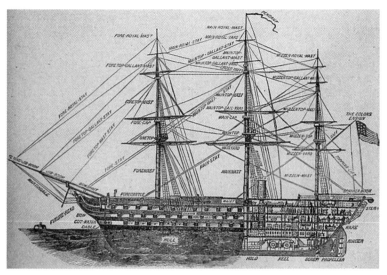

Parts of a schooner.
Webster's Practical Dictionary, *1906, WikiMediaCommons.*

For international trade, the East Coast still had the advantage. Trade from those East Coast US cities was with Europe, Africa, the Mediterranean, and even the Far East—as there was yet to be a Panama Canal.

This Schooner

The *Ada F. Whitney* was a 312-ton, three-masted schooner. It was built in Thomaston, Maine, in 1870, registered the following year in her home port there, and owned by W. M. Whitney & Co. From the American Bureau of Shipping records, we learn she was constructed of oak and yellow pine with a single bottom and iron fittings. Her assigned signal letters were "J. H. S. D."[2] This was an agreed-upon system of identifying a ship's name with corresponding books listing codes and names.

Her namesake is not revealed here, but there was an Ada Francis Whitney (née Parker), born August 26, 1864, in Malden, England, and wife of Frank Ami Whitney. Seems likely.

Her masters were listed by the American Bureau of Shipping simply as "W. O." On the voyage of September 22, 1885, her captain was R. Gilchrist.

Final Voyage

On that fateful September day in 1885, the *Ada F. Whitney* was doing what so many other "work horse, eighteen-wheeler" schooners were doing along America's Atlantic coast: hauling large loads from one port to another. On the morning of September 22, she was on her way from Boston, Massachusetts, to Brunswick, Georgia. At the time, she was "in ballast," meaning she had delivered her cargo in Boston and had no cargo to pick up and was on her way to Georgia for a different loading of cargo.

The *Annual Report* sets the scene:

> In the forenoon of that day, *Ada F. Whitney* was passing off the North Carolina coast when the weather worsened. At about noon, during the prevalence of a fresh easterly gale, with rain, the three-masted schooner *Ada F. Whitney* was driven ashore on the North Carolina Outer Banks, about two and a half miles south of the Poyners Hill Station, near the present-day village of Duck, NC.
>
> The crew of the United States Life-Saving Service Poyners Hill Station No. 9 had watched her movements for some minutes before she struck. The schooner appeared to be unmanageable from the loss of canvas. When, therefore, it became obvious that she would soon be ashore, the surfmen set out with the beach apparatus, and in half an hour were on the scene. This was with great difficulty encountered in getting there, the high tide of the morning having covered the beach and left it in a very soft and bad condition. By the time of their arrival she had driven in to within 120 yards of the shore and swung broadside to, with the seas breaking over her deck and the spray flying half-mast high. She was dangerously also rolling very deeply.[3]

The first shot from the Lyle gun lodged the shot line in the mizzen-topmast shrouds, an ideal start. However, a basic understanding of how the beach apparatus process works is necessary to follow what happened next.

The Beach Apparatus

Greater detail is provided in the opening chapter of volume 1 as well as chapter 1 of this volume, but in order to understand what the Poyners Hill crew faced, a simple understanding is helpful. The lifesaving device rescuing the shipwreck survivors is the breeches buoy. It rides on the "zip line" of the hawser. This hawser *must* be kept extremely taught in order to keep the buoy and survivor above the lethal waves they are escaping. In a drill, this is easy to do; the wreck pole does not move. However, a shipwreck in violent surf *does* move; and it moves *a lot*. In the case of this chapter's focus, the wreck was moving toward the lifesavers. Each foot of that movement slackened the tension on the hawser. Consequently, it required constant adjustments of the beach apparatus components. The

THE UNITED STATES LIFE SAVING SERVICE.

Graphic illustration of executing the breeches buoy beach apparatus rescue from the cover of Scientific American, *Special Edition, February 6, 1892.* **Author's document and photo.**

fall line must constantly be retightened. In some cases, it even required digging up the sand anchor and relocating it.

Working in this storm, with the added seemingly never-ending job of the more constant relocations of the beach cart, lines, sand anchors, and crotch pole, all seven of the schooner's crew landed safely on shore. That is what the US Life-Saving Service does, but that is not all.

The survivors are taken back to the station and given dry clothes, food and drink, succor and first aid, if needed. Also, if needed, they are provided a place to stay until they can be picked up.

From the *Annual Report*:

> While the rescue was in progress the district superintendent, Mr. T.J. Poyner, and Messrs. John C. Gallop and Josephus Baum, residents of the vicinity, joined the party and lent valuable aid. The keeper of the Caffeys Inlet Station, to the south, also came up and rendered good service. The latter had been watching the vessel from his station and started with the apparatus as soon as she struck, but finding travel so bad with the heavily loaded cart he had pushed forward alone on horseback leaving his men to follow, and arrived in time to get the people ashore. The captain and mate were taken in charge by Superintendent Poyner and conducted to his home, while the rest were given quarters at the station, where they remained five days.[4]

The Good and Bad of the Ending

The *Annual Report* concludes: "During the succeeding night the schooner worked closer in and bilged [was flooded]. On the following day, when the station crew boarded her to recover the crew's effects, she was full of water and in such condition as to preclude the possibility of saving her. The station crews a few days later assisted in saving the water casks and part of the rigging, the anchors and chains and other heavy articles being recovered by the Baker Salvage Company, of Norfolk. The wreck was condemned and sold at auction."[5]

The good: the crew were all saved. The bad: the ship was nearly a total loss. As usual, the crews of America's forgotten heroes succeeded by saving lives—and then by doing far more.

Busy Outer Banks Lifesavers

Amazingly, on the same day, the very next entry into the *Annual Report of the Operations of the United States Life-Saving Service for the Fiscal Year Ending June 30, 1886*, reads as follows (verbatim):

> [September 22] At about 4 o'clock in the afternoon, during the prevalence of a northwest gale, with heavy rain, the lookout of the Big Kinnakeet Station, (Sixth District,) [now village of Avon, Hatteras Island] coast of North Carolina, observed a small schooner in Pamlico Sound, about four miles from the station, scudding under bare poles* directly for the beach. The surfboat was immediately got out and hauled a mile through the woods to the landing-place on the west shore. This task was not an easy one, as the thick growth of trees impeded the men in their movements and made the work slow and toilsome. About the time that the life-saving crew launched their boat the vessel, which could now be plainly seen with part of her sails blown away, let go both anchors, which brought her up a short distance from the shore. Her crew of two men landed safely on the beach and were taken by the surfmen to their homes. The schooner proved to be the *Oran*, of and for Hatteras, North Carolina, from Tar River, in the same State, with a cargo of wood. She rode out the gale without further harm and subsequently resumed her voyage.[6]

---

*Ebenezer Cobham Brewer defined scudding in his 1894 *Dictionary of Phrase and Fable*: "In seaman's language, to 'scud' means to drive before a gale with no sails, or only just enough to keep the vessel ahead of the sea; 'scudding under bare poles' is when the vessel is being driven by the wind so violently that no sail at all is set. Figuratively, it means to cut and run so precipitately as to leave no trace behind." www.infoplease.com /dictionary/brewers/scudding-under-bare-poles.

CHAPTER 14

THE WRECK OF BRIG
VERA CRUZ VII, MAY 8, 1903

PORTSMOUTH LSS STATION

*Conflicting accounts, accusations, and counteraccusations saturate this wreck
story in confusion, but one thing is certain: this was the largest number of
persons rescued from a single vessel ever, anywhere. And it happened on the
North Carolina Outer Banks. This record remains today. But it is a very
strange story!*

What Is Known: Basic Facts

The sailing vessel, referred to in some accounts as a barkentine but in
most as a brig, was of Portuguese registry, under the command of Julio
M. Fernandes. She had sailed from the Cape Verde Islands bound for
New Bedford, Massachusetts, with 399 passengers. The vessel wrecked
on Dry Shoal Point, three miles east-southeast from the United States
Life-Saving Service Station on Portsmouth Island, at 2:00 p.m. on
May 8, 1903. There was no storm.

CAPE VERDE ISLANDS

The history of Cape Verde is typical and yet unique for its location. For three centuries, the islands were a setting for the transatlantic slave trade, exile for political prisoners of Portugal, and a place of refuge for Jews and other victims of religious persecution during the Spanish-Portuguese Inquisition.[1]

The Ship

The *Vera Cruz VII* was a large vessel at 605 tons, either a barkentine or a brig (see sidebar below). Her master was Captain Julio M. Fernandes, whom author Sonny Williamson reports in his work *Shipwrecks of*

BRIG VS. BARKENTINE

Brig

BRIG

Brig, a two masted vessel square rigged on both masts. The brig is a very old and efficient sailing rig, and the class was still in use up to the very end of commercial sailing ships. They were very common in European waters.

Barkentine (also spelled Barquentine)

BARQUENTINE

Barquentine, a vessel with the foremast rigged square, and the other masts rigged fore and aft. Superior for coast waters.[2]

Ocracoke Island had "left the country, without being caught, in a sperm oil barrel aboard a New Bedford whaler."[3] More aspersions will be cast upon him by additional sources. One report said the *Vera Cruz VII* was "an older ship," but few other details can be found about this vessel.[4] Almost all accounts give the crew numbering at twenty-two with a total of 399 passengers. The cargo was listed as 214 barrels of sperm whale oil, but her primary cargo was obviously the passengers who were laborers for hire in Massachusetts. A National Park Service publication from the Cape Lookout National Seashore also claims the *Cruz* carried "illicit liquor."[5] The fact that this is "Vera Cruz" number 7 makes one wonder about the first six.

What Is Known: The Noncontroversial Details

The vessel *Vera Cruz VII* departed Brava, Cape de Verde Islands, on April Fool's Day (a foretelling?) 1903, bound for New Bedford, Massachusetts. Its primary mission was to deliver approximately four hundred Portuguese African workers to New Bedford. Approaching the American East Coast, while the ship was not in distress, "Surfman Washington Roberts [of the Portsmouth Life-Saving Station, Portsmouth Island] had just reported a large sailing vessel coming ashore while trying to enter Ocracoke Inlet from the ocean," recorded the *Annual Report of the Operations of the United States Life-Saving Service for the fiscal year ending June 30, 1903.*[6] She stranded 300 yards offshore, a considerable distance for the lifesavers to cover. A different account explained what happened next: "The crew [of the *Vera Cruz VII*] sent a distress signal and the surfmen of the Portsmouth Life-Saving Station quickly responded. When they arrived at the wreck, the captain [Fernandes] asked the Surfmen to transfer all 23 women, 3 of the children, and 10 men to the Life-Saving Station. However, the other passengers and crew members remained on the ship."[7] This would just be the beginning of a troublesome strangeness.

The crew of the Portsmouth Island US Life-Saving Service Station No. 28. Surfman Washington Roberts (far left) was on the Vera Cruz VII *rescue episode.*
Courtesy of the US Coast Guard.

It Gets Stranger

Four hours later, with 366 passengers still aboard, the vessel sent a second distress signal to the Life-Saving Station. The surfmen were asked to quell a disturbance among the passengers. Strange. The *Report* does not detail the causes or results. We do know that the brig remained stuck on the shoals all night with the rowdy crowd still aboard.

The next morning, the weather worsened, putting the *Vera Cruz VII* and her occupants in jeopardy. The increasing winds and rising seas prompted Keeper Ferdinand G. Terrell to begin the massive rescue. Due to the sheer number of people, the lack of shipwrecked victims' discipline, the urgency of the rising tide, and the distance from the ship to shore, the lifesavers decided to temporarily remove as many as possible to the nearby Dry Shoal, a shallow area offshore of the village that was dry at low tide. Incredibly, the eight surfmen, using both station's surf-boats, and assisted by seven village Good Samaritans and their fishing boats, 371 passengers were relocated. Most of the ship's crew remained onboard, however.

But the tide was still rising. Even more help was needed and needed quickly. More villagers from Portsmouth responded with more boats. "It took the lifesaving crew 41 trips in the station's open surfboats to bring the 398 passengers and 22 crew to the safety of the shoal. They also removed the body of a passenger who had recently died on board and buried him where they landed," the *Annual Report* states.[8]

By midnight, all survivors were safely moved to shore. But bigger problems would immediately arise: Where would they put up all those people and how would they feed and care for them? For how long? Portsmouth, its surfmen and its citizens, all became lifesavers now facing a gargantuan task.

IT WASN'T HOLLYWOOD; IT WAS REAL

One of the local Portsmouth village volunteers was Isaac Willis O'Neal. He was so inspired by that experience that eight years later he joined the United States Life-Saving Service and served at the very Portsmouth Station from 1911 to 1913.

Page Two

When the US Life-Saving Service began in the early 1870s, the station buildings were designed to house two different crews: the six to eight surfmen and their keeper in one room every day and for the occasional shipwreck survivors, the ship's crew in another room. These were the days of sailing ships, mostly the cargo-carrying schooners that had crews of merely a handful, five to ten. There was no such thing as "passenger ships," so Portsmouth Station, like all the others, was woefully unprepared for this blitz of survivors.

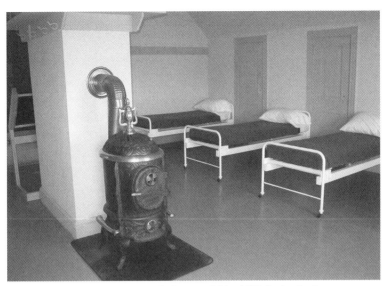

Life-Savers' crew sleeping quarters in the Portsmouth Island Life-Saving Station.
Author's photo.

The small, isolated Life-Saving stations were always located in or near equally small, isolated coastal villages. These villagers were very familiar with shipwrecks and typically would do whatever they could to assist. Four hundred, however, was asking a *lot*! As fate would have it, the once-thriving village of Portsmouth had already begun to decline. Many of its residents simply moved away to the mainland, abandoning their houses, which remained vacant.

The Unusual Gets More Unusual: An Odyssey

Twenty-three women and three children were initially housed in the Life-Saving station, which itself made crowded quarters for the surfmen also staying there. This was an unusual situation. Meanwhile, the remaining group of male passengers, as well as the vessel's crew, remained onboard the brig. Then the hurried evacuation as just described occurred. This is where the numerous vacant houses became a blessing, for all of the remaining survivors at least had a roof over their heads. More events were to come.

The *Annual Report* continues, "It was now the 12th of May and the Life-Saving Station crew and good people of Portsmouth had housed these 420 unlucky travelers for three nights while feeding them a total of 2,540 meals and using four and ½ barrels of flour in the process."[9] A National Park Service article tells us that "The three days of expenses reported by Keeper Terrell totaled $179.15," which would be well over $6,000 today.[10]

Also, on May 12, 416 passengers were transferred to the US Revenue Cutter Service *Boutwell*, which took them to nearby New Bern, North Carolina.

USRCS *BOUTWELL* HISTORY[11]

Cost $70,000 (= about $2.5 million today)

1873, May 28: launched from Buffalo, New York

1873, October 29: commissioned seven officers and thirty-one enlisted men; stationed in Savannah, Georgia, and cruised monthly to Jacksonville, Florida.

1881: driven ashore in hurricane

1898: stationed in New Bern, North Carolina

1907, July 26: decommissioned in Baltimore, Maryland

1907, October 23: was sold

Since the port city of New Bedford, Massachusetts, was under suspicion due to "cumulative evidence that the laws were being evaded"[12] there, and these Portuguese passengers were bound for that port, the US Immigration Service sent an inspector to New Bern, North Carolina, as a precaution. It was already known that the captain was an experienced smuggler with an undesirable reputation and had mysteriously escaped from his own country.

Thus, arriving from Baltimore after the great travail to reach New Bern, was Inspector Bertram N. Stump. He opens his detailed 881-word report to the commissioner general of immigration in

Washington, DC: "Sir: In the matter of the stranded passengers and crew of the barkentine *Vera Cruz VII* which sailed from Brava, Cape de Verde Islands, April 1, 1903 stranded at Ocracoke, North Carolina, May 8, landed at New Bern, N.C., May 12, 1903 I have the honor to reply as follows."[13]

He arrived on May 13 and immediately took full charge. As his first mitigating act, he "at once authorized the leasing of a vacant house as a temporary hospital, and Acting Assistant Surgeon Primrose, stationed at New Bern, N.C., was authorized to purchase cots, blankets, and a supply of necessary medicines."

The next day, starting at 8:00 a.m. and continuing until 6:00 p.m., he registered all the passengers, classified them into groups, and began an official manifest. All of that day long, he also treated the "Many cases of dysentery [that] occurred during the time."

On May 15, all the registrations were completed. On May 16, the lifesavers landed the vessel's mate and one seaman and brought them to the Portsmouth Station so that all could begin the next phase of their odyssey.

"At 6 p.m. Sunday, the 17th instant, all arrangements having been concluded for transportation to New Bedford, Mass., by immigrant train," at a ticket cost of $12.30 per person, or $415.00 in the dollar value of 2023. This train was comprised of eight coaches and one baggage car, and was stocked with seventy-five loaves of bread and "sufficient canned meats to give them all breakfast the next morning at 9 a.m. en route."

On their way to Washington, DC, the next day at noon, "I [Stump] issued all we [the train passengers] had left, consisting of crackers." The train rolled on: reaching Baltimore, Maryland, passing Jersey City, New Jersey, where supper is provided to all, and they are served breakfast as the train passed New London, Connecticut, and from there to Providence, Rhode Island. Finally, finally, four hundred–plus African Portuguese workers reached their final destination of New Bedford, Massachusetts. They had gone through a shipwreck, fights onboard, multiple stages of rescue, lodging, food, medical treatments, two

SCORECARD

It can be a little difficult to follow these dates and events in May of 1903. Here is a brief summary:

May 8: *Vera Cruz VII* wrecks at Dry Point, Portsmouth, North Carolina

May 9: United States Life-Saving Service lands 371 passengers on the Dry Shoal

May 10: not recorded; obviously busy at station and in village dealing with survivors

May 11: LSS station takes care of some of the crew and baggage

May 12: 416 people are transferred to *Boutwell* to go to New Bern, North Carolina

May 13: US Immigration inspector Stump arrives in New Bern

May 14: US Immigration inspector Stump registers and treats all

May 15: the registration and manifest are completed

May 16: the LSS lands its first mate and one sailor to the station

more different sailing vessels, and a long, long train ride, with great expenses being generously made for them by the US Life-Saving Service, the US Revenue Cutter Service, the US Immigration Service, and the good hearts of the humble people of the remote Outer Banks village of Portsmouth.

Now, The Controversial Details

From research by Ocracoke premier historian Philip Howard: "Although Captain Julius M. Fernandez, 'a notorious smuggler, not only of dutiable goods but of men whom the laws of this country would prevent from landing,' claimed he was seeking fresh water, 'many believe he was trying to land his passengers in a secluded area, in an attempt to avoid customs and immigration officials.'" He adds that "Captain Fernandez reportedly 'left the country, without being caught, in a sperm oil barrel aboard a New Bedford whaler.'"[14]

From the National Park Service:

> Rumors of smuggling operations surround the *Vera Cruz VII*.
> For one, Ocracoke Inlet is far outside the traditional shipping
> route from Cape Verde Islands to New Bedford, MA. Addi-
> tionally, only 225 of the 399 passengers were listed on the ship's
> manifest. Some of these passengers are reported to have said
> that Captain Julius M. Fernandez promised them passage into
> the United States, with or without passports. Other sources
> suggest that a large number of fishing boats were seen in the
> area a few days before the wreck and, perhaps, they intended to
> smuggle immigrants through the North Carolina sounds.
>
> Some sources suggest that the ship was wrecked on purpose
> in an attempt to smuggle immigrants (and liquor) into the
> United States. Unfortunately, the captain of the *Vera Cruz VII*
> eluded authorities on the mainland.[15]

CHAPTER 15

SCHOONER
HESTER A. SEWARD,
JANUARY 6, 1895

HAPPY NEW YEAR?

A boatload of shingles was going down, not up. The captain feared that "Hatteras will batter us."

The Promise

This is the story of a New Year's shipwreck with a happy ending, as well as an impromptu stay on Hatteras Island for the six crew members aboard the schooner *Hester A. Seward*. Hauling timber from South Carolina to Maryland, the voyage began with a promise, and almost ended in disaster.

Timber has been part of South Carolina's economy since the late seventeenth century. Over time, timber grew into a major employer with millions of dollars in invested capital that, in the process, altered the landscape of South Carolina.[1] The hardwood trees there were prized for making durable roofing shingles. From the *Annual Report of the Chief of Engineers to the Secretary of War for the Year 1895*, we learn that in that year, South Carolina exported 238,350 tons of timber for "shingles, cross ties & other articles" valued at $1,683,000 (more than $53 million in today's dollars).[2]

The small schooner, *Hester A. Seward*, had taken on a load of these shingles in Georgetown, South Carolina, bound for roofing new houses in Baltimore, Maryland. It should make a Happy New Year for many new homeowners there, as well as the crew and owners of the *Hester A. Seward*, the Kirwan Brothers Company. But a promise is only about a potential happening.

The Ship

The *Hester A. Seward* was a small vessel, only a two-masted, 150-ton schooner. She was built ten years prior, in 1885, at Taylor's Island, on the shores of Chesapeake Bay along the Eastern Shore of Maryland. During its early history, Taylor's Island was an important center for farming, ship building, and seafood. The schooner was owned by a Mister T. J. Seward, postmaster of Hill's Point Post Office in Dorchester County. The vessel was homeported in Baltimore. On its fateful final voyage, the *Seward*'s captain was Dixon Younger.

Wreck and Rescue

Amazingly, this was not the only shingle-laden small schooner owned by T. J. Seward that was lost on the Outer Banks of North Carolina. The two-masted, 141-ton schooner *Francis E. Waters* in 1889 had also taken a cargo of Georgetown, South Carolina, shingles bound for Baltimore. It also was a total wreck, this time at Nags Head, all lost including six lives—but that is the later story in chapter 25 of this volume!

The weather for Sunday, January 6 of 1895, off the Outer Banks was typical of that time—a heavy gale had sprung up and the high winds had produced rough seas, as always. Struggling slowly against these forces on her northbound journey, trying to clear the dangerous coast around Cape Hatteras, the *Hester A. Seward* finally sprang a leak. Knowing this could quickly become fatal, Captain Younger immediately

United States Life-Saving Service Station Hatteras Inlet, on the south (west) side of Hatteras Inlet.
Courtesy of the US Coast Guard.

ran for what he hoped would be the safety of Hatteras Inlet. But, as the merciless, shallow sands unseen below so often did, the bar there grabbed the schooner and held her stationary as a target for the pounding surf. As usual, the surf won, and the schooner sank in what turned out to be a fortunate spot: several United States Life-Saving Service stations were nearby.

The Hatteras Inlet Station was the closest, and a surfman on beach patrol had spotted the wreck and reported it to his keeper, James W. Howard.

Score card: The Changing Names and Locations of Life-Saving Stations

Like so many other matters then and now, the United States Life-Saving Service was an evolving organization. The following were developments along the North Carolina coast alone: the first seven stations were built in 1874; eleven more were added in 1878; between 1880 and 1888, six more were added; and the final four were built during the period 1894 to 1905—for a grand total of twenty-nine. During these evolutions, six of the stations were renamed (some more than once) and many were slightly relocated. Two were actually changed from one side of an inlet to the other. Hatteras Inlet was one of these. Today, the Hatteras Inlet Station is near the southern tip of Hatteras Island, but the original Hatteras Inlet Station was built in 1883 at the eastern end of Ocracoke Island. This is the location of this rescue story. Some of the pilings for the pier of the original station were visible until recently as the Hatteras-to-Ocracoke ferry arrives. The Outer Banks is an extremely dynamic environment!

Rescue Continues

Keeper Howard instantly launched the station's surfboat. Reaching the wreck after a rough four-mile trip, the lifesavers found that a pilot skiff had been near the wreck and had safely taken off all six crew.

PILOT BOAT

"A marine pilot boat is a vessel that's specifically used to ferry helmsmen or marine pilots from harbors to ships that need piloting, or vice versa. The concept of boats for pilots is quite old, predating the heydays of the Greco-Roman empires."[3] This particular type of boat was a skiff, which is a shallow, flat-bottomed open boat with a sharp bow and square stern.

Howard offered assistance, but it was not needed at the time. Shortly following was the arrival of the Durant Station crew from Hatteras Island in their sail-oar equipped surfboat. Keeper Zera G. Burrus of this station was requested by the *Seward* crew to take them to his station, and following standard procedures, they spent several days there, quickly provided dry clothes, and taken care of in the typical US Life-Saving Service manner.

United States Life-Saving Service Station Durant on Hatteras Island, north (east) side of
Hatteras Inlet. No longer exists. On the left is the original station. On the right is its converted
form as a motel after being decommissioned in 1939.
Courtesy of the US Coast Guard.

The captain and crew of the *Hester A. Seward* concluded with this
letter of acknowledgment and thanks (presented verbatim):

HATTERAS, NORTH CAROLINA,
January 6, 1895[4]

SIR: The master and crew of the schooner *Hester A. Seward*,
of Baltimore, MD, who were wrecked at Hatteras Inlet on
the above date, wish to express out [*sic*] gratitude and thanks
to the keeper and crew of Durant's Life-Saving Station for
the prompt and faithful manner in which they responded
in making the effort they did. Had it not been for the pilot
boat he would have been of good service to us; but under the
circumstances, could not reach us in time, as the pilot boat was
on hand, lying in wait to pilot my schooner in. Keeper Burrus
met us one-half mile from the wreck, and we were transferred
to his boat, taken to Durant's Station, kindly treated, furnished
with dry clothing, and properly cared for. We hope no blame
will rest on him or crew, as they did their duty. Yours truly,
DIXON YOUNG, *Master*; T. D. GRIFFISS, *Mate*.

The vessel splintered and all uninsured cargo of shingles and timbers
was lost; but starting the New Year with six lives saved—that is a
Happy New Year!

CHAPTER 16

STEAMSHIP *BREWSTER*

THE IRONIC WRECK AND RESCUE, WITH THANKS

Another victim of Cape Hatteras's Diamond Shoals, the German steamship's fate had been predicted by a local woman's dream. Once again, multiple US Life-Saving Service stations coordinated the rescue. Heroes were born. All thirty-three ship's crew were thankfully saved four days after Thanksgiving, 1909. But there is also great irony here.

The Ship

The *Brewster* was built in 1903 by Burmeister and Wain in Copenhagen, Denmark, and owned by H. H. Schmidt. She was a 1,517-ton steamship and had a registered homeport of Hamburg, Germany. She had a crew of thirty-three. Her value was about $36,000 (around $1 million today). At the time of their last voyage, the ship's officers were Germans, and many of the crew this time were Jamaicans, due to her port of embarkation and her cargo. On November 29, 1909, the German steamship *Brewster*, on a trip from Port Antonio, Jamaica, to New York, carried a large cargo of bananas, pineapples, oranges, and coconuts valued at $7,000 then ($200,000 today). Locally, she was referred to as "the banana boat" (not to be confused with the same moniker used for the Norwegian freighter *Cibao* that wrecked on Ocracoke on December 4, 1927, with more than sixteen thousand bunches of bananas).

The Locale

Strangely, it appears at first, these two aids to navigation, the Cape Hatteras Lighthouse and the *Diamond Shoal* Lightship, contributed to the cause of the *Brewster*'s wrecking. The first irony.

In spite of the warnings of these two lights, shipwrecks occurred. That is when the indispensable United States Life-Saving Service stations came into the picture. Seven of North Carolina's twenty-nine stations were in this locale.

Original Diamond Shoal *Lightship LV-71 torpedoed by a German submarine in World War I.* **Monitor National Marine Sanctuary; public domain.**

THE MODERN LIGHT STATION

Submerged into fifty-foot-deep Atlantic waters, the Diamond Shoals Light hovers approximately 120 feet over the water and is a striking and solitary sight in an otherwise deserted, open ocean region. Diamond Shoals Light was one of six "Texas Tower"–style lighthouses that were erected in the 1960s in six different offshore locales along the East Coast. Completed and activated in 1966, and later automated in 1977, the unmanned lighthouse provided additional guidance for offshore mariners until 1996, when Hurricane Fran blew through the region and caused devastating damage to the structure.

The light station was eventually deactivated five years later in 2001, and within several years, the light was removed, and the Diamond Shoals Light essentially became a rusty and mostly forgotten relic in the water.

The future is looking brighter for Diamond Shoals Light, however, as it was eventually purchased in 2012 by a private citizen with a goal of restoring it to its original condition.[1]

Wreck and Rescue

The wreck was discovered at daybreak on the morning of November 29, 1909, by surfman 2, O. O. Midgett, of the Cape Hatteras Life-Saving Station. He immediately reported this to acting Keeper Baxter B. Miller of his station. As was standard operating procedure, Keeper Miller alerted three more nearby stations by telephone for assistance—Big Kinnakeet with Keeper A. T. Gray, Creeds Hill with Keeper E. H. Peel (perhaps Peele), and Hatteras Inlet (then located on Ocracoke, not on Hatteras Island, as today) with Keeper D. W. Barnett. That help and cooperation would very much be needed, as it turned out.

The Cape Hatteras station immediately launched its twenty-six-foot *Beebe-McLellan* (sometimes spelled Mclellan) surfboat, powered by what the surfmen called "arm strong engines" (rowed with oars). The Creeds Hill station did the same. The Hatteras Inlet Station, however, was able to launch their larger, thirty-four-foot power lifeboat. On the way out, Captain Peel's Creeds Hill surfboat sprang a leak and had to be abandoned. Before sinking four miles offshore, its crew was rescued by Captain Miller's Cape Hatteras surfboat and then transferred to the larger Hatteras Inlet power lifeboat. Lifesavers rescuing lifesavers! More irony.

The *Brewster* had grounded around 6:30 p.m. the previous day (Sunday, November 28), so it had been well battered by the time these lifesaving crews could reach her. When they did, "The seas were breaking over the vessel fore and aft, and it was therefore out of the question to board her."[2] Then, Ocracoke author Philip Howard explains, "Recognizing the perilous situation, Capt. Peel and Capt. Miller urged the crew of the *Brewster* to abandon ship. The steamer's captain, F. Hinz, and the remaining 27 sailors refused to leave the stricken vessel. Meanwhile, seas and winds increased. For an hour the lifesavers, wet and cold, pleaded with the *Brewster*'s crew to leave their ship."[3]

Consequently, the surfmen knew that the only safe way to affect the rescue would be to place their boats on the lee side of the *Brewster*, thus being out of the wind and not being pushed into her. Trying to pull alongside was to risk wrecking the surfboats, so another SOP technique was used. The *Brewster*'s crew were instructed to drift a line to the surfboat via a buoy. Then sailors must jump in the water one at a time so they could be hauled by clinging to that line to the safety of the lifesavers' boats. After a group of about a dozen loaded were into the surfboat, they were transferred to the larger lifeboat. Then another load in same way. The entire crew of thirty-three were saved: sixteen in the Hatteras Inlet power boat, twelve in the Cape Hatteras surfboat in tow behind the power boat and five that had been rescued by the Diamond Shoals Lightship.

The United States Life-Saving Service did not stop with the successful rescue itself, as we have seen. All of those "after things" happened as usual. In the fortunate case of the *Brewster*, all that was needed was dry clothing—thankfully. They were given shelter for three days, after which they were transferred to the Revenue Cutter *Onandaga* for transportation to Norfolk.

Painting titled The Wreck of H. P. Kirkham, *by Rodney Charman, depicting a United States Life-Saving Service surfboat approaching a distressed sailing vessel to rescue survivors.* **Egan Maritime Institute. egan@eganmaritime.org.**

Amazing Premonition

Elizabeth "Bett" Linton (1856–1910), later O'Neal, was born in Wysocking, Hyde County, North Carolina. That small community was on the inner coast of North Carolina, but no longer exists (see map on next page). It was close enough to Ocracoke Island that Bett made her living as the hired cook for the Hatteras Inlet Station, at that time located on Ocracoke. Hiring cooks was a common practice at most US Life-Saving Service stations.

> In November 1909, Bett dreamt that a number of German men came ashore at Ocracoke. Dreams were often interpreted by islanders as harbingers of things to come [it happened famously to Rasmus Midgett—see sidebar on next page]. The next morning Bett cooked a great many pineapple cakes for the surfmen at the station. When asked why all the cakes, Bett explained that she was certain they would be having company soon.[4]

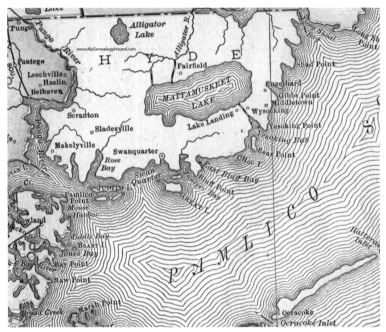

A map of Hyde County, North Carolina, showing the village of Wysocking, 1911.
Courtesy of Rand McNally; public domain.

RASMUS'S DREAM

A granddaughter of Rasmus Midgett, Mrs. Hazel Foster, was interviewed by Cape Hatteras High School students Belle Stowe and Helen Midgett for the school magazine, *Sea Chest,* in 1976. She related the story that one night at his station he had a dream. When he got up, he told the station keeper "we'd better get ready because there's going to be a wreck today." They all laughed at him all day long—until a ship came ashore! When he later reported another shipwreck dream in which he even detailed how he found a platter with certain initials engraved in it, everybody got ready. There *was* a wreck, and he *did* find a platter with those initials!

Only days later, thirty-three people suddenly became company to the station where she cooked. Many of them were Germans, as she predicted. On top of that, pineapples were a large part of the wrecked ship's cargo!

Firsthand Accounts

From a Coast Guard Surfman on the Rescue
In January of 2018, Ocracoke author Philip Howard recounted a revealing 1939 interview with Isaac (Big Ike) O'Neal (1865–1954), who served with the United States Life-Saving Service from 1904 to 1917. O'Neal starts, "While in the service at Hatteras Inlet Station, we had one very rough trip off Diamond Shoals trying to save the crew off of the Steamship Brewster." He then goes on to describe the rescue in which he participated, as we have seen. Then, he simply ends with the understatements typical of the Service and Coast Guard, "We towed the captain's boat to the beach and then transferred the 28 men to the Cape Point boat and then took them to the Cape Point Life-Saving Station. We then went back to Hatteras Inlet Station. My station keeper was Captain Dave Barnett."[5]

From the Ship Brewster's *Crew*
> SIR: We the undersigned, members of the German steamer Brewster . . . beg to express our appreciation of the gallant conduct of the crews of the Cape Hatteras, Creeds Hill, and Hatteras Inlet Life-Saving Stations. . . . We must say that their conduct on this occasion is worthy of the Greatest praise, and the manner in which the rescue was carried out worthy of American seamen… and assure you that we will never forget same. F. HINE, Master; W. DUHRING, Chief Engineer; H. CLAKSEN, Second Officer; O. WALAAS, Supercargo.

From Local Witnesses on the Beach

SIR: We, the undersigned citizens of Cape Hatteras, Dare County, State of North Carolina, having witnessed the rescue of the captain and crew of the steamship *Brewster* . . . believe this to be one of the bravest acts of heroism ever accomplished by the Life-Saving Service . . . we respectfully ask as a matter of justice to said acting keeper and crew of the Cape Hatteras Life-Saving Station and the keeper and two of the crew of Creeds Hill station, that they be awarded medals of gold. Trusting that this letter will meet your favorable consideration, we remain. Yours, very respectfully, C. H. GRAY, *United States Commissioner*; C. C. Miller, *Notary Public*; F. P. WILLIAMS; O. M. SCARBOROUGH

From a Local Fisherman Out in His Boat at the Time

SIR: I was out to the shoals on the day mentioned fishing from a power boat, and after the Cape Hatteras crew started to the stranded ship, I took them in tow and brought them as near the ship as I dared to go. I remained near the vessel until the crew was taken off and saw all the difficulties under which the life savers worked; also, their strenuous and heroic struggle against adverse conditions which were at times almost impossible to overcome. . . . I have had experience at surfing [meaning being in a boat on the ocean, not the modern meaning] all my life, ad I can not [*sic*] speak too highly of these brave men. I wish to add my voice in praise of their noble work. Very respectfully, H. L. Gaskill.

From US Coast Guard: E. H. Peel, B. B. Miller, Awarded 6 December 1911

On 6 December 1911 E. H. Peel, keeper of Creeds Hill (N. C.) Life-Saving Station and B.B. Miller, Surfman No. 1 and acting keeper of the Cape Hatteras (N. C.) Life-Saving Station, each received the Gold Lifesaving Medal for their assistance in rescuing the crew of the German steamer *Brewster*.

In addition, nine lifesavers received Silver Medals for this same rescue: W. H. Austin, W. L. Barnett, D. W. Fulcher, Y. O. Gaskins, I. L. Jennett, E. J. Midgette, O. O. Midgett, H. S. Miller, and U. B. Williams.

The Final Irony

Only eight years after Americans saved the lives of Germans off the North Carolina coast, German submarines in World War I would be ambushing and killing American sailors by the hundreds.

The Happy Ending, with Thanks Being Given

When the *Brewster* finally broke apart, copious numbers of coconuts, pineapples, oranges, and bananas washed up on the shore of the Outer Banks. Islanders gathered the fruit, including bunches of bananas, which they rinsed off with fresh water and hung up to ripen. So many bunches of bananas were retrieved by Ocracoke islanders that most of them could not be eaten before they began to rot.[6]

VII.

SOME FOR THE RECORD BOOKS

CHAPTER 17

THE SINGLE MOST IMPORTANT SHIPWRECK IN AMERICAN HISTORY— CUE SUMNER KIMBALL

That headline might seem audacious, but it becomes clear when compared to the screaming 1951 magazine article headline: "THE CATASTROPHE THAT SHOOK AMERICA AND LED TO ESTABLISHMENT OF ALL-YEAR BEACH CONTROL BY OUR COAST GUARD."[1] That article was written by Bill Sharpe, the editor of *The State* magazine. Sharpe's article appeared in the November 3, 1951, issue. This magazine would later become the extraordinary *Our State: Celebrating North Carolina* magazine on newsstands today.

The Background

Since colonial times, America's coasts were plagued by dreadful shipwrecks. They were frightfully common and extracted enormous amounts of damage and loss of life. We earlier witnessed the slow development. By now its biggest scourge was the cronyism infestation.

A Turning Point

Shipwrecks, deaths, and destruction continued unabated. The tragic situation came to a head on the North Carolina coast in late 1877 and early 1878.

On November 24, 1877, the US Army steamer *Huron* wrecked off Nags Head in a violent storm. While only yards from the beach, 103* lives were lost to drowning. The Nags Head Life-Saving Station two miles away was closed for the season. Then only twenty miles farther north and only two months later, the steamer *Metropolis* wrecked off Currituck Beach in another tempest. The rescue was bungled by the crew from Currituck Beach Station No. 4 due to inexperience and lack of preparation. Another eighty-five lives were lost as crowds on the beach watched the shipwreck victims drown.[2]

Wreck of the U. S. Steamer Huron— Large Number of Lives Lost.

WASHINGTON, Nov. 24.

The observer at Kitty Hawk reports at 11:35 A. M. to the Chief Signal Officer as follows: "The United States man-of-war steamer Huron struck two miles north of No. 7 station at 1:30 A. M.; her foremast and maintopmast are gone. The steamer is at Ocowan Creek. Assistance is needed immediately. The sea is breaking over her, and several have already washed ashore drowned. The number on board is about one hundred and thirty-five. She has no cargo.

LATER.—At 3 P. M. the surfmen returned to Kitty Hawk and reported that the Huron had gone to pieces. Thirty were saved and all the others perished. No assistance was rendered.

STILL LATER.—Four officers and thirty men, from the Huron, were saved. Capt. Ryan was lost. The signal observer at Kitty Hawk reports that assistance is wanted immediately. The men are only half clothed and the dead are uncared for on the beach. The others who perished are still in the breakers.

The Huron was an iron screw propeller, built four years ago, and of 521 tons measurement. She had been out from Fortress Monroe only twelve hours when the disaster befel her. Cautionary signals were displayed when she left.

The Huron was commanded by Captain George P. Ryan. There were fifteen marines on board the vessel. The scene of the disaster was 12 miles from Kitty Hawk.

Period newspaper article on the sinking of the Huron. Outer Banks Coastal Life. www.outerbankscoastallife.com/contact.

The Final Straw

Headlines of the *Metropolis* disaster exploded in newspapers all over America. The articles were filled with anger. The news outraged our entire nation. Demands for immediate improvements had the

---

*There is a discrepancy of one in these figures. The first, 103, is by expert North Carolinian historian David Stick.

politicians retreating. Thomas Nast's political cartoon certainly captured the critical essence of the situation.

Here are excerpts from Bill Sharpe's actual November 3, 1951, issue article:

> Nothing good could come out of such a ghastly, pitiful wreck as that of the *Metropolis*, it seemed. The steamship came ashore in a heavy sea below Whaleshead (Currituck) Light January 31, 1878, and 102 lives were lost.
>
> Everything about the tragedy was shameful. The owners were charged with concealing defects in the ship, inspectors charged with collusion, the chartering company was accused of overloading her and the captain was accused of imprudent handling of his ship. The Life-Saving crew reached the wreck late, and then without sufficient equipment.
>
> Worst of all, natives of the Bank as well as passengers were accused of inhospitality and looting. Coming on the heels of the scandalous wreck of the warship *Huron* in 1877 off Kitty Hawk, the disaster threw the county into an uproar. The *New York Tribune* carried columns of the story on its front pages, and even months later reverberations . . . in the form of charges, counter-charges, investigation and reports . . . were being heard.
>
> But no matter. As long as men trod that lonely, violent beach, they will always remember the *Metropolis* as one of the too-often times when man's mistakes and inadequacies and greed coincided with a cruel mood of nature to shock the nation with a brutal episode of the sea.[3]

The Phoenix Arises

It was time for a new and improved United States Life-Saving Service. Ironically, it would eventually become *the most* heroic organization in American history. Much of that was due to one man.

Until the Civil War, the United States had only one national maritime organization: the Revenue Marine. It had been fathered by Alexander Hamilton and became official in 1790. In 1863 the name was changed to the United States Revenue Cutter Service (USRCS). Its singular mission was ocean-based law enforcement. It was neither charged with nor equipped or trained for life-saving rescues. That long void remained. Finally recognized in 1871, a US Life-Saving Service (USLSS) was established only as a branch of the USRCS. It was headed by Sumner Kimball from 1871 until 1878.

As a result of the *Huron-Metropolis* uproar, in 1878 the US Life-Saving Service was made a separate and equal organization to the US Revenue Cutter Service, and both remained under the Treasury Department. The new Service with a new mission needed a dynamic, powerful, and competent "straight-laced" administrator. Kimball was asked to be that superintendent.

Well aware of the poor reputation, Kimball was extremely guarded in his response. In essence, he said he would take over if, and only if, he could do it his way, have no interference, and have official backing. Having considered the secretary's proposal carefully for a week, Kimball

Sumner Kimball, later years.
Courtesy of the US Coast Guard.

accepted the promotion on the following terms. "Mr. Secretary," his own words firmly stated, "I shall accept your offer upon one condition. If you will stand by me, after I have convinced you that I am right, I shall attempt to bring about the reforms you desire. But I want to warn you that the pressure will be tremendous. Congressmen will come to you in long processions and will attempt to convince you that I am wrong and that the service is being ruined. It will require an uncommon display of backbone on your part, but if you will stand firm and refer all complaints to me, I promise you that I shall put the service where you want it and where it ought to be."[4] So it would be.

Born in Maine on September 2, 1834, and raised there, Sumner Increase Kimball became a lawyer in 1858. He was elected to the Maine House of Representatives the next year, became a clerk in the United States Treasury Department in 1862, and became superintendent of the USRCS in 1871. He always had a stellar reputation for honesty, competence, and accomplishments. He personally remained out of the spotlight and simply focused on organization efficiency. He remained as the US Life-Saving Service Superintendent until 1915 when it became the United States Coast Guard. For thirty-seven years, he was the sole USLSS super.

Historian Dennis Noble goes on to conclude, "Kimball realized that to create a professional service, and one that was in large part located in small communities, his crews would have to be above petty politics and be seen as a service to the community and the nation."[5] *That* is precisely what today's United States Coast Guard is. And *that* is why the *Metropolis* was "The Single Most Important Shipwreck in American History." It ushered in Sumner I. Kimball.

Kimball's Accomplishments

There have been a scarce number of government officials in the entire history of the United States of America that could match the comprehensive level of positive accomplishments of United States Life-Saving Service Superintendent Sumner Increase Kimball. The entire list would be too long here; so, only the major highlights.

That list starts with his removal of incompetent politicians and the scourge of cronyism—an enormous achievement by anyone at any time!

> Kimball, using his own political know-how and reinforced with Faunce's report, proceeded to completely remake the lifesaving network. He succeeded in gaining an appropriation

of $200,000 and Congress authorized the Secretary of the Treasury to employ crews of surfmen wherever they were needed and for as long as they were needed. Kimball instituted six-man boat crews at all stations, built new stations, drew up regulations with standards of performance for crew members, set station routines, set physical standards, and, in short, set the organization on the road to professionalization. . . . The Service's reputation for honest, efficient, and non-partisan administration, plus performance of duty, can be largely attributed to the efforts of this one man.[6]

One of Kimball's first acts was to order inspections and implement the needed changes. He literally "wrote the book"—*Regulations for the Government of the Life-Saving Service of the United States*. It starts with introduction, paragraph 2 "A rigid observance of these regulations is required from all persons connected with the service; and it is further made their imperative duty to report forthwith to the Secretary of the Treasury any negligence, disobedience, or infraction thereof which may come to their knowledge."[7]

Some important excerpts:

Articles of Engagement for Surfmen

From *Regulations for the Government of the Life-Saving Service*, 1884, Form 1803:

> And we do hereby further covenant and agree to hold ourselves subject to any proper call, by signal or otherwise, for service at any shipwreck, or to assist any vessel in distress, or to rescue, or assist in rescuing, any person from drowning, during any portion of said term of one year not embraced in the "active season," and at such times to do our utmost in saving life and property, and to hold ourselves subject to the said regulations, rules, and discipline of the Life-Saving Service, and to the lawful commands of the officers placed over us.[8]

Strictness of the Service—Rejected Personnel

The board next visited the Sixth District, in which they examined seventy-nine keepers and surfmen, of whom sixty-four were accepted and fifteen were rejected, four of the latter being keepers. Of these four keepers, two were rejected as having no knowledge whatever of the duties required of them, one being a blacksmith and the other a teacher by occupation; the third as lacking experience as a surfman; and the fourth as physically disqualified.

Starting in 1876, Kimball instituted the extremely detailed *Annual Report of the Operations of the United States Life-Saving Service for the Fiscal Year Ending June 30,* of that year and for each remaining year until 1915 when the Service became the United States Coast Guard. These were three-hundred-plus-page books containing everything of note that happened at every station in the country. They are now a gold mine of original documents for researchers.

> Each year, with the help of the US Government Printing Office, Kimball and O'Connor published the *Annual Report* of the Operation of the United States Life-Saving Service. In the florid language of the Victorian era this tome not only held pages of statistics on the operations of the Service but also gleaned from the Wreck Reports of the various stations the most heroic rescues that had been accomplished during the past year. Kimball also used the Report as his "bully pulpit" to lobby for what he wished Congress to fund in the ensuing year. A copy of the *Annual Report* was placed in the hands of every member of Congress and was widely distributed to Public Libraries throughout the nation. In an age prior to electronic media, it soon became a much-anticipated publication.[9]

Sumner Increase Kimball's Greatest Gift to America

He started his model of strictness, efficiency, competence, standardization, and honor that became the US Coast Guard and remain its hallmarks today.

Consider for a Moment:

Today's total military population (Army, Navy, Air Force, Marines, and Coast Guard) is approximately two million, including reserve units. The total Coast Guard personnel is only fifty-six thousand, which is 2.6 percent of the total US military. The US Army has bases all over the world. The Army's Fort Bragg (changed name to Fort Liberty in 2023), for instance, alone has a population of 238,600. That one base has more than four times the population of the entire national Coast Guard.

From the Coast Guard website, we learn that "the Coast Guard protects and defends more than 100,000 miles of US coastline and inland waterways and safeguards an Exclusive Economic Zone (EEZ) encompassing 4.5 million square miles stretching from North of the Arctic Circle to South of the equator, from Puerto Rico to Guam, encompassing nine time zones—the largest EEZ in the world."[10] These figures change annually.

On an average day, the Coast Guard:

- conducts forty-five search and rescue cases;
- saves ten lives;
- saves more than $1.2. million in property;
- seizes 874 pounds of cocaine and 214 pounds of marijuana;
- conducts fifty-seven waterborne patrols of critical maritime infrastructure;
- interdicts seventeen illegal migrants;
- escorts five high-capacity passenger vessels;
- conducts twenty-four security boardings in and around US ports;
- screens 360 merchant vessels for potential security threats prior to arrival in US ports;
- conducts fourteen fisheries conservation boardings;
- services eighty-two buoys and fixed aids to navigation;
- investigates thirty-five pollution incidents;
- completes twenty-six safety examinations on foreign vessels;
- conducts 105 marine inspections;

- investigates fourteen marine casualties involving commercial vessels;
- facilitates movement of $8.7 billion worth of goods and commodities through the nation's Maritime Transportation System.

Sumner Increase Kimball died in the city he had worked in most of his life, Washington, DC, on June 20, 1923, at age eighty-eight, having done one of the most important things ever for the United States. He made America vastly safer for maritime travel and, as a bonus, now more secure.

Thank you, Superintendent Kimball.

Kimball's early home in Maine.
Maine Memory Network, collections of Sanford-Springvale Historical Society, courtesy of MaineMemory.net, item #22844.

CHAPTER 18

THE IMPROBABLE RESCUE OF THE WRECKED SCHOONER *CHARLES S. HIRSCH*, OCTOBER 29, 1908

This episodic story has every element of an exaggerated Hollywood movie: a ship's masts snapping off in a storm; a series of nor'easters one after another; cold, dark October nights; no lighthouses around to help; days fighting an uncontrollable vessel; a captain lost and confused; three United States Life-Saving Service stations responding with full crews and equipment; and multiple failed rescue attempts. It includes everything that could go wrong. That is, until the storm warrior heroes—who could always surmount the insurmountable odds—saved lives!

But it is a true story with documented details. Read on.

The United States Life-Saving Service stations' crews of Paul Gamiels Hill, Kitty Hawk, and Caffeys Inlet could have been the poster children for the theme "against all odds." Typical of the Service's forty-four-year history of persistence and diligence to duty, the keepers and surfmen would overcome "Murphy's Law" time after time. By today's standards, most of us would find this impossible. But that was a time when "ships were made of wood and the men were made of steel."

The Ship

The *Charles S. Hirsch* was a four-masted schooner of 530 tons burden owned by the Hirsch Lumber Company of New York. On this trip, she carried a crew of eight men, including the captain, as follows: Frank Wall Hunter, master; Charles O. Olson, mate; Fred L. Hoffses, engineer; Edward J. Christiansen, Albin Julgen, Torres Gundersen, and Ludvik Helgesen, seamen; and the cook.

The Beginning

The large *Charles S. Hirsch* left Brunswick, Georgia, on the morning of October 18, bound for Baltimore, Maryland, with a cargo of 318 Georgia pine pilings. These were enormous "processed trees" stripped of limbs and bark measuring eighty to ninety feet in length and twenty inches around. Eleven days later, she will be gone.

PILINGS

"Timber piles were the first driven piles. They have been used for centuries to support man-made structures. They are still used the world over to support a variety of structures and for marine applications. . . . Original drawings prepared in 1896 of the San Francisco Ferry Building show it resting on 5,000 redwood piles, 14 inches in diameter which were driven down 80 feet into the San Francisco Bay mud. Investigation of the piles in 1981 showed the piles were in perfect condition." This we learn from the Timber Piling Council.[1] For our purposes, at this time in these coastal places, most of the pilings were used for the construction of docks, wharves, piers, boardwalks, fish houses, screw pile lighthouses, and other marine structures.

The *Annual Report*[2] takes seven long paragraphs and three full pages with more than 1,300 words to describe the storm and the constant fighting of the captain and crew for control of the schooner. Suffice it here to say that it was an extremely difficult situation, fraught with danger and probable demise of all of the night of the October 29. As the sun rose on the morning of the October 30, "the wind had freshened up to 20 knots, and it had begun to drizzle, making a mist over the water. Day was breaking, however, and through the occasional rifts in the scurrying fog the sailors could see to windward long lines of foam-crusted seas, which warned them of their proximity to the shore."[3]

NOR'EASTERS AND ACTIVE SEASON

Originally, the United States Life-Saving Service stations were only open and active nationally during what they called "the storm season." The USLSS "storm season" was from September 1 to May 1, then a series of different dates until finally year-round.

The storm season, especially the winter, took place in those months that produced nor'easters (storms with northeast winds). They were far more numerous than hurricanes and often just as destructive. Winter may have a dozen or more storms, whereas there may be one hurricane every three to five years—or, often, much longer.

A hurricane would last several hours, while a nor'easter would last days at a time. It could produce similarly destructive winds—but far more waves, rain, and flooding.

In a valiant attempt to turn the vessel into the refuge of what Captain Frank Wall Hunter thought was Cape Henry, Virginia, Murphy's Law struck. Wind, sails, and waves all went the wrong way; the battered *Charles S. Hirsch* struck hard aground.

This was the captain's explanation: "The schooner paid off northwest, but seemed to hang, and as I did not want to lose too much ground or strain my steering gear, I next called to the mate to slack the spanker peak. As she still did not pay off, I then told him to lower his spanker away. I, at the same time, ran to leeward and let go the mizzen sheet. As the vessel still did not answer her helm, I began to suspect that something was wrong with her steering gear, and was doing everything possible to bring her about."[4] Simple, eh?

Panic ensued because "The seas were running high when she took bottom, and they now broke over her decks and the houses fore and aft, the spray flying high up in the rigging."[5]

Captain Hunter called all hands on deck for safety and to make a plan. But the broken schooner was taking on water so fast that all was abandoned in consideration of the salvation of individuals. Then, the unbelievable happened.

> Some twenty minutes after the schooner fetched up, the deck load began to work loose, and soon the piles stacked under the starboard side were chafing the rigging as they rose and fell with the seas, tearing it asunder. Freed from their fastenings to windward, the masts could not withstand the terrible pounding and the pressure of the piles on the leeward rigging, and three of them—the mainmast, mizzenmast and spanker mast—snapped off simultaneously, the two last named going overboard and the mainmast swinging around against the foremast, where it hung suspended by the rigging.[6]

Although Captain Hunter thought he was off the Virginia coast, he was much farther south— actually being off North Carolina, near the town currently known as Duck. Lucky for him and his crew, there were several United States Life-Saving Service stations in the vicinity.

All US stations had the same daily duties and weekly drills to hone their expertise. Watch was kept from the station tower every day from sunrise to sunset. At night, each station sent two surfmen to the beach, covering the miles between them. Thus, the US Life-Saving Service had the beaches covered around the clock: *Semper Paratus*.

SHIP'S SHROUD

Shrouds

Diagram of a sixteenth-century ship's shrouds. WikiMediaCommons.

Hundreds of fictional movies that show sailing ships of the time have unwittingly convinced viewers that the shroud on a vessel—the seeming net of ropes going up the mast—were only for sailors climbing to get to the sails. In reality, however, this was simply a by-product. The main and critical purpose was to brace and support the mast. Notice that the shroud is always *behind* the mast. Remember, the wind is pushing the sail forward; it can be quite strong at times. So the shroud is a brace of *backward* force to counter the *forward* force of the wind. Without the shroud, the wind could snap the mast.

So it was that surfman 1, Andrew Scarborough, on beach patrol from the Paul Gamiels Hill Life-Saving Station, was the first to spot the struggling schooner. This was about 5:30 a.m., so per his training, he watched and observed, trying to determine or anticipate what may happen and, if the vessel were to come ashore, where it may do so. Cleverly, he put a stake in the sand to mark the place before he returned to the station several miles away to report his findings to Keeper Thomas Harris. Before he left, surfman Paul D. Beals, the number 3 man at the same station, came in from the south patrol and met him. Beals stayed for the watch. Through their usual teamwork, they had this area covered.

Years of routine practice kicked in immediately: the Paul Gamiels Hill Station sprang into action, quickly on their way with the beach cart and its beach apparatus. As required by the strict *Regulations for the Government of the Life-Saving Service of the United States*, Keeper Harris telephoned his neighboring stations: Captain Tillett of the Kitty Hawk station, six miles south, to come with his men: and Captain Snow of the Caffeys Inlet Station, six miles north, to come to assist if needed. This had long been a common-sense procedure; the Life-Saving Service always worked as teams, both within the station and between stations, as is continued to this day by the United States Coast Guard.

The Multiple Rescue Attempts Begin: First Murphy's Law

"The vessel lay broadside to the beach and pounding heavily, with the seas almost hiding her from view. Within fifteen minutes the Lyle gun was fired with 5 ounces of powder, laying a No. 9 line across the vessel just forward of her spanker mast. After the sailors had taken refuge on the quarterdeck, 6 of them, it appears, climbed into the spanker rigging."[7]

The basic idea of the breeches buoy rescue was for the lifesavers to send a line to the stricken vessel. This was done by firing a twenty-pound projectile (shot) to the vessel via a thin line. A sailor onboard needed to secure the line and then pull it in to retrieve the real working part: a pulley (block) with a much larger line already running through it (whip line). Once this was attached high up on a mast (see details in the diagram on page 11), the lifesavers could start the saving process.

When the line was fired, the sailors jumped down from the rigging on the deck to grab the line. But in their understandable haste to secure the whip line to the mast, they crossed the lines. Once tied to the mast, the lines would not work—the lifesavers were helpless. There was no way, or time, to communicate the problem to fix to the situation. The alternative? Cut that line and fire another. So, Keeper Harris sent two surfmen back to the station to get another whip line.

Meanwhile, true panic has set in for the schooner's desperate sailors. Earlier, when they realized the rescue could not take place, they had all climbed into the rigging. Not long after, the masts all snapped— with men high up on them. Two fell into the sea, one was carried away by the raging surf, and the other, miraculously, safely mounted a drifting spar in the water "where he remained for fifteen or twenty minutes, and then climbed back on board with the help of a shot line that had fallen near him."[8]

Rescue Attempt Number 2

Always expecting the unexpected, and "always ready," Keeper Harris sent for a surfboat in case the breeches buoy did not work. A second Lyle gun projectile with shot line attached was fired. It was a perfect shot within easy reach of the huddled mass of sailors. But it got tangled in the wreckage and the sailors could not haul in the life-saving whip line. Murphy's Law number 2.

"Failing the second time in their efforts to get the apparatus in operation, the sailors returned to the stump of the spanker mast, around which they clung, some of them lashing themselves fast. Several of the Life-Savers who were present on the beach testified that while the sailors were in this position the seas repeatedly buried them out of sight. That they managed to hold on was a matter of astounding surprise to the veteran surf fighters."[9]

Rescue Attempt Number 3

This attempt was almost identical to the previous one—a number 9 shot line with four ounces of black powder in the Lyle gun to propel the shot was used—and it landed, once again, where the previous one had. This time, however, "changed the fortunes of the shipwrecked men. They had some trouble in getting the whip on board, due to the wreckage and current, but they at last succeeded in fastening both whip and hawser to the spanker stump, securing the hawser some 2 feet above the tail block. After that the rescue was only a matter of minutes. Six men in all were brought ashore, the captain being the last to leave the ship."[10] The whip line should have been tied much higher up to work, but there was no "higher up."

Life Line, *a well-known painting by Winslow Homer, 1884.*
Courtesy of the Philadelphia Museum of Art—Kathleen A. Foster, chief curator.

Six sailors saw their imminent and probable demise erased by the incredible work, persistence, and skill of one small group of "America's forgotten heroes."

Those six were part of the 177,286 lives saved by the United States Life-Saving Service from 1871 to 1915.

Accomplished, so often, "against all odds."

CHAPTER 19

TRACKING DOWN THE FAMOUS USLSS QUOTE ABOUT WHAT THE BOOK SAYS ABOUT GOING OUT

We do *know the correct actual quote. We* do *know who said it. What we do* not *know is what shipwreck generated it, where and when it was, and which station was responding to it. In researching all the possible wrecks listed in the* Annual Report of the Operations of the United States Life-Saving Services *volumes, a smoking gun* was *found.*

America's Forgotten Heroes

The United States Life-Saving Service (1871–1915) is one of the least known yet most inspiring and heroic aspects of American history. Compounding this unfortunate unfamiliarity are the common misconceptions and numerous incorrect facts held by the public.

The Misquotes

Undoubtedly, one of the most mistaken references is that of the famous quote of the "Old Salt Captain" who (supposedly) barked out something like, "Regulations say we have to go out, but don't have to come back." There are *many* (many) variations of this—some more distorted than others. One particularly dreadful source has a keeper "somewhere on the Atlantic coast" in "a timeframe of the mid-1870s" in the surfboat with his distressed crew, holding up the book of regulations and telling them, "It says you have to go out but you don't have to come back." Even sadder is that the quote is sometimes credited to the entirely wrong person.

This misinformation started long ago, in almost Hollywood exaggeration. The *Congressional Record*—no less—had this story peppered with errors (as depicted in this excerpt, with the original spelling and punctuation maintained):

> Semper paratus [*sic*] always prepared always ready is their motto. It was old Capt. Pat Etherdige [*sic*], that valiant officer in charge of the Nags Head station of yester-year who contributed a priceless saying that has become a legend in Coast Guard history. A wreck offshore in the deep of the night. Frantic signals were coming in from the stricken ship. It was a sea in which only the stoutest boat could survive, and only stout-hearted men could face. For a moment there was hesitation on the part of a newly married surfman who cried out, "Captain none of us will ever come back." Old Captain Pat, stern old long bearded man of the sea, without education replied that he would read what the regulations had to say about such a situation. The story goes that when he opened the book it was upside down. "The regulations say," said he, "when you get call you must go out there. I can't find where they say anything about how you are going to get back. Come on men and follow me." And they went out and they brought back 32 human beings who were snatched from the jaws of death.[1]

The Errors

- The official Coast Guard motto is "Semper Paratus." The direct Latin translation is "Always Ready." There is no "always prepared."

Latin for "always faithful," *semper fidelis*, has been the Marine Corps motto since 1883.

- The name "Etherdige" is misspelled. It should be "Etheridge."
- All United States Life-Saving Service personnel were required to pass a civil service test, which required literacy.
- Patrick Henry Etheridge was *never* keeper of the Nags Head Station. He was keeper at the Life-Saving stations of Creeds Hill (1884–1888) and Cape Hatteras (1891–1909).
- Much of the account appears to be dramatic fiction.

The Actual Facts

Here is the actual original quote and its source:

> *The Blue Book says we've got to go out and it doesn't say a damn thing about having to come back.*
>
> —Patrick H. Etheridge, keeper from 1891 to 1909,
> US Life-Saving Service Station Cape Hatteras.[2]

Here is the official explanation, taken from my book *Shipwrecks of the Outer Banks: Dramatic Rescues and Fantastic Wrecks in the Graveyard of the Atlantic*:

> From May 6, 1891, until October 31, 1909, Patrick Etheridge was keeper of the Cape Hatteras Life-Saving Station (not to be confused with the lighthouse). An eyewitness at the time tells the story:
>
> "A ship was stranded off Cape Hatteras on the Diamond Shoals and one of the life-saving crew reported the fact that this ship had run ashore on the dangerous shoals. The old skipper [Etheridge] gave the command to man the lifeboat and one of the men shouted out that we might make it out to the wreck, but we would never make it back. The old skipper looked around and said, 'The Blue Book says we've got to go out and it doesn't say a damn thing about having to come back.'"[3]

United States Life-Saving Service Station keeper Patrick Henry Etheridge.
Outer Banks History Center.

Etheridge was not exaggerating. *The Regulations of the Life-Saving Service of 1899* stated:

> In attempting a rescue, the keeper will select either the boat, breeches buoy, or life car, as in his judgment is best suited to effectively cope with the existing conditions. If the device first selected fails after such trial as satisfies him that no further attempt with it is feasible, he will resort to one of the others, and if that fails, then to the remaining one, and he will not desist from his efforts until by actual trial the impossibility of effecting a rescue is demonstrated. The statement of the keeper that he

did not try to use the boat because the sea or surf was too heavy will not be accepted unless attempts to launch it were actually made and failed, or unless the conformation of the coast—as bluffs, precipitous banks, etc.—is such as to unquestionably preclude the use of a boat.[4]

Unfortunately, this quote has been badly mangled a huge number of times. It has also been erroneously attributed to others. The above, however, is from the official Coast Guard website and from an *eyewitness*.

The Real Quest

It is one thing to cite the correct quote with the correct person who said it, but there is an even deeper mystery here. In all the literature, records, and documents that I have seen, nowhere does it say which wreck this was or when it occurred.

The only "knowns" from the eyewitness were that the wreck was on the Diamond Shoals and that the surfboat was launched. We do *not* know which shipwreck it was, when it happened, whether it was the Inner Shoals or the Outer Shoals—or even which station it was. Patrick Etheridge had also been the keeper of Station Creeds Hill from August 27, 1884, until April 2, 1888. The Diamond Shoals would also have been an area of responsibility for Creeds Hill, who were very often requested by Station Cape Hatteras to assist. But there were *no* shipwreck accounts in the *Annual Reports* for Creeds Hill during that time period. So, it had to be at Station Cape Hatteras.

The Possibilities

In searching all of the *Annual Reports* during the time period from May 6, 1891, to October 31, 1909, that Patrick H. Etheridge was keeper of the Cape Hatteras LSS Station, a smoking gun was found. (Quotes following are from the official *Annual Report* of that year. Text in brackets are the author's edits.):[5]

Schooner *Martha*: March 4, 1893, zero lives lost. [Can eliminate; breeches buoy rescue was made, not by surfboat.]

Barkentine *J. W. Dresser*: July 23, 1895, zero lives lost. [Could be; wrecked on "outer Diamond Shoals during heavy weather."]

Steamer *Glanayron*: May 22, 1896, zero lives lost. [Could be; "wrecked 7:45 p.m., outer Diamond Shoals in heavy weather." Three stations responded, decided to wait until morning.]

Steamer *Hesperides*: October 9, 1897, zero lives lost. [Can eliminate. Wrecked in "hazy weather, SW point of Diamond Shoals." Report describes easy launching of surfboat.]

Schooner *William H. Kenzal*: April 5, 1900, (unknown) lives lost. [Probably eliminate. Strangely, there is no account for this wreck in any volume of the *Annual Reports*. Even expert David Stick could not find it!]

Steamer *Virginia*: May 2, 1900, six lives lost. [*The most likely*. Full explanation to follow.]

Schooner *Hettie J. Dorman*: May 5, 1900, zero lives lost. [Can eliminate. Although wrecked on Outer Diamond Shoals, cause was striking a submerged vessel, no storm.]

Steamer *Palestro*: August 9, 1900, zero lives lost. [Probably not. "Stranded on Outer Diamond Shoal during thick weather." Probably means fog or heavy rain but, apparently, no storm.]

Schooner *George R. Congdon*: January 31, 1901, zero lives lost. [Can eliminate. "Stranded on beach."]

Steamer *Northeastern*: December 27, 1904, zero lives lost. [*Highly likely*.] From the *Annual Report*:

> At 11 p.m., during a strong SSW wind, with a very high sea and thick fog, the *Northeastern*, a freight steamer of 2,206 tons, carrying 22 men, struck upon the outer point of Diamond Shoals, about 9 miles from either station, ultimately breaking up and becoming a total loss. Her signals of distress were observed at both stations at about 4 a.m., and rockets were sent up in response, while the keepers held consultation

by telephone. Owing to the dangerous surf it was impossible
to launch a boat to go to the rescue and, in fact, the weather
was so thick that it was not possible for the lifesavers to know
that a vessel was upon the shoals. The weather continued
thick until the morning of the 28th, when the wreck could
be sighted. Keeper Etheridge, of Cape Hatteras station, then
called away the surfboat, and the crew endeavored to launch,
but at each attempt the boat was hurled back upon the beach
by the resistless breakers.[6]

Schooner *Cordelia E. Hays*: January 15, 1905, zero lives lost. [Not
likely, since it wrecked on the Inner Diamond Shoals.]
Schooner *Robert H. Stevenson*: January 13, 1906, twelve lives lost.
[Can definitely eliminate. No station ever saw it, so there was no
USLSS response.]
Schooner *Hilda*: February 6, 1907, seven lives lost. [An excellent
candidate.]

Following is the log of attempts to rescue the crew of the three-masted
schooner *Hilda*, February 6, 1907. She grounded on the Inner Diamond
Shoals five miles offshore in a heavy gale about 4:00 a.m. A heroic
effort was made by crews from both stations to save those on board but
all seven perished:

2:15 a.m.—Surfmen B. F. Etheridge and U. B. Williams of Cape
Hatteras Station discover vessel in the direction of Diamond
Shoals. Burned three Coston signals.
2:30 a.m.—Keeper P. H. Etheridge, in the lookout tower of his
station, could see the vessel in the moonlight. Was slowly
moving southward.
4:00 a.m.—Vessel stopped, presumably anchored. Made no
signal of distress. Lifesavers fired rocket to let her know they
had her under surveillance.

6:00 a.m.—Lookouts at both Cape Hatteras and Creeds Hill stations reported distress signals from vessel. Rockets fired in response.

6:30 a.m.—Cape Hatteras surfboat launched.

7:20 a.m.—Creeds Hill surfboat launched.

8:00 a.m.—Two surfboats met near Inner Diamond Shoals. Northwest wind blowing at gale force. Sea very rough. Temperature below freezing and still falling. Vessel a three-masted schooner hard aground on inner shoals five miles from Cape Point and surrounded by huge breakers for half a mile in all directions.

8:15 a.m.—Surfboats attempted to go through breakers to stricken vessel but thrown back by raging sea. Vessel now sunk, waves sweeping over her fore and aft. One man seen clinging to remnants of cabin.

9:00–12:00 a.m.—Repeated attempts made to reach vessel. All unsuccessful. Surfboats frequently almost submerged by tremendous breakers.

12:00 noon—Having exhausted every means of rescue and in constant danger of capsizing, surfboats head for shore.

12:30 p.m.—Mast of Creeds Hill surfboat breaks off. Boat wallowing in waves. Impossible to use oars because of size of waves and force of wind. Mast finally hauled aboard and patched up.

1:30 p.m.—Cape Hatteras surfboat reached shore safely.

4:00 p.m.—Damaged Creeds Hill surfboat finally beached near Cape Point.

February 7, 1907:

6:00 a.m.—Crews from both stations again assemble on beach to attempt rescue. Weather murky.

7:00 a.m.—Sky clears. Wind still blowing strong. Surf high. Schooner has completely disappeared, presumably broken up with loss of all hands.

Steamer *Brewster*: November 29, 1909, zero lives lost. [Would have been another most excellent possibility, except it was a month after Patrick Etheridge left the Cape Hatteras station! Very famous wreck. The acting keeper, Baxter Miller, received Gold Lifesaving Medal.]

And now, the time, place, circumstances and *the* shipwreck that *most likely* allowed United States Life-Saving Service Cape Hatteras Station Keeper Patrick Henry Etheridge to utter that most famous line.

Steamer *Virginia*: May 2, 1900, six lives lost. [The most likely.]

The *Virginia* was a large 2,314-ton vessel. On the fateful day of May 2, 1900, she had been bound from Daiquiri, Cuba, to Baltimore, Maryland, with a cargo of iron ore. Captain Charles Samuels of London, England, was sailing master with her crew of twenty-four men.

Around 2:00 p.m. that day, Captain Samuels ordered the sounding lead to be thrown, for he knew he was approaching the dreaded Diamond Shoals of Cape Hatteras, North Carolina, and that history had repeatedly taught that no chances were to be taken there. The

Actual photo of the steamer Virginia, *1909, from postcard.*
Public domain.

first sounding showed fifty fathoms of water, very safe indeed. So, he altered course to a little closer to the cape. For three and a half hours it was clear sailing, but still constant soundings were taken. The problem, which would have been innocuous anywhere else, the *Annual Report* tells us, was "The wind was light from the northwest and the sea was rather rough, while the weather was hazy, resembling a fog, and consequently objects were not visible at any considerable distance."[7]

As suddenly as it happened to the great RMS *Titanic*, the lookout at the bow alerted imminent danger, in this case by crying out "breakers ahead!" The *Virginia* ran aground and quickly put her engines in reverse to get off the grounding. Unlike the *Titanic*, however, the *Virginia* was given a second chance. About that time, Captain Samuels had just returned to the bridge from his supper. He believed they should continue and countermanded the previous order and rang the bell for "full speed ahead." Almost immediately, the *Virginia* ran so violently aground that she split and began filling with day-old May Day Atlantic water. She lay nine nautical miles from the Cape Hatteras Life-Saving Station in one direction and the same distance for the Creeds Hill Life-Saving Station, making her extremely difficult to reach. The deadly Diamond Shoals wasted no time claiming another victim. She broke the ship into three pieces! As the disaster unfolded, the first two lifeboats to be lowered were smashed to pieces but were empty. The next was successfully launched with fifteen crew who rowed safely away from the wreck. Another lifeboat was launched with seven crewmen but soon capsized and six were drowned.

There now remained only five persons on the wreck itself. The *Annual Report* sadly continues, "The steamer's hull was awash, and there was no better place of refuge than the main rigging, to which the survivors speedily betook themselves. All about them was the impenetrable haze or fog, while their eyes rested upon a most disheartening scene below… The vessel was broken into three pieces, and through the rents in its jagged sides the water hissed and foamed, and at intervals spouted upward in great volumes 15 or 20 feet high . . . [now] nothing showed above the sea but the two masts, the bridge and funnel, and a few feet of a flagstaff far aft. All this dreadful havoc had been wrought in little more than 30 minutes."[8]

This story, like so many in this forgotten history, gets worse, more disheartening, and harder to believe. The remaining crew knew they were out of sight of any help from land, so they decided to set a signal fire, since nightfall was now approaching. But those supplies were in a different part of the three broken ship sections. They spent the dark night alone and unseen.

The next morning, desperate, they rigged a zipline to the bridge, a section that was more above water and had more room. The forecastle was another broken-off section that held the lifegiving supplies. Now with increasing hopelessness, they risked all to swim to the forecastle and they managed to procure some kerosene and some material to burn. But the day had dawned hazy, lessening any chances of being seen, so they waited until dark to light a signal fire. They spent another frantic night fighting for salvation. The tide had risen, the wind had increased, and frequent sudden rain showers had all conspired to put out their signal, yet they persisted. Yet, another night passed.

Awakening to dwindling hope, they were out of ideas, food, and strength. Here, almost unbelievably, we should hear the Lone Ranger's theme song playing, for their signals had been seen by surfmen of both Life-Saving stations. At 7:00 a.m., Keeper Patrick H. Etheridge of Cape Hatteras and Keeper Homer W. Styron of Creeds Hill launched their rescue boats. "The wind was now blowing a gale from the northward, and the sea was running high, but there was no faint heart among the life-savers, although they knew full well the peril of their undertaking."[9] The five shipwreck victims were saved but under the most strenuous and dangerous conditions.

And now, the smoking gun:

From the *Annual Report of the Operations of the United States Life-Saving Services for the Fiscal Year Ending June 30, 1909*: "To have attempted such a feat during the second night, when the uncertain light was seen which raised a bare suspicion of a disaster, would have been, as one of the most competent witnesses declares, simply foolhardy, and without justification of the dangers involved."[10] We must repeat, with emphasis added, "*as one of the most competent witnesses declares, simply foolhardy.*" Once this "most competent witness" expressed his doubt of success, it seems fairly obvious that this is when Keeper Patrick Etheridge must have replied, "*The Blue Book says we've got to go out and it doesn't say a damn thing about having to come back.*"

VIII.

AGAINST ALL ODDS

CHAPTER 20
SCHOONER
THOMAS J. MARTIN,
JANUARY 9, 1883

Overcoming insurmountable odds was what the United States Life-Saving Service routinely surmounted to rescue "those in peril on the sea." Such was the case in the rescue of the schooner Thomas J. Martin, *January 9, 1883.*

The wreck of the schooner *Thomas J. Martin* on the Outer Banks was in many ways a typical scenario of shipwrecks and surfmen's rescues of the late 1800s. In the "storm month" of January, being the "pitchest" of black nights, the Graveyard of the Atlantic weather threw the small vessel out of control and ran it hard aground near the present town of Duck, North Carolina. The lifesavers from nearby Caffeys Inlet Station soon spotted her distress on routine beach patrol. The surf was too violent to launch their surfboat, and the night was too black to use the Lyle gun to shoot her a line; so, once again, the lifesavers were faced with a dilemma.

The Economics

Trade between the North and the South of the United States during the 1700s, 1800s, and early 1900s was mostly confined to East Coast

Atlantic shipping, and was almost always done by the hard-working "blue collar" vessel of the times: the schooner. The origin of the term "schooner" is not certain but probably derives from the Scottish term that loosely means "skipping over water," such as skipping stones, which every boy has done numerous times in his childhood. Compared to the lumbering, heavy ships preceding them, the schooner may have felt like it was skipping over the water.

Although the South was largely agricultural, it tended to be mostly large plantations rather than small farms. Consequently, what is not generally known today is that the North necessarily had many small farms for local produce. One of the most important ingredients for these farmers was fertilizer. By the 1880s, commercial fertilizer was being produced that contained three main elements: nitrogen, phosphorus, and potassium.

The first large-scale phosphate mining in the United States was in the vicinity of Charleston, South Carolina, in the counties of Charleston, Colleton, and Beaufort. Mining started in 1868 and continued until 1938.

PHOSPHATE

The term *phosphate rock* (or *phosphorite*) is used to denote any rock with high phosphorus content. The largest and least expensive source of phosphorus is obtained by mining and concentrating phosphate rock from the numerous phosphate deposits of the world. Some phosphate rock is used to make calcium phosphate nutritional supplements for animals. Pure phosphorus is used to make chemicals for use in industry. The most important use of phosphate rock, though, is in the production of phosphate fertilizers for agriculture. Virtually all common fertilizers have an "N-P-K" rating. Phosphorus is the "P" in fertilizers. Phosphorus is involved in numerous plant functions, but its most important role is helping plants capture the sun's energy and begin the photosynthesis process.[1]

The Beach Patrol Daily Duty

In chapter 1 of my book *Shipwrecks of the Outer Banks: Dramatic Rescues and Fantastic Wrecks in the Graveyard of the Atlantic*, I describe these procedures. Here, I offer a brief summary: For the beach patrol, two men from each station were sent to the beach at the same time. They would walk in opposite directions, heading toward their neighboring station. They would meet the neighboring station's beach patrolling surfman halfway, chat, and exchange beach checks to prove to their keepers that the patrol was complete.

"Beach check," replica. Author's photo.

Every beach check in the entire Service bore three numbers: the district number (of thirteen) in the US, the station number within that sistrict, and the surfman number (1–8) within that station. Consequently, every beach check was unique—there was only one combination of those three numbers in that order.

The Wreck and Rescue

So it was that the schooner *Thomas J. Martin*, whose homeport was Bridgeton, New Jersey, with a crew of eight, was bringing a load of phosphate rock from Charleston, South Carolina, to New York. Unfortunately, this voyage was scheduled for January of 1883. Not long after weighing anchor in Charleston, the *Thomas J. Martin* was sailing into the dark, blustery night off of the North Carolina coast. Around 1:00 a.m., the weather worsened, blowing the north-northeast winds that were typical for that time of year along the Outer Banks, which were frothing up the sea. She was out of control and stranded about four hundred yards from shore and half a mile to the north of the Caffeys Inlet Station, now renumbered Station No. 10.

CAFFEYS INLET STATION KEEPER MALACHI CORBELL, EARLIER

From the US Coast Guard History Program: Keeper Malachi Corbell saved two African American fishermen whose boat capsized near Caffeys Inlet, North Carolina, and in June 1877 became the first member of the US Life-Saving Service to win the Congressional Lifesaving medal. He was awarded a Silver Lifesaving Medal.

On regular northbound beach patrol from Station Caffeys Inlet on the night of Tuesday, January 9, 1883, the station patrolman was over two miles north of the wreck when he discovered her, which was about twenty minutes after her stranding. "He at once fired his red Coston light and ran for the station, where he arrived at two o'clock, badly exhausted with the speed of his course," we learn from the *Annual Report of the Operations of the United States Life-Saving Services for the Fiscal Year Ending June 30, 1883.*[2]

Years of daily training, standard at every United States Life-Saving Service station, immediately kicked in. Keeper Daniel B. Austin immediately shot up some rockets, "both as a signal of cheer for the ship and to recall the patrolman on the south beat for service with the rest of the crew."[3] The *Annual Report* that year further states, "The night was so black and thick and the surf so high, that it was judged prudent to operate with the wreck [Lyle] gun rather than the boat, and this, with the beach apparatus, was accordingly taken, the rescuing party arriving abreast of the wreck by half past two."[4] That means all hands with necessary lifesaving equipment on the two-ton wreck cart had been on scene seventy minutes after the wreck was spotted, ready to serve "so that others may live."

Mother Nature, however, was not cooperating. It was so utterly dark that the lifesavers could not even see the wreck. This made the Lyle gun attempt unfeasible, since there was no target and no known distance. Furthermore, the surf had become so turbulent that it precluded the use of the surfboat. In complete frustration, the only course left for the life-savers was to wait. Even then, however, it would not be idly. The *Annual Report* continues: "In the enforced interim of waiting, the keeper left one man with orders to build a fire upon the beach, and hurried back with the remainder of the crew to fetch the surf boat for use if it should be required."[5] This was typical for this Service, who was always prepared for all contingencies.

Shortly before dawn, the weather cleared enough for the wreck to be seen. The Lyle gun was planted, aimed, elevated, and fired, and it produced a near perfect attempt, placing the shot and shot line in the forward rigging. As usual, immediately following, the whip line was sent, then the hawser, and finally the instrument of salvation: the breeches buoy.

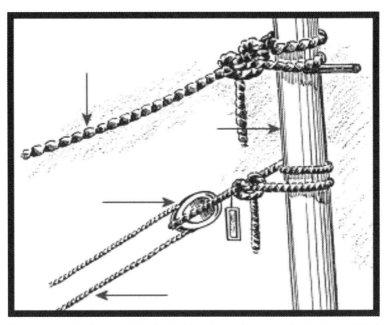

Illustration showing the setup of attaching, first the whip line (lower) and then the hawser (upper) as high as possible on a mast.
Courtesy of the US Coast Guard.

Setting up all the equipment aboard the wrecked vessel itself requires 100 percent effort of the ship's crew. The efforts of the *Thomas J. Martin*, crew, however, was not up to Keeper Austin's standards and were so dismally slow that it was light enough to safely launch the surfboat, which keeper Austin did! The Caffeys Inlet lifesavers made speedy work of the rescue, the eight men on board being brought ashore on the first trip and most of their baggage on the second. By half past 7:00 a.m., all hands were in the station, where the rescued men received proper attention; five of them were fed and sheltered at the station for a day and a half, after which they left for their homes; the other three remained for eight days. That is what this Service did.

But that is not all. They were also very frugal. "At one o'clock on the day of the rescue the life saving [*sic*] crew again went out in the surf boat, taking with them the schooner's mate, and made an effort to recover the shot line, which had been left attached on board."[6] Rough seas made the attempt unsuccessful, so they tried again three days later, but it proved to be so entangled that it was let go.

As almost a postscript, the *Annual Report* ends with "Two patrolmen from the two stations on either side of Caffeys Inlet [Poyners Hill to the north; Paul Gamiels Hill to the south], not meeting with the patrols therefrom, pushed on to see what was the matter, and finding them at the wreck turned in and rendered good service. The colored cook of the Caffeys Inlet Station, Appollus Owens, also volunteered, and helped all he could."[7]

Another successful, joyous, difficult rescue by the United States Life-Saving Service—a huge piece of heroic American history that hardly anyone has ever heard of.

CHAPTER 21

STORM-TOSSED SCHOONER
ARIO PARDEE

It would be extremely difficult to top the amazingly painful story of "Dunbar Davis's Longest Day."[1] Beginning on Tuesday, August 29, 1893, fifty-year-old Keeper Davis of Oak Island Station, North Carolina, spent fifty-five consecutive hours without sleep, food, or water while responding to five different wrecks, one after the other, mostly on his own.

However, almost unbelievably, the 198-ton, three-masted schooner *Ario Pardee* would endure an incredible 152 hours in five consecutive storms before finally becoming a total loss at the Wash Woods Life-Saving Service Station. This would be nine years before Dunbar Davis's soggy saga at Oak Island and at the extreme opposite (southern) end of the Outer Banks.

Ship Master Henry A. Smith and crewmen John W. Comer, Ole Jensen, John Force, and Thomas B. Allen not only outdid Dunbar Davis's marathon but also exceeded it by a factor of ten!

The trip's itinerary was very simple: Perth Amboy, New Jersey, to nearby Chester, Pennsylvania. This was approximately ninety miles and almost any sailing ship of the day could easily make that trip in a day or two at most.

The Odyssey Begins

Usually, one thinks of the Greek poet Homer when hearing the word odyssey. It is most correctly used, however, since *Merriam-Webster* defines an odyssey as "a wandering or long voyage usually marked by many changes in fortune." This voyage of the schooner *Ario Pardee* is a classic example of that.

In the *Annual Report* of 1885, the captain writes, "I sailed December 8, 1884, from Perth Amboy, with a crew of five men, all told, on the schooner *A. Pardee*, of Perth Amboy, bound from the port of Rondout, New York, to Chester, Pennsylvania, with a cargo of cement."[2]

INCORRECT DATE

Although this is from the captain's own report, the December 8 date is clearly incorrect. All records indicate the odyssey lasted ten days, not the thirty-two days total if she left on the eighth. Furthermore, Outer Banks author and historian David Stick, renowned for his thorough and meticulous research, puts the date as December 18. The original date of Captain Smith's 1884 document is easily explained as a simple typo or one keystroke error in a transcript.

"Sailed at 7 a.m. Wind northwest. Passed Sandy Hook [New Jersey] 11 a.m. When abreast of Long Branch, the wind shifted to north, and commenced to snow. At 6 p.m., wind blowing a gale from the north, took in sail, and run the vessel before the wind under a reefed mainsail and jib."[3] Then he calmly adds, "Gale lasted fifty-six hours." The strong north wind was blowing and pushing the *Ario Pardee* to the south, in precisely the opposite direction the captain wanted to go.

This endured from 6:00 p.m. Monday, all through that night, then all the next day and all night Tuesday, and all day and night Wednesday, then all day Thursday before finally ending at 2:00 a.m. into Friday early morning. This, however, was just the *first* storm.

It boggles the mind to imagine what these five men were doing all that time. Captain Smith does not say, nor does the *Annual Report of the Operations of the United States Life-Saving Service for the Fiscal Year Ending June 30, 1885*, which only describes the lifesavers' rescue.

Using the modern definition of "gale," this means sustained winds ranging from thirty-nine to fifty-four miles per hour. At its maximum, such winds can produce ocean wave heights from eighteen to thirty-two feet. Only winds produced by what is technically named a "storm" or a "hurricane" will exceed that.[4]

For fifty-six straight hours, then, the schooner was tossed about, perpetually unstable and out of balance. As Captain Smith describes, "we had continuous high seas, washing everything movable from deck; stove [archaic term meaning "bashed in" or "smashed"] water casks and split sails."[5]

Walking or even standing would be like imitating a drunken sailor. Sleeping would be well-nigh impossible. Eating was almost out of the question, for no cookstove could be lit for danger of burning down the wooden ship. What was left? Warm beer, stale ship biscuits, and perhaps some cold canned goods.

A Second and Third Gale

In spite of all, Smith says not a word. Instead, his very next sentence is, "Afterwards took a gale from south, lasting about twenty-four hours, and run before that."[6] He meant to sail away from the storm, keeping the stern in front of the storm. "This tactic requires a lot of sea room, and the boat must be steered actively."[7] He does not say what happened or what they did during that time, just that it is another full day of storms. We do not know exactly where the *Ario Pardee* is, and Smith probably doesn't either.

Presumably, shortly after that, Smith does not say how long, but simply, "Then took a gale northwest and run that out." Nor does he say how long this third gale lasted or how they handled it, other than "running it out." But the good news, finally it might seem, was that the winds had

The five fathom light ship; the vessel in the picture is the similar but more modern LV-108 (or LS-108), which served from 1924 until 1942.
US Coast Guard Lightship Sailors Association and Friends Association, Inc.

calmed down enough for Captain Smith to take control of the schooner, so he "made what sail we could and run for land."[8] The battered but manageable vessel made it to the lightship off Five-Fathom Bank. "Located in the Atlantic Ocean to help guide vessels to the Delaware Bay, the original lightship was recommended for establishment in 1826. Over the years several ships endured the rough weather, heavy seas";[9] it was replaced several times.

Almost Unbelievably, Yet More Storms

About five miles out from lightship LV-40 (the fourth such vessel, serving from 1877 until 1904), Smith was struck by yet another gale—this being westerly, it pushed him toward the Delaware shore. The *Pardee* hove to and rode out this storm for another twelve hours. At least then Captain Smith knew where he was, and it was dreadfully off course.

After passing another half day going nowhere, the winds abated, allowing Smith to make sail and head for land. Nothing would be that easy on this day, however. Coming tantalizingly close to a safe landfall, *Pardee* made it to the Indian River Inlet, heading for the Delaware Breakwater, when it was struck by strong north winds. At this point being about five miles from Cape Henlopen to his northwest, the winds "blew away jib. Hove the vessel to again, wind blowing a gale and snowing."[10]

Beginning of the End

Could it get any worse? You will guess by now that it certainly would. It did. By the next day, the schooner was seriously damaged, broken, and leaking badly. It was time to run up the proverbial white flag. Due to extremely overdue good luck, the steamer *Chattahoochie* was nearby. Smith contacted her and asked if she could take him and his crew off.

Captain J. W. Catherine of the *Chattahoochie* of the Savannah Line reported spotting the disabled vessel at 2:30 p.m. and that she was flying her ensign upside down, an international maritime signal of distress. The *New York Times* article of December 28, 1884, reported that the *Pardee* was rolling in such a dangerous manner that it was impossible to get alongside. The article continued ominously, "For several moments the occupants of the [life]boat seemed in much greater danger than the people on the schooner."[11] Sailor Thomas B. Allen of the *Pardee* was finally rescued, but it was then getting dark, and rain and sleet began, so the steamer withdrew. At that time, sailor Allen reported that the *Pardee* already had four feet of water in her hold.

Sadly, Smith reports, "The steamer made two attempts to take us off. They got one man by life buoy and line. The sea running very high and night coming on, she left us."[12]

Captain Smith had one less crew and a broken and sinking ship that was still in a storm. With no other options, he heaved to again and endured the final battering *for another sixty hours*!

At midnight, *ten days later*, Smith happily reported, "we sighted a bright red light ahead and saw breakers. Let go both anchors. In a short time saw lights on shore and heard guns fired at intervals during the night. Heard two shots pass over the vessel but could not find any line. At daylight 2th we discovered that we were near a lifesaving station and saw signals by flags. We had no code to answer signals. Set our ensign in distress."[13] The bright red light was actually the Currituck Beach light, and the guns fired during the night were the Lyle gun from Wash Woods Service Station.

From the *Annual Report*, "Just before midnight of the 28th the south patrol of the Wash Woods Station (6th District), North Carolina saw a schooner close in, about a quarter of a mile south of the station. The sea was running high, and the weather was thick and foggy. He hurried to the station and reported his discovery to the keeper, who at once turned out the crew and had the beach apparatus hauled down the shore to a point abreast of the vessel and placed in position."[14]

The *Annual Report* continues, "By this time the crews of the False Cape [Virginia] and the Currituck Beach Stations [North Carolina] arrived on the ground to render assistance." The surf boat was soon successfully launched, and the lifesavers were able to board the wounded schooner. Keeper Corbel provided each of the vessel's crew with a cork life preserver, placed them and their baggage in the boat, and, by 9:00 a.m., had them all safely landed.

Then Captain Smith, in his *Report* log concludes, "Vessel still afloat, but sea running very high. At 10 a.m. vessel parted chains and came ashore, and soon began breaking up. Vessel was about a quarter of a mile from shore, in two and a half fathoms of water, when we were rescued by Captain Corbel [keeper of the Wash Woods Station, usually referred to by all as "Captain"] and his brave crew, and only for their aid we would most likely have all been lost. We, the master and crew of the schooner *Ario Pardee*, desire to return our most sincere thanks to Captain Corbel and his men for their timely rescue of us from our perilous position and their kind treatment of us since."[15]

The Wash Woods Life-Saving Station, original photo from January 1885.
Courtesy of the US Coast Guard; public domain.

The *Pardee* crew were sheltered at the Wash Woods Life-Saving Station for another twelve days. As was standard operating procedure at all US Life-Saving Stations, the survivors were given a place to stay, dry clothes, meals, and any needed first aid. Captain Smith had lost his shoes and was provided a pair from the station's stock, which was supplied by the Women's National Relief Association.

The vessel and cargo were a total loss. Ship Master Henry A. Smith and crewmen John W. Comer, Ole Jensen, and John Force were alive and had survived an impossible string of 152 hours of storms.

Holidays?

Far too many days, twenty-two of them, after leaving port in Perth Amboy, New Jersey, their arduous storm-tossed schooner trip was over. Ironically, along the way they had passed sixty-five United States Life-Saving Service Stations: forty-one in New Jersey, six in Delaware, thirteen in Maryland, and five more in Virginia. Also, they would have passed too many lighthouses to list here!

Some of the better known of those Life-Saving stations included the following (those italicized were featured in this story):

New Jersey—*Sandy Hook*, Monmouth Beach, Atlantic City, Ocean City, and Cape May;

Delaware—Lewes, *Cape Henlopen*, Rehoboth Beach, and the still-existing Little River;

Maryland—Isle of Wight, Ocean City, Wallops Island, and Smith Island; and

Virginia—Cape Henry, Virginia Beach, and *False Cape*.

Today, we know that a holiday is a joyous, fun celebration and/or a vacation. This grueling odyssey was clearly the opposite of that. However, when it is realized that the word "holiday" comes from the old English "holy day," this takes on an entirely different meaning. Yes, the crew had missed the holidays of Christmas Day and New Year's Day. But they arrived home through the grace of God just as a New Year was beginning. Surely a holy day for them.

CHAPTER 22

SCHOONER *LEONORA*

YET ANOTHER TRAGIC
LESSON UNLEARNED

In this story, almost everything that could go wrong to help thwart the life-savers' rescue did. Lesser men certainly would have failed, but these stalwart surfmen succeeded against all odds. Their persistence, endurance, and sacrifice are unimaginable to most of us today. But they reflected these dauntlessly. And for what? So that others may live.

Poor decisions and panic on vessels facing shipwreck, combined with sudden and extreme changes in conditions, have always made it necessary for United States Life-Saving Service crews to be ready and prepared for almost any situation. These modest stations, although located miles apart on the sands of the treacherous North Carolina coast, always made it standard operating procedure to assist each other when the cry "ship ashore!" was sounded.

All of this was true for the unfortunate wreck of the old schooner *Leonora* and the Life-Saving stations of Cape Hatteras and Creeds Hill. It is, yet again, another account of not only the avoidable loss of a ship but also the loss of lives—that is, the ship's crew and captain. Oh, how the surfmen wished ships' crews would listen and learn from them.

The Ship

"The *Leonora* was a three-masted schooner of 458 tons, formerly the whaling brig *Leonora*, of New Bedford, built in 1874 [the same year that the first seven United States Life-Saving Service North Carolina stations were established]. At the time of the disaster described here she was owned by the Gilbert Transportation Company, of Mystic, Connecticut, and was registered in New London. She left Round Pond, Maine, on what proved to be her last voyage, December 2, 1907, with a cargo of fish scrap consigned to parties in Charleston, South Carolina. There were seven men in her crew, all told, as follows: W. K. Gillchrist, master; Fred Reed, mate; Harry Steab, Peter Smith, John _____ (a Canadian), and Otto _____ (a Norwegian), seamen; and Rudolph Almeida, cook. As indicated, the surnames of two of the seamen could not be ascertained. Steab and Almeida were the only survivors of the shipwreck."[1]

A Series of Mistakes

As is the case in so many other situations, a disaster is often the result of a series of poor decisions rather than a single incident. The first mistake made was converting *Leonora* from her original configuration of a whaling brig to a schooner. These are two entirely different designs: whaling brigs are for the open ocean, for sailing deep waters for years at a time. Schooners are for quick coastal trade in shallow waters. Such a conversion required compromises, some of which contributed to *Leonora*'s fatality.

The second big mistake was keeping the vessel in service long past her useful—and safe—lifespan.

It is worthy of remark that in four of the six instances in which loss of life occurred during the year within the domain of the service in connection with disasters to water craft the vessels involved were old—a circumstance that, one may conclude from the evidence filed in the Department, had something to do

with the outcome of the casualties as regards the accompany-
ing fatalities . . . [among the four such vessels] was the *Leonora*,
thirty-three years, also be mentioned that the four vessels named
constitute the entire number of the large or documented class to
suffer shipwreck during the year with fatal consequences.[2]

Trouble Begins

All the way from her Maine departure until reaching Cape Hatteras on
Sunday, January 6, *Leonora* enjoyed fair winds and following seas. But
then and there, Cape Hatteras started to display her iconic and infamous
weather—a storm was brewing. All Atlantic coast ship captains were
aware of the dreaded Cape Hatteras and the lethal Diamond Shoals. We
assume that Captain Gillchrist was also thusly conscious. Or was he?

As the fury of the storm increased, conditions for the *Leonora* worsened. She had already "shortened sail" by reefing, furling, and changing
to smaller sails. But it was not enough.

"She had been leaking hours before the weather had grown so tempestuous as of itself to menace her safety" was a testimony given by one
of the only two survivors, seaman Steab. The *Annual Report* goes on to
say, "Her anchors were let go about 9 o'clock on the night of the 7th,
at which time she was half full of water, the crew having been pump-
ing for thirty-six hours without being able to free her."[3] This was the
third—and most costly—mistake.

The next day, things went from bad to worse. One negative event
after another built to the inevitable. All of the few remaining sails were
blown away and the schooner was "under bare poles, and completely at
the mercy of the elements."[4] There could not have been a more helpless feeling: a waterlogged vessel with no sails—meaning no control or
guidance—in a violent storm at night and entrapped in the worst possible place—in the coils of the dreaded Cape Hatteras Diamond Shoals.

Captain Gillchrist was facing the inescapable and painful decision that
ships' captains caught in storms near dangerous shores have long had to
make—that is, to "give up the ship" and beach her. This was his plan.

"When the vessel got into 8 fathoms, however, about 9 p. m., the mate prevailed upon him [the master] to drop the anchors and try to ride it out, expressing the belief that when day dawned their condition would be discovered from the shore and a tug be sent to their assistance."[5] This was the fourth mistake. It was a fatal decision. Why would an experienced seafarer let a lesser sailor override his decision? Perhaps it was the terror of the situation, or a ray of hope with which to counter the gloomy dread. Or maybe it was just a mistake in judgement.

The Wreck

Only one outcome could occur under such conditions. And it did. Amazingly, however, there was still a faint possibility of salvation. The Cape Hatteras beach patrol by surfman E. F. Stowe had not only spotted the distressed vessel but had also signaled it, letting the crew know that help was nearby and on the way, when necessary. But it got worse: "After some delay, spent in searching for a torch, the sailors [on the *Leonora*] burned an answering signal, and receiving no response from the beach they would have signalled [*sic*] again, but when they returned to the cabin, where it seems the necessary combustibles were stored, they found the place flooded."[6]

With only minutes remaining, the crew scrambled from one haven to the next. As the vessel was being swept over completely by the raging surf, the crew first headed for and up the fore-rigging. As the rigging began to collapse, they came down, reached the main mast, and began to climb. As the storm brought it down also, carrying the mate overboard with it, the remaining crew headed to the back and climbed out in desperation on the spanker boom.

"What now remained of the stricken ship did not last more than fifteen minutes longer. It appears from the evidence that Steab and Almeida—the only survivors—succeeded in getting on the shoal, from which they were eventually rescued, by holding on to drifting wreckage, but whether they were on the schooner when she broke up or were washed overboard previous to that time is not shown."[7] Keeper Patrick

Etheridge of the Cape Hatteras Life-Saving Station explains, "We heard a man hallooing, and I knew some of the crew were on the island. This island is a shoal that made up last summer off the cape. It is bare at half tide, and at high tide the seas break all over it. There is a slue 10 or 15 feet deep and 200 or 300 yards wide separating it from the mainland. The shoal changes during gales, at times entirely disappearing."[8] It was pure luck that they made it there at that particular moment.

The Incredible Rescue

Meanwhile, the Creeds Hill Station patrol by Surfman R. W. Basnett had also spotted the schooner's distress light signal and reported it to Keeper Peele. Both stations sent crews to the beach and tried to see through the storm and the darkness to determine what to do.

"The boat was taken to a spot 14 miles from Hatteras station and placed on the beach, ready for launching."[9] This simple statement is very typical of such reports, which often have "an economy of words." That was all it said. Fourteen miles! That is, fourteen miles on foot, on the

The United States Life-Saving Service Creeds Hill 1878 Station No. 24. Second from the left, in the double-breasted jacket, is Keeper Eugene Peele. The fifth adult from the left is Surfman William "Bill" Styron, who is detailed in graphics from the Virginian Pilot.
National Park Service, Cape Hatteras National Seashore.

sandy beaches with wash over everywhere, in the middle of the night, in the middle of a horrific storm with howling winds. How tortuous that must have been. And that just begins the arduous rescue in the surfboat powered by what the surfmen called "Armstrong engines." The two survivors on "the island" were rescued. They were brought back to the Cape Hatteras Life-Saving Station and given first aid, food and water, dry clothes, comfort, and a place to recover. But even then, the rescue work was not finished.

Both stations had surfmen remain guard on the beach all night looking for more possible survivors washing ashore. None were found. However, the next day, January 9, the bodies of all the lost sailors were recovered: three of those by the surfmen of Creeds Hill, one by the men of the Big Kinnakeet Station, and one by the crew at Gull Shoal—nearly twenty miles north of Cape Hatteras. Nothing more was said in this *Report*'s economy of words.

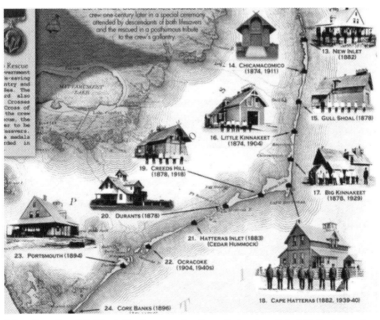

Map of a section of the North Carolina coast that shows the locations of the Life-Saving stations mentioned in this book.
Created by Bruce Roberts and Cheryl Shelton-Roberts.

The Lessons

Any wreck involving the loss of life had to be thoroughly investigated by the Service following the incident. These reports were then officially filed. The investigating officer for this particular incident concluded his report with the following: "when [the captain] found she dragged he should have slipped his chains and gone on the beach. She would undoubtedly have gone to pieces in a few minutes after striking, but the life-saving crews would have been there and would probably have saved more, if not all, of the crew."[10]

These were incredible efforts made to save lives despite horrendous conditions. Yet, somehow, America has forgotten these peaceful heroes.

SERIOUS ELECTRICAL STORM OFF HATTERAS

Norfolk, Va., Oct. 25.—The most serious electrical storm ever recorded on the Hatteras coast prevailed there for two hours beginning at midnight, William Styron in a surfman, while patrolling the beach, was struck by lightning and instanly killed. The bolt struck Styron in the head and came out of his boots, literally tearing the body to pieces. The body was subsequently found and was today prepared for burial.

From the Hatteras life saving station today it was declared that never in the history of man at that point was there such severe thunder and lightning as prevailed between midnight and 20'clock this morning. Between midnight and 90'clock today there had fallen at Hatteras more than three and a half inches of rain —a literal cloudburst. But for the sparsely settled county much havoc and loss of human life would have resulted from the storm. The lightning struck in many places. Trees were torn to pieces and the ground in many was torn up.

The storm was felt at points along the entire North Carolina coast. The rains for 24 hours have been severe in all parts of eastern North Carolina, with washouts reported in some places. The rain of the past 24 hours has brought the total pracipitation at Wilmington, N. C., up to nearly ten inches during the month of October. Lumberton, Nag.s Head, New Bern, Washington, Elizabeth City and other points throughout eastern North Carolina report heavy rain.

Copy of the newspaper article reporting the startling and tragic incident of Creeds Hill surfman William Styron. **Creedmoor News** *(NC), October 30, 1919; public domain.*

CHAPTER 23

SCHOONER *NATHANIEL LANK*, 1891

HATTERAS ISLAND

All of Mother Nature's forces were going against the lifesavers. The dual crews of the Hatteras Island's Gull Shoal and Chicamacomico Life-Saving stations faced numerous insurmountable odds. Once again, they routinely surmounted them all. Elements of this story include triumph, tragedy, persistence, bad luck, and an easily solved mystery.

Although there were other circumstances leading to shipwrecks during the days of sail, the most common reason by far was encompassed in a single word: storms. Storms produced forces that thwarted the skills of masters and crews, or that overpowered even the strongest of hulls, wood or steel. After all of the fight, effort, time, and energy expended by the ship to win the struggle, the final desperation was its wreck. There was nothing the lighthouses could do about that; this was the time for the lifesavers.

These same powerful forces were the ultimate challenge faced by the brave and wiry "storm warriors" and "recue heroes" known to mariners, worldwide, as the surfmen of the United States Life-Saving Service. This particular case involved the crews of the schooner *Nathaniel Lank* and the Life-Saving Stations of Gull Shoal and Chicamacomico.[1] All three crews—two Life-Saving stations and one ship crew—had a singular objective: save lives.

Another Hatteras Island Wreck and Rescue

The *Nathaniel Lank*, a typical cargo vessel of the times, had filled her hold with tons of sugar while at dock in St. Thomas and was bound for the Delaware Breakwater.

> The National Harbor of Refuge and the Delaware Breakwater Historic District encompasses a series of seacoast breakwaters behind Cape Henlopen, Delaware, built between 1828 and 1898 to establish a shipping haven on a coastline that lacked safe harbors.[2] The breakwater would literally "break the water"—that is, it would eliminate the waves in the surf, producing a smooth surface in the port.

Such a voyage of about 1,600 miles (or 1,390 nautical miles) takes a number of days. At an average speed of seven knots, sailing straight twenty-four hours a day, and under perfect sailing circumstances will require about eight days. A lot of weather can happen in that time. Sure enough, at 4:00 a.m. on Thursday, January 22 of 1891, the *Nathaniel Lank* became one of the many victims of an Outer Banks storm.

The Ship

The *Nathaniel Lank* was a three-masted schooner with a register of 288 tons. Her homeport was Wilmington, Delaware. At the time of this incident, she had a crew of eight, a cargo of sugar, and was captained by N. J. Sipple of Frederica, Delaware.

The Wreck

From the *Annual Report of the Operations of the United States Life-Saving Service for the Fiscal Year Ending June 30, 1891*: "The weather was thick and rainy, accompanied by a fresh gale from the south-southeast, and the sea was running high and rough. She struck about 200 yards from the beach, a little south of the halfway point between the Chicamicomico [*sic*] and Gull Shoal Stations, just within the latter's precinct."[3] These were neighboring stations, with Chicamacomico Station No. 18 being approximately six miles north of Gull Shoal Station No. 19. The south beach patrol surfman from Chicamacomico and the north beach patrol surfman for Gull Shoal quickly discovered the wreck and "at once hurried to their respective stations with the alarm, and, after a brief consultation between the two keepers by telephone as to what appliances [meaning the surfboat and/or the beach apparatus cart] each should take with the view of working in concert, they set out with their men to the scene of the wreck."[4] To be fully prepared, the keepers decided that Chicamacomico would bring their beach apparatus and Gull Shoal would bring their surfboat.

The Rescue

As had become standard operating procedure, the keeper within whose precinct the wreck landed would fire off flares. As a reminder, this had multiple purposes: If the flare was fired off by a surfman on beach patrol, it did two things: (1) it let the shipwreck crew know they had been spotted and that help was on the way and (2) it alerted the station to make ready for the rescue. If it was fired from the station itself, (1) again, it let the shipwreck crew know they had been spotted and that help was on the way and (2) tells the surfmen on beach patrol to rush back to their stations to help begin the rescue. So, Keeper David M. Pugh did just that by firing two rockets.

   The two life-saving crews arrived abreast of the wreck about the same time. The choice of which rescue method to use quickly became

LIFE-SAVING STATION KEEPERS AND CREWS IN 1891 AT GULL SHOAL AND CHICAMACOMICO[5]

United States Life-Saving Service Gull Shoal Station No. 19

Keeper: David M. Pugh

Surfman No. 1: Rasmus Midgett

Surfmen: E. S. Midgett, Ira Midgett, Davis L. Gray Sr., George L. Midgett, Gilbert B. Midgett, and Homer W. Midgett.

United States Life-Saving Service Chicamacomico Station No. 18

Keeper: Josiah H. Wescott

Surfman No. 1: William B. Midgett

Surfmen: Benjamin W. O'Neal, Charles Schroder, Joseph Midgett, Benjamin Paine, Edward S. Midgett, and John Payne.

(Now it is easy to see why we say, "The Midgetts are big around here!")

apparent. The surf was entirely too high to try launching the surfboat, so the safer method was to set up the beach apparatus, and Keeper Wescott of Chicamacomico rendered his beach apparatus to Keeper Pugh of Gull Shoal and, in proper military fashion, placed himself and his crew under Pugh's command.

They all began to synchronize the rapid movements of setting up the beach apparatus, as they had practiced every Thursday. Each surfman had a specific task and all were done simultaneously: the Lyle gun was placed, aimed, and elevated. The black powder charge was inserted in the muzzle. The faking box with the shot line was placed adjacent to the Lyle gun, its top was removed, and it was inverted and angled into position. Several feet of the shot line were wetted and then it was bent, or tied, to the twenty-pound shot. The hole for the sand anchor was being dug. The whip lines were being unreeled from the cart and faked out on the beach. The breeches buoy, the crotch pole, the sand anchor, and the fall line were laid out in place. The hawser remained coiled up in the beach cart. When all was ready and safe, the keeper fired the Lyle gun.

Keeper Pugh's first shot landed toward the rear, or stern, of the vessel between the main mast and the mizzenmast. However, the crew had all assembled at the front, or bow, of the schooner around the forecastle and bowsprit. The surfmen then observed that the schooner's crew of sailors were making no efforts to go to the stern to retrieve the shot line. It was common to have to fire multiple shots, so, in seeing this, Keeper Pugh fired a second shot sometime later that successfully landed within easy reach of the sailors.

Then it was supposed to be the simple task of sending out the whip lines and the hawser so that the breeches buoy could start hauling over sailors one at a time. Of course, it was not to be so simple.

Once the shot line reached the ship, it was up to sailors there to haul it in. That is because tied to the thin shot line is the more robust whip line. When the whip line reached the vessel, it could then be mounted to a mast via a pulley (or block). The whip line passed through the block and thus formed two lines, both ends in the hands of the lifesavers on shore. By tying the stoutest of all lines, the hawser, to one whip line, and pulling toward shore on the other whip line, the hawser could be sent to the shipwreck and tied off to the mast. Finally, the breeches buoy was tied to the whip line and went out to the shipwreck ready for a survivor to climb in.

The bad luck began when the shot line was being hauled into the shipwreck; it snapped in two. Prepared and experienced with adversity, this did not stop the momentum of the lifesavers. Pugh quickly and accurately fired a third shot to the end of the flying jib and it was obtained by the sailors. The *Annual Report* tries to politely explain the next series of snafus, "Greater caution was not observed by the latter in hauling the whip off, and being aided in this as much as possible by the surfmen, who would walk with both parts of it along the beach to windward to offset the current, and then suddenly slack out, they finally succeeded in getting the block into their hands and making it fast to the flying jib boom."[6] The lifesavers did it all. Now, the hawser could be sent out and the breeches buoy began saving lives.

Seven of the eight crew members safely landed ashore by 9:00 p.m. The missing man was *Lank*'s captain, Sipple. He had been seen going to the stern of the schooner and climbing into the rigging of the mizzenmast. The survivors gave no reason for this action, causing somewhat of a mystery. However, when it was realized that Captain Sipple had made this risky move just after the first shot was fired, it became clear that this was the definitive work of a master mariner; he saw that his men were making no effort to retrieve the shot line, which would be their salvation, so he went after it himself. Noble and heroic. Unfortunately for Sipple, the *Nathaniel Lank* was rapidly sinking, as well as going to pieces. The captain was then cut off from the successful breeches buoy on the opposite end of his ship. The *Annual Report* details his dilemma: "The only way at that time to have got forward would have been by the spring stays between the mastheads, and he was doubtless in no condition then to attempt such a perilous feat. It was equally impossible to reach him with a boat, or for anyone to go off the buoy from the shore with any prospect of aiding him, as the surf was dashing wildly over the submerged hull between the bowsprit and the rigging, where he was."[7] By around 10:00 p.m., Captain Sipple made a desperate attempt to go forward but was swept away by the violent surf.

Amazingly, his lifeless body washed ashore thirty minutes later. "Immediate efforts were made to resuscitate the body, but without success. It had been too long in the water and life was extinct. As the head and face were badly bruised it is quite likely that he was knocked insensible by contact with the wreckage very soon after being washed overboard."[8]

Newspaper Accounts

Bare-bones reports were typical of newspapers at the time, probably because there were so many shipwrecks. The one excerpted below is so expressive and detailed that today's reader can share the 1891 reporter's words directly—the *Delaware Gazette and State Journal*—Wilmington, of January 29, 1891, read as follows:

THE LANK'S SURVIVORS

Four Seamen and the Body of Their Dead Captain Reach Philadelphia

Tuesday morning's Philadelphia press says Henry King, Peter Aucker, Robert Grier, and P. Sandriage, four suffering and half-clad sailors arrived at the Sailors Home early Monday morning in quest of a resting place nearly exhausted from exposure in want of food and rest. They were some of the survivors from the Philadelphia schooner Nathanial Lank [owned by ex-governor Hall] which was wrecked off Cape Hatteras Thursday last, and telling a thrilling story of their struggles to escape being washed overboard by the enraged sea which swept that remote spot where the vessel met her end. . . .

All four of the sailors say that bad luck has followed them ever since they joined the unfortunate schooner and they have met with nothing but hardships. On the voyage from Jacksonville to Demerara the craft sprung a leak and all hands were at the pumps day and night until their destination was reached. On leaving Demerara, homeward bound, the same trouble was again experienced and the captain had to put into St. Thomas for repairs. On the night the *Lank* struck it was thick and hazy on the land and Captain Sipple had calculated himself to be further off shore.[9]

Perspective

During the twenty-year period from 1871 until 1891, there had been 5,943 shipwrecks on American shores. The combined value of ships and cargo lost was listed as more than $96 million in 1891. That is equivalent to approximately $3 *billion* today. However, the lifesavers accounted for saving $72 million in 1891 property, or $2.2 million now.

The most amazing figures, though, were typical of the Service's entire record. From 1871 to 1891, the year of this chapter's shipwreck, the lifesavers responded to 49,920 persons in peril on the sea, of which they saved 49,320; that is a 99-percent success rate. Their own loss of life in these extremely dangerous conditions, nationwide, was less than 1 percent.

But somehow America forgot.

CHAPTER 24

WRECK OF THE SCHOONER *HENRY P. SIMMONS*, THE FIRST IN A TRILOGY OF THE OCTOBER 1889 STORM

"A PECULIARLY HARROWING ONE"

The Henry P. Simmons was one ship in a trilogy of ships that were engulfed in the unholy terror of a great Outer Banks Atlantic rage known simply as "The October 1889 Storm." It would involve one short of a dozen ships, two US states, and multiple Life-Saving stations, and it would endure for nearly a week. Some were saved and some were lost.

October 23, 1889, was in general a very tempestuous month, but there can be little doubt that the most destructive storm experienced on the Middle Atlantic coast of the United States during the month was that which reached the shores of Virginia and North Carolina on the afternoon of the 23d and raged with great violence. . . . In three instances there was lamentable loss of life, the particulars of which are here given. The vessels involved were the schooners *Henry P. Simmons, Francis E. Waters,* and *Lizzie S.*

Haynes, all three being wrecked within a few miles of each other, the first two in the night of the 23d and the *Haynes* on the following day. The case of the *Simmons* was a peculiarly harrowing one.

So began the *Annual Report of the Operations of the United States Life-Saving Service for the Fiscal Year Ending June 30, 1890*, for the Sixth District.[1]

The Context

Although the wreck and attempted rescues of the schooner *Henry P. Simmons* were, indeed, peculiarly harrowing, the story cannot be told in isolation—it was a tragic part of a much larger event. There are no records of a hurricane hitting the central US coast on October 23 of 1889, but whatever it was and wherever it came from, a massive monster of a storm hit the area of the North Carolina–Virginia state line, stayed for nearly a week, and ravaged a small flotilla of ships. Typical of a nor'easter.

Along North Carolina

Wrecking within miles of each other on the northernmost coast of North Carolina were the *Francis E. Waters* (chapter 25), the *Henry P. Simmons* (chapter 24), and the *Lizzie S. Haynes* (chapter 26). Two additional North Carolina wrecks nearby that day were the three-masted schooner *Annie E. Blackman*, twenty-five miles to the south, and the 250-ton, three-masted British schooner *Busiris* that wrecked somewhat further to the south near the Poyners Hill Life-Saving Station No. 9.

For the wreck of the schooner *Annie E. Blackman*, excerpts from the *Annual Report of 1890* provide this summary:

The three-masted coal-laden Schooner Annie E. Blackman, of Somers Point, New Jersey, was lost at sea, some two or three miles off New Inlet, North Carolina, at half-past 3 o'clock in the morning of this date, October 23, 1889.... By this time the gale was blowing with terrific force, and the vessel, practically unmanageable, labored so heavily in the tremendous seas which constantly swept her decks that she began to leak. She drove steadily toward the beach. and when yet far beyond the scope of operations of the lifesavers, and invisible from the shore owing to the thick weather, was tripped by an unusually heavy sea and thrown upon her beam ends. Her crew of seven men were soon struggling in the storm-tossed sea, and, with the exception of the captain, who had fortunately taken the precaution to put on a cork life-belt earlier in the night, undoubtedly sunk in a very short time, as they were probably clad in heavy oil-skins and rubber boots. The captain floated through New Inlet, which is not far to the northward of the station of that name, (Sixth District,) and, at 5 o'clock, drifted ashore, or, rather, into shoal water. . . . Investigation proved that the station patrols had faithfully performed their duties, and that, under the conditions of the weather, it was utterly impossible for the surfmen to have seen the schooner, and even had she been discovered no boat could have gone to the relief of the crew. That six men were drowned is very deplorable.[2]

Along Virginia

Just to the north of these, the Virginia coast claimed the sloop *General Harrison*, the British steamship *Baltimore*, the schooner *Welaka*, and the original grounding place of the schooner *Henry P. Simmons*. One Virginia account also includes the coasting schooner *Frank O. Dame*. This, however, is clearly an error, as several reports, including the *Boston Globe*, report the wreck as taking place on October 12, not October 23:

> NORFOLK. Va, Oct 14—The British steamer Teviotdale, from Galveston, arrived this morning, having on board the captain and crew' of the schooner Frank O. Dame of Boston, from Brunswick. Ga, for Philadelphia, with railroad ties. The Dame became water-logged and was abandoned Oct 12 in lat 35s 26", long 76' 15", her crew being taken off by the steamer. MOVED ABOUT IOO FEET. Steamer Spartan Hauled Astern Towards Deep Water.[3]

The story of the Bridgeton, New Jersey, sloop (a sloop is a fore-and-aft rigged boat with one mast and a single jib), *General Harrison*, is one of the shortest and happiest. Her crew saw the storm coming, anchored the *General Harrison*, and then went ashore in the sloop's boat. The oncoming storm caused the sloop to drag anchor and come ashore northwest of the Cape Henry Life-Saving Station (Virginia) midmorning the next day. All were safe and the vessel was able to be refloated.

The incident of the British steamer *Baltimore* was an equally short and happy story. She had simply run aground on an outer sandbar, sustained no damage, and was safely hauled off with all well.

The short story of the 433-ton schooner *Welaka* was truly sad. Sailing from Georgia, it had earlier encountered a two-day storm that damaged the vessel. While trying to make repairs at sea, she was hit with the October 23 storm and ran aground amid the rest of the melee. The British steamship *Spendthrift* began to tow *Welaka* off the sandbar, but the towline broke and caused the two vessels to collide. The schooner's captain had had enough, and simply abandoned her and sailed off on the *Spendthrift*. So much for the rest of the cast.

Now for the "Peculiarly Harrowing One"

The *Annual Report* again introduces this epic and harrowing narrative: "The low beaches of Virginia and North Carolina were literally strewn with wrecks, and the hardy crews of the Sixth District were kept exceedingly busy saving life and property. The storm had come with such suddenness that many coasters were unable to reach a harbor, and this will account for the great number of casualties."[4]

The Ship

The *Henry P. Simmons* was a three-masted, 648-ton schooner with a length of 152 feet. She was built by the Morris & Mathis shipyard at Cooper's Point in Camden, New Jersey, across the Delaware River from Philadelphia in June of 1884 with hull number forty (of 216 built) and

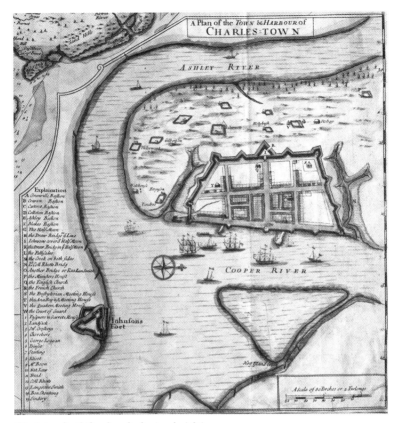

Charleston, South Carolina, harbor in colonial times.
Public domain.

owned by Robert. C. Grace, who was also her master and commander
on this fateful voyage. She had a crew of eight sailors and a cargo of
South Carolina phosphate rock, used in making commercial fertilizer.
She had departed Charleston, South Carolina, on October 17 with her
heavy load, bound for Baltimore, Maryland.

The Wreck and Rescue

The tragic account of this harrowing encounter was told by the sole
survivor of eight crewmen: Robert Lee Garnett. I recount it here in
excerpts from the *Annual Report*.[5]

Seaman Garnett began his account by making note of their great progress and smooth sailing. He related that "on or about October 17th" they departed Charleston bound for Baltimore. He was relieved to report they had safely traversed the dreaded Diamond Shoals and were only around ninety miles from the safe harbor of the Chesapeake Bay when "with no prior indication that a storm was approaching, a sudden strong easterly gale struck the schooner and by 8 o'clock that evening was blowing in gusts of hurricane intensity." The winds struck so quickly and so strongly that the sailors' efforts to take in sail, standard procedure for the first action taken in such a situation, was denied. Instead, they only had time to lash the helm midships, and then, for fear of immediately being washed overboard, they scurried up into the rigging. Now, with no steering, no crew to handle the lines and the sails, and in the midst of a ferocious hurricane, the devastating outcome was inevitable.

But it took another two and a half hours for the *Henry P. Simmons* to run aground. Amazingly, this gave the crew time to occasionally descend from the rigging and feverously work the pumps in a singular effort to keep their ship from sinking. When it finally hit bottom, the *Simmons* was driven ashore near the North Carolina–Virginia state line. This was between the US Life-Saving station Wash Woods, in North

Wash Woods United States Life-Saving Service Station, National Park Service, Cape Hatteras National Seashore.
Public domain.

Carolina, and the US Life-Saving station False Cape, in Virginia. The schooner struck so viciously that "The top of her cabin was swept away by one of the first breakers that stuck and she soon settled in the sands until her hull was completely submerged—nothing but the three masts was left above water," Garnett said.

The torrential rains that typically accompany a hurricane continued all night, which is how the crew spent that night in the rigging. The torrents were so heavy the men could not see where they were. Thoughts must have been running through their minds: Are we close enough to shore to wade in? Is there a Life-Saving station nearby? Is there any help around? Why have we not seen a distress flare or signal rockets? Why have we not heard the report of the Lyle gun? How long can we hold on?

Unfortunately, the last question was answered around 3:00 a.m. when, cold, weak, and exhausted, the ship's steward let go and fell into the sea and was swept away. The *Annual Report of the Operations of the United States Life-Saving Service for the Fiscal Year Ending June 30, 1890*, eloquently but graphically paints this picture:

> When day dawned the scene from the rigging of the wreck was a wild and terrifying one. The wind still raged and the waves broke into surf as far offshore as the eye could see through the pelting rain and spoon drift, while to the leeward lay the low sand hills, which ever and anon came into sight and were then hidden by the towering billows that madly chased one another shoreward, and were there scattered with thunderous roar into a smother of foam and spray upon the desolate beach.[6]

Ever vigilant, the Life-Saving Service crew were performing their routine duties. The Wash Woods Station patrolman, returning from his north route, reported a faint light far offshore, but the raging storm made it impossible to discern what it was. The first morning patrol could now see a sunken vessel, but it was a great distance offshore. The *Annual Report* explains, "Under these conditions patrol duty was attended with the greatest difficulty and danger, the men having in places to wade hip-deep and being frequently driven to the knolls for safety."[7] This accounts for the extreme difficulty the lifesaving crew experienced to reach a place opposite the wreck with their bulky equipment, which they finally managed to do, arriving around 10:00 a.m.

By then, according to Garnett's statement, as the lifesavers set up their equipment, the second mate fell in. An hour later, a third seaman fell. Before the day ended, another was lost. It was then determined that the vessel was one thousand yards to sea—far out of the Lyle gun's range and in impossible conditions for the surfboat. The ultimate scenario of frustration for the lifesavers is expressed well in the *Annual Report*: "Here, on the one hand, was a sunken vessel with her crew in the rigging, looking imploringly to the shore for help, and, on the other, a band of sturdy men skilled in the handling of boats in the surf and equipped with the most approved appliances for the saving of human life from the perils of the sea, but withal powerless to save. Yet this was the exact situation."[8]

The operation was then into its second day. Beginning at daybreak, "Three attempts were made on this date 26th to reach the Simmons but every time the boat was driven back full of water," the prior *Annual Report* of 1890 states.[9] Two more crewmen without hope or life fell in as no abatement of the weather occured. Finally, however, by evening, the winds and seas began to calm.

Yet still another day. Now, there was but one sailor left in the rigging and it was still not known if he was alive or dead. So, at 5:00 a.m. on the morning of October 28, the surfboat was again readied and manned "by the picked crew of oarsmen from the Wash Woods and False Cape crews including Keeper O Neal of the last-named station and with the veteran keeper Malachi Corbel at the steering oar a bold and successful dash was made through the heavy line of breakers on the bar," the 1889 *Report* continues.[10] The lifesavers reached the vessel, climbed aboard, and, as the 1890 *Report* happily told:

To the great relief of every man in the boat a faint response came to the keeper's hail, and presently there crept out into view the form of the sole survivor of the dreadful tragedy. He had been ensconced within the sheltering folds of the mizzen gaff topsail, and this protection, with the aid of a splendid physique, had enabled him to withstand the great hardships to which he had been exposed. He had been without food of any kind for over four days, his only sustenance having been rainwater caught in the sail, and his survival was simply marvelous.[11]

The Exhausting Conclusion

The remarkable Robert Lee Garnett was succored at the Wash Woods Station and incredibly had recovered enough in two days to leave for home in Virginia Beach. Five bodies were eventually recovered and given proper burials. Captain Grace's body was claimed by his family.

This rescue would have been a "particularly harrowing one" in and of itself, considering the great distance from shore with the hurricane winds and waves. Yet this was merely *one* of multiple wrecks that multiple stations with multiple Sixth District Life-Savers responded to over multiple days near the end of 1889. The year 1889 presented a total of thirty-six disasters through which the Sixth District stations saved well over $500,000 worth of ships and cargo (almost $17 million today), responded to 248 persons onboard, saved 229 (92 percent success), and succored sixty-five persons for 298 days.

The lifesavers who responded to the *Henry P. Simmons* were a part of the United States Life-Saving Service—that amazing, remarkable, incredible, fantastic, and heroic United States Life-Saving Service.

CHAPTER 25

SCHOONER
FRANCIS E. WATERS,
PART II

THE STORM OF OCTOBER 23, 1889

Few sailing vessels have been a part of a series of strange, odd, and improbable events as did the schooner Francis E. Waters. *Or maybe not.*

A String of Odd Occurrences

The first oddity was that it was owned by T. J. Seward, who seems to have been the postmaster of Hill's Point Post Office, Dorchester County, Maryland, at that time. One would not expect a postmaster to be the owner of a ship—and the *Waters* was only his first. Perhaps this unique circumstance was due to Maryland's position at the center of American shipbuilding at the time.

Seward evidently had connections to the timber industry in South Carolina. So, on October 23, 1889, the *Francis E. Waters* departed the port of Georgetown (originally spelled "George Town" from the 1670 English colony) with a cargo of shingles. It was bound for its homeport of Baltimore, Maryland, but wrecked in a raging Outer Banks storm off the North Carolina coast. In itself, this so far does not seem to be so odd. However, a similar schooner, only six years later, the *Hester A. Seward*, also owned by T. J. Seward and carrying shingles from Georgetown to Baltimore on January 6, 1895, wrecked at the Outer Banks at a total loss. It also, like the *Francis E. Waters*, involved a crew of six, but with one major difference in outcome: all six were all saved.

The Second

The wreck of the schooner *Francis E. Waters* was in a triumvirate of shipwrecks on that Thursday night of October 23, 1889, all around the North Carolina–Virginia state line, involving multiple United States Life-Saving Service stations in response. Wrecking within miles of each other were the *Francis E. Waters*, the *Henry P. Simmons*, and the *Lizzie S. Haynes*. The other two stories are so detailed and dramatic that they deserve a separate telling, which has been addressed elsewhere. There were actually two additional wrecks nearby that day, but the three-masted schooner *Annie E. Blackman* was twenty-five miles to the south and the 250-ton *Busiris* wrecked somewhat farther to the south at Poyners Hill, each coming under separate jurisdictions.

The full stories of the *Henry P. Simmons* and the *Lizzie S. Haynes* are told in chapters 24 and 26, respectively.

The Ship of This Story

The *Francis E. Waters* was a two-masted, 141-ton schooner built in 1882 and homeported in Baltimore, Maryland. She was owned by T. J. Seward (and G. F. Seward, presumably related) and on October 23, 1889, was transporting a cargo of lumber and wooden shingles loaded in Georgetown, South Carolina, bound for Baltimore, and valued at $3,000 (more than $90,000 today). On her fateful voyage, she had a crew of six and was captained by L. S. Tall.

The Wreck and Rescue Efforts

The US Life-Saving Service Nags Head Station No. 14 was located seven and one-quarter miles northwest of the Bodie Island Lighthouse (or "Light Station" in official parlance). Van Buren Etheridge had been appointed keeper in 1881 and was serving at this time and continued to do so until 1915. From 12:00 until 3:00 a.m. in October, surfman 5, Elisha Twine, was on the northbound beach patrol. He met the south-bound surfman from the Kill Devil Hills Station No. 13, which was five miles farther north, exchanged beach checks, and then returned to his station. He reported in Keeper Etheridge's wreck *Report* "seeing lots of sumthing [*sic*] drifting in the surf all the way on his beat but the night was so dark he could not tell but very little about what it was." From 3:00 to 7:00 a.m., the next beach patroller from Station No. 14, surfman 2, Samuel T. Forbes, was unable to complete his patrol due to extremely high tides, but said he was able to see "lots of lumber and shingles."[1]

Interesting later photo of the Nags Head Life-Saving Service Complex. The larger two-story structure is the new 1912 station. The original, circa 1874, is the smaller building, second from left. It was one of the first seven built in North Carolina but, sadly, no longer exists. The tower is for signal flags, not radio.
LeRoy S. Hulan, United States Coast Guard; public domain.

The 1878 Kill Devil Hills LSS Station No. 13. It would later give vital assistance to the Wright brothers.
National Park Service, Cape Hatteras National Seashore.

On what was a strikingly dark night, the *Francis E. Waters* had successfully cleared the biggest hurdle of her voyage—the dreaded Diamond Shoals—and could now continue north. "By sundown the wind backed to the northeast and increased to a gale of terrific violence, the night becoming, in nautical phrase 'as dark as a pocket.' This, together with a tempest of driving rain and the blinding spray flying shoreward from the crests of the breakers, produced atmospheric conditions upon the shore absolutely impenetrable to human vision."[2] This, coupled with an extraordinarily high tide, impeded the surfmen's patrols and rescue efforts. In a most frustrating way, those on shore knew nothing of the disaster until the next morning, when the schooner was discovered bottom up in the breakers—an enormous disaster, for sure. This was discovered by a beach patrol from the Kill Devil Hills station, since the Nags Head patrol was unable to complete their route. The Kill Devil Hills surfman immediately reported this to his keeper, Jesse Partridge, who just as quickly telephoned the Nags Head keeper, V. B. Etheridge, for the wreck was within their area of responsibility. Etheridge instantly deployed his crew onto the scene. In his report, Keeper Etheridge said the wreck, which they discovered at about 6:00 a.m., was two and three-quarter miles north-northwest of his station. What they faced was beyond exasperating—the schooner was upside down at an unknown distance from shore but enveloped in a raging surf being a "half-buried hull against and over which the surf was dashing incessantly. A man could not have maintained himself there for a moment."[3] No crew could be seen. A heartfelt sense of helplessness fell over the entire lifesaving crew, for they now knew they would not be able to do what they trained and lived for—saving lives in peril on the sea. In desperation, they were reduced to being mere scouts to locate dead bodies from the surf and sands. One African American sailor's body was soon found amid tangled wreckage that had washed ashore, which was "decently interred later in the day, there being no marks upon it which might lead to its identification" (same *Annual Report*).[4] All that remained to do was salvage some of the cargo, of which they managed to collect about a third. Nothing more, until a second body, seaman R. W. Lecompte of the *Francis E. Waters*, was found by the Gull Shoal Station thirty miles south, two weeks later.

The *Annual Report* ends sadly:

> This is all that is definitely known, and the incidents of that dreadful night will be forever shrouded in mystery. We can only conjecture. . . . But theorize as we may, there can be no doubt from the established facts, especially the locating of the anchors

offshore and the recovery of Lecompte's body at so great a distance from the dismantled hulk, that the supreme moment involving the practical destruction of the schooner and the loss of her crew, came before she reached the breakers and far enough away to prevent her being seen through the storm by the beach patrol. . . . There can be no alternative than to class the loss of the crew of the *Francis E. Waters* in the list of fatalities—fortunately not large—which have occurred within or near the scope of the operations of the Service yet have been beyond the power of its agency to avert.[5]

Third Oddity: Have Shipwreck, Will Travel

The wreck of the *Francis E. Waters* sat on the beach at Nags Head until a storm in May of 1978 picked it up and floated it southward, crashing it through and splitting in two Jennette's Pier. The storm then carried the wreck south to the Oregon Inlet. The city moved it

The ship on display at the Nags Head Municipal Building; is it the Francis E. Waters? *Author's photo.*

back to Nags Head to rest outside city hall. Journalist Kip Tabb traces this odyssey very well:

> The shipwreck that has come to rest beside the Nags Head Town Hall is now just a skeleton, the bones of the ship that once plied the ocean off the coast of North Carolina.
>
> It had been a part of the Nags Head beach for some time before it found a home at Town Hall, alternately appearing then disappearing based upon the vagaries of wind, tide and sand. In 1978, a storm freed the wreck from the sand and it once again was afloat upon the sea—unfortunately in this case, floating into Jennette's Pier, which was a wooden structure at that time.
>
> After the storm, Nags Head brought the wreck back to the Town Hall, where it has remained until today.
>
> Initial research on the vessel indicated it was the Francis E. Waters, a two-masted schooner that sunk on October 23, 1899.
> . . .
> Unfortunately, the bones of the ship that rests beside Nags Head Town Hall, may not be—probably is not—the Francis E. Waters.
>
> In 2014, a new study of the wreck was initiated under the supervision of Dr. Nathan Richards, who at the time was the head of Maritime Studies at the Coastal Studies Institute. What the study concluded was that the shipwreck seemed larger than the dimension of the Francis E. Waters and that the ship had been misidentified.
>
> The researchers pointed to two other possibilities—the Florence Randall and Thomas Goddard.[6]

Yet another Outer Banks shipwreck mystery? Perhaps the final oddity and even irony is that after being harshly covered by the violent surf of the Outer Banks Atlantic Ocean, which was the end of its existence, it was named "Waters."

CHAPTER 26

SCHOONER
LIZZIE S. HAYNES

THE "STRIKE THREE" SHIPWRECK IN THE GREAT OCTOBER STORM OF 1889

A three-ring circus of eleven shipwrecks were in concert along the Outer Banks of North Carolina during October 23 and 24 of 1889. In the center ring was the trilogy of the Henry P. Simmons, *the* Francis E. Waters, *and the* Lizzie S. Haynes. *This report focuses on the third member.*

The origins, ferocity, and partial results of this great October 1889 storm have been earlier expounded in the accounts of the *Henry P. Simmons* (chapter 24) and the *Francis E. Waters* (chapter 25). The storm began suddenly on October 23 and raged on violently until the 27th. The *Simmons* and the *Waters* were taken down late the first day and the *Lizzie S. Haynes* went down very early the next day.

The Ship

The *Lizzie S. Haynes* was a very large 437-ton, three-masted, "work-horse" schooner. She was 140 feet in overall length, 32.9 feet at the beam (in width), and had a draft (in depth) of only 12 feet. She was

The Altoona *was a three-masted schooner similar to the* Lizzie S. Haynes. *It also wrecked later at Cape Hatteras.*
National Park Service, Cape Hatteras National Seashore.

built in 1881 in Wiscasset, Maine, and had a homeport of Bath, Maine. The *Haynes*'s official number was 140455, and her official letters were J.V.K.B.

WISCASSET, MAINE

Located on Maine's southern Atlantic coast, the seaport became a renowned center for shipbuilding, fishing, and lumber. Wiscasset quickly became the busiest seaport north of Boston and remained so until the early 1800s.[1] "It was a very prosperous era with so many ships registered here, that it was said you could walk from deck to deck all the way across the harbor and masts were everywhere the eye could see."[2]

"Up the street, the Federal-style Nickels-Sortwell House, now owned by Historic New England, is a testament to the days between the late 1700s and the early 1800s when shipbuilding and international shipping brought newfound wealth to Wiscasset."[3]

The Last of the Three October 23 Wrecks

On this voyage, the *Lizzie S. Haynes* had a crew of seven men with a cargo of Georgia yellow-pine lumber, which was very popular and much in demand at the time. She had taken it on in Savannah, bound for Baltimore, Maryland. This triumvirate of schooners had much in common: all three of these vessels had cargo taken on in South Carolina ports and all were bound for Baltimore. All would also share a grisly fate at the same time and place.

The calamity of the *Lizzie S. Haynes* began when she was dutifully spotted around 8:00 a.m. by the beach patrol of the United States Life-Saving Service Oregon Inlet Station No. 16, despite the torrential rain. She was out a mile or two, north and east of the surfmen. As the out-of-control schooner inevitably drifted closer to shore, the surfmen on beach patrol could see that the crew had already escaped to the rigging, thereby sealing the schooner's fate, but, hopefully, not theirs. Specifically, as the *Annual Report of the Operations of the United States Life-Saving Service for the Fiscal Year Ending June 30, 1890*, reads, "Two men could be seen in the fore shrouds, three in the main, and two in the mizzen."[4]

Score Card

Locating the "Oregon Inlet Station" can be understandably confusing. As reported in my first book on the Service,

> The origins of Station Oregon Inlet are shrouded. The name first appears for a station near the inlet in 1874 as a US Life-Saving Service station but named Bodie Island Station. It was located on the south side of the inlet. In 1883, the station on the north side of the inlet, "Tommy's Hummock," was renamed "Bodie Island Station." At the same time, the original Bodie Island Station, still located on the south side, was re-named "Oregon Inlet Station." In 1888 it was moved farther westward, but still on the south side. Less than a decade later, it was totally destroyed by a

storm. A new station was built there and became operational in 1898. It was abandoned in 1988; the current station, now back on the north side, opened in 1990.[5]

So, our Oregon Inlet Station at the time of this story was *on the south side*, which is the picturesque but currently abandoned "Old Oregon Inlet Station" at the south end of the amazing Marc Basnight Bridge over Oregon Inlet. A 501(c)(3) nonprofit organization was formed in 2024 to rescue and repurpose this home of historic Hatteras heroes. Its name is the Outer Banks Coast Guard History Preservation Group.

US Life-Saving Service Standard Operating Procedure Rescue Begins

The Oregon Inlet Station keeper, Samuel J. Payne, quickly recognized the difficulty of the situation. As was standard operating procedure (SOP), he immediately telephoned the keeper of his neighbor station to the south, Pea Island. This one was commanded by the legendary Captain Richard Etheridge.[6]

Just an hour after the Haynes was spotted, the Oregon Inlet crew was in position with their lifesaving equipment abreast of the impending wreck and ready to spring into their well-drilled action. As was the case so often in these violent storms, the lifesaving crew would, first, take few and critical minutes to rapidly and efficiently set the sand anchor, position the Lyle gun, and lay out all the remaining apparatus. However, usually then the shipwreck would drift and be pushed along by the heavy surf. So, the lifesavers would have to undo all they had done, relocate, and begin again. Very often this was reenacted multiple times before a shot could be fired. Finally, the *Lizzie S. Haynes* became stationary. "She struck at twenty minutes to 10 o'clock, three hundred yards from the beach, at a point three and three-quarter miles below Oregon Inlet and a little less than two miles north of the Pea Island Station. She was thus within Etheridge's beat," the *Annual Report* continues.[7] The cooperation between the stations and the races of the crews was exemplary, for they all had the singular mission of "saving lives in peril on the sea."

Initially, it appeared that the wreck would land within the Oregon Inlet Station's domain, what today's Coast Guard would call their area of responsibility (AOR), so Keeper Paine had requested that Keeper Etheridge's crew only bring a spare number 7 shot line, the medicine chest, and a bag of blankets. Not having to drag the unwieldy beach apparatus cart, the Pea Island crew reached the scene of the actual wreck first. But now things had changed. A part of the Life-Savers success, universally, was thinking, predicting, and reacting. Etheridge did all of these and expected the wreck to be pushed even farther south, closer to his station, so he sent his crew back to retrieve their beach apparatus cart. Etheridge himself continued on north to assist the Oregon Inlet crew. But predictions can easily turn out to be incorrect or incomplete.

The Center Ring

All of this was taking place immediately following the agonizing response to the wreck of the *Henry P. Simmons*, followed promptly by the awful discovery of the fatally and lifelessly overturned *Francis E. Waters*. Then, only twenty-five miles to the south, was the bizarre incident of the three-masted schooner *Annie E. Blackman*, which was also ensconced by this behemoth of a storm and "invisible from the shore owing to the thick weather, was tripped by an unusually heavy sea and thrown upon her beam ends."[8] The seven crew were swept across the decks into the raging sea and six were gone instantly. The captain had earlier put on a cork life belt that kept him afloat above the towering surf. Incredibly, he drifted through New Inlet and landed safely to a beach, tied himself to a telegraph pole, and was discovered by the New Inlet Station the next morning.

"Hardly had the captain of the schooner *Annie E. Blackman* been carried to the Life-Saving station, when the schooner *Lizzie S. Haynes* was discovered in the same vicinity. Her three masts broke off near the vessel's deck and, with a crash that was heard above the roar of the wind, fell into the ocean."[9] The falling masts up which the crew had escaped had carried all seven of the crew violently to the deck, throwing one overboard to be lost. This occurred as the Oregon Inlet crew and the Pea Island crew were rushing to the scene from opposite directions and they witnessed the horror, as described by the *Annual Report*: "This appalling and exciting incident infused fresh energy into the little band of jaded life-savers as they pressed forward, and within five minutes from the time of their arrival the Oregon Inlet crew had thrown a line over the wreck."[10] Even more serious challenges were to befall the lifesavers; the schooner's cargo of lumber was filling the seas with deadly shrapnel along with broken spars, torn sails, and rigging that could easily entangle the beleaguered lifesavers. Now, only two survivors could be seen on deck, which turned out to be the captain and the steward. Quickly, a line was fired to them via the Lyle gun, but the thin line broke as they began to retrieve it. A second line was fired. It was successfully obtained by the two men, but due to the amazing number and degree of difficulties in the situation, it was not until 4:00 p.m. that the breeches buoy was able to be delivered, and the captain and steward were safely brought to shore, reluctantly leaving a delirious sailor who refused to leave the ship. The survivors were succored at the Pea Island Station.

True to their sworn duty to never give up, the Life-Saving crews of both Oregon Inlet and Pea Island waded out to the schooner by midnight. There they discovered two bodies; one gone, the other mostly—but eventually lost after two hours efforts. As the *Annual Report* explains: "Thus, five of the little band of seven men composing the schooner's crew, who but a few hours before were in the full flower and promise of manhood, became the victims of the storm."[11]

The ecstasy of saving lives and the agony of losing them.

The following is the captain's letter:[12]

OREGON INLET, NORTH CAROLINA,

November 1, 1889.

Mr. S. I. KIMBALL,

General Superintendent U.S. Life-Saving Service,

I desire to express my thanks for the prompt service rendered by the keepers and crews of the Oregon Inlet and Pea Island Life-Saving Stations at the wreck of the schooner Lizzie S. Haynes on Pea Island, October 24, 1889, and would state that no default on the part of the life-savers or defect in the working of their gear was responsible for the loss of life that occurred on that day.

W. A. SAWYER,

Late Master of Schooner Lizzie S. Haynes.

VICTIMS OF THE STORM.

Several Schooners Wrecked and a Number of Lives Lost During Last Week's Gale.

NORFOLK, Va., Oct. 28.—A special from Kittyhawk reports the following vessels lost in last Wednesday's storm in that vicinity: The schooner Francis S. Walters, of Baltimore, was found floating bottom up at Nags Head, and her entire crew were drowned. The schooner Frank M. McGear was wrecked near Whale's Head, but her crew was saved. Five of the crew of the Lizzie S. Haynes, wrecked near Body's Island, were drowned, but the captain and steward were saved. Two of the dead bodies were washed ashore and buried. The schooner A. E. Blackman capsized two miles off shore, and the only man saved was Captain Charles Edwards, who swam to New Inlet.

NORFOLK, Va., Oct. 29.—Intelligence from the wreck of the Jersey schooner George T. Simmons states that the last of three men lashed in the rigging for three days and nights has perished. The whole crew was lost.

An original newspaper account of the shipwreck and rescue, Ann Arbor Register, *1889.*
Ann Arbor Library; public domain.

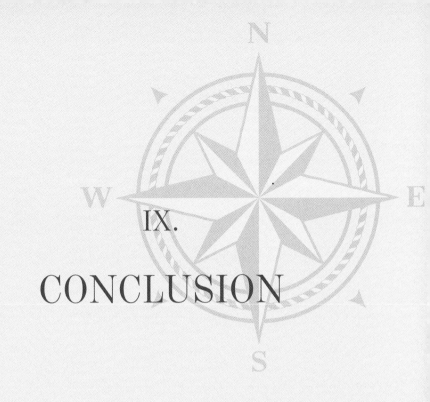

IX.

CONCLUSION

CHAPTER 27

THE WRECK AND RESCUE OF THE SCHOONER *A. B. GOODMAN*

THE US LIFE-SAVING SERVICE GOING ABOVE AND BEYOND, "AGAINST ALL ODDS"

In the annals of the forty-four-year history of the United States Life-Saving Service, 1871 to 1915, there are thousands of successful rescue stories. Most of those thousands are dramatic stories. Many are very dramatic. A select few are so unbelievably heroic in overcoming seemingly impossible and insurmountable odds that they go beyond being against all odds. The wreck and rescue of the schooner A. B. Goodman *is one of those stories. Yet it is only a small part of what are now America's forgotten heroes.*

The Setting

Of course, this epic episode occurred in the dreaded Diamond Shoals off the infamous Cape Hatteras. The two-masted schooner *A. B. Goodman*, homeported in Seaford, Delaware, had departed the major US port of Baltimore, Maryland, with a cargo of guano, bound for New Bern, North Carolina. The guano, seabird and bat dried excrement fertilizer, added to the troubles of the coming storm. In his article for the *Northern Mariner* magazine, "A Load of Guano: Baltimore and the Fertilizer Trade in the Nineteenth Century," author Pete Lesher explains, "Guano was a cargo of last resort for captains and shipowners. The yellowish dust would cover every part of the ship during loading. The noxious odor of ammonia that was released by the guano during handling dried out noses and irritated eyes; crew who were working to place the cargo in the hold were often unable to remain in the hold for more than five minutes at a time. The cargo also presented a fire hazard."[1]

A FEW WORDS ABOUT GUANO (BUT JUST A FEW)

Talking about animal poop might seem humorous or distasteful, but it was very serious business to American agriculture then. "It's easy to forget how large the United States is for one country, especially when you compare it to a continent like Europe that's made up of so many smaller countries. According to a neat overlay map posted to Reddit, you can fit 30 European countries into the continental US."[2] The incredibly vast, uncultivated lands with a relatively sparse population was quickly exhausted by enormous farms, ranches, and plantations. America then had no large supplies of naturally sourced fertilizer. Europe had been using guano for many years, primarily importing it from Peru's plentiful supply. Why our ship was departing Baltimore was because this was a major US port of commerce. Peru's guano was imported by businessmen there to resell, mostly to the South.

Outer Banks weather in March and April can be unpredictable, sudden, and violent. Before the *A. B. Goodman* could reach its destination in New Bern, North Carolina, it encountered a ferocious gale rounding Cape Hatteras, the centerpiece of the Graveyard of the

Atlantic. The area had long ago earned a bad reputation by all mariners; the author of the *Annual Report of the Operations of the United States Life-Saving Service for the Fiscal Year Ending June 30, 1881*, which details the wreck, paints an even more dismal and unpleasant picture of the land area there:

> The point at which the disaster took place was about three miles from shore, and six miles east of Life Saving Station No. 22 (6th District), North Carolina. This station is built upon the rise of an eminence known as Creeds Hill, and its north patrol reaches for 6 miles around the edge of the dreaded cape. Looking from the station, the view toward the cape presents to the eye the aspect of an immense desert of sand, strangely and fantastically sprinkled all over with gnarled and twisted trunks of black, dead trees. In winter, or during the inclement season, nothing more dismal could well be imagined than this Sahara, with its thin remnant of a former vegetation killed by the salt tides. The level is only diversified by occasional mounds of sand, and, here and there, pools of sea water, left by some overflow in the hollows. Behind, or to the west, a forest of pines and live oaks, dense and almost impenetrable, stretches away northward to Hatteras light house. All around the cape for two miles, in storms at flood tides, a heavy sea swings across the low and somewhat shelving beach, in among its bordering hummocks, and back again with violence, ploughing gullies as it runs. The surf makes the sand a quag, quick-sands form in the gullies, and the solitary patrolman, making his way along the top of the beach in the darkness by the dim light of his lantern, faces the chances of destruction, being liable to be swept off his feet by the rush or refluence [archaic nautical term meaning "flowing back"] of the surf, sucked down in the gullies by the quick-sands, or struck by some fragment of wreck-stuff shot forth by the breakers. Yet this dreadful watch is made necessary by the presence of shore of a nest of shoals, range after range, which are the terror of

navigators. The first, a mile wide, stretches from the point of the cape between two and three miles seaward, covered with a depth of only seven feet of water, which in storms are miles of raging foam. This formation is, in fact, a submarine prolongation of the cape. Beyond it, separated by half a mile of channel, is another formidable shoal, the Diamond, two miles long; and beyond this again, another range of shallows, the outer shoals. For 6 or 7 miles out from shore, these terrible bottoms spread their ambush for shipping, and hence the watch in this locality for vessels in danger requires to be particularly kept around the point of the cape, no matter at what toll or hazard to the sentinel.[3]

The Ship

There is scant information available today about the vessel. We do know that the *A. B. Goodman* was a small, two-masted schooner with a crew of five on this voyage. We know she had a crew of five, but only learned the names of four of them: Captain Steward; First Mate A. A. Thompson from Bethel, Delaware; Seaman James Walston from nearby Galeston, Maryland; and Seaman Louis Beck who was the only loss.

The schooner's homeport was Seaford, Delaware, which is located on the Nanticoke River. That river flows directly into the Tangier Sound, which, in turn, flows directly into the Chesapeake Bay. The major port of Baltimore, Maryland, is just north on the opposite shore of the bay, an easy trip for the *Goodman*.

The Shipwreck

On Monday, April 4, 1881, at about 6:30 p.m., the *A. B. Goodman* ran hard aground on the outer edge of the inner shoal of Diamond Shoals. It struck so violently that it immediately sank, with her hull completely underwater and only her two masts above the ocean. She shipped the sea so rapidly that the crew of five only had time to scamper into the rigging, the only temporarily safe place.

THE DIAMOND SHOALS

Since this dreaded part of the Atlantic Ocean is talked about so frequently, here, just a short reminder should suffice. "Shoals" can be loosely defined as underwater sand dunes and/or sand bars. Their dangers presented are several: they are not seen; they are in shallow water; and they are constantly changing and therefore can only be charted one way because it will be different on the way back.

The Diamond Shoals is a huge area of ocean bottom offshore of Cape Hatteras, North Carolina. It is a complex of inner shoals, outer shoals, and gullies in between, all extending twenty miles out to sea and can be miles wide—well beyond sight of land, making captains think they must be safe. An additional danger, ironically, is that there are two light stations there: the famous Cape Hatteras Lighthouse on land at the cape, but also the Diamond Shoals Lightship on the outer edge of the shoals. A great number of nighttime sailors confused which light was which and plotted a course that ran them aground there.

The 1878 Bodie Island Life-Saving Station shown here was virtually identical to the 1878 Creeds Hill Station. The latter is extinct; the former is the only 1878 remaining in North Carolina. **National Park Service.**

United States Life-Saving Service keeper Benjamin Baxter Dailey—born May 23, 1844; died November 19, 1914 (aged seventy). With wife and dog, Buxton, in North Carolina. **Courtesy of Pat Rosen, Dailey's great-granddaughter.**

The surfman on beach patrol from Station No. 22 Creeds Hill was severely hampered in his lookout duty by the rain, squalls, heavy winds, gray skies, dim light, and later darkness, salt-spray from the angry surf, and now even snow! Thus, it wasn't until 10:00 p.m. that he reported what might be a vessel in distress. Due to the weather conditions and the distance, he was unable to make a positive determination. Station Keeper Benjamin B. Dailey was up at dawn the next day to verify. Sure enough, a vessel was foundering on the Diamond Shoals. Immediate action was required.

The Episodic Rescue Begins

The beginning of this real-life drama is unfathomable to modern minds. In almost Hollywood fashion, the men resigned themselves to the inevitable. They knew this day might come when they signed up to be lifesavers. They knew they might risk all—and lose—so that others may

KEEPER BENJAMIN B. DAILEY: A FEW NOTES

Benjamin Dailey's official badge.
United States Coast Guard.

Keeper Dailey was the hero of the astounding barkentine *Ephraim Williams* rescue off of Cape Hatteras in December of 1884. Dailey—whose name is consistently misspelled in the *Annual Reports* as "Daily"—was then the keeper of the Cape Hatteras station. It was a common practice of the United States Life-Saving Service to rotate keepers at nearby stations (a continuing tradition of today's US Coast Guard). Keeper Dailey is buried in the Dailey Family Cemetery in Buxton, North Carolina, synonymous with Cape Hatteras. The complete, incredible story of the *Ephraim Williams* saga is in volume 1.[4]

live. They knew that the odds were in their favor when the "book" said they had to go out; but it was eerily silent about coming back. Now, it was very evident that the mighty surfmen were being placed in a position of being against all odds.

For this is what they all also knew: they knew the wind that day was blowing powerfully seaward, away from land; they knew their surfboat was a small, flat-bottomed craft that would be skipped over the water like a boy bouncing stones; they knew that being pushed out into that violent, rolling, massive sea with towering waves would give them almost no chance of survival; and they knew all of this in their hearts and their heads before entering the surfboat.

The "they" were "Keeper, B. B. Dailey, and Surfmen Thomas J. Fulcher, Damon M. Gray, Erasmus H. Rolison, Benjamin F. Whidbee, Christopher B. Farrow, and John B. Whidbee, the last named a substitute for a member of the crew absent on leave. One of the crew, Z. Basnett, was left in charge of the station," as listed in the *Annual Report*.[5]

Times were different then; our culture and our values were different then. Before launching the surfboat, the group gathered together. In a calm, silent, foreboding resolution, they made a compact with the Almighty and prepared for the After. They each made out a simple, short will. Then these real-life men, sworn and dedicated to duty and the welfare of their fellow man, emptied their pockets of the few remaining possessions—a watch, a wallet, a few coins, perhaps a pen knife—and gave them to Surfman Basnett to keep back at the station for family and relatives.

Then, they launched their surfboat into destiny.

The First Likely End

The initial launch was into a relatively calm surf, so the start wasn't so bad. But soon that changed for the worse—much worse. The *Annual Report* describes the situation: "Heaps of rough water incessantly tumbling, and thickets of bursting foam, filled the offing, and the current running one way, while the wind was the other, made an ugly cross sea."[6] They were fighting the wind, the waves, the channels, the shoals, exhaustion, and their fears—all while rowing manually and mightily. *After two hours*, they reached what was left of the wrecked schooner. They had made it; they had gone out. Lesser men would have conceded their loss and given up completely. Not these men. But it could have ended there.

The Second Likely End

Yes, they had made it to the wreck, but the conditions were preventing them from making the rescue. Against the wind and the currents, they tentatively approached, seeing the survivors in the main crosstrees, but were about to be smashed upon the wreck themselves, and so they pulled back their rescue boat. After regrouping, they tried again. Once more they were pushed back. They tried a third time, unsuccessfully. Then a fourth time. Lesser men would have ended all attempts there.

The Third Likely End

As I write this in my home on Cape Hatteras Island, a big storm is approaching. My sympathy for these men is becoming empathy. The most likely of the endings is about to happen.

Frustrated with the lack of success, Keeper Dailey knew from his training and experience that the most prudent tactic now was simply to wait. So, he "hailed the wretched group up on the mast, telling them to keep good heart and that they would be rescued as soon as possible."[7]

He then had his crew maneuver the surfboat about three hundred yards to the stern, or rear, of the wreck and then they dropped anchor. Simply sitting and waiting in that violent storm and watching the *Goodman* survivors literally hang on for dear life must have been excruciating for the surfmen who had dedicated their lives to saving others.

After another hour of waiting to reach these men who had wrecked at 6:30 p.m. the day before, Keeper Dailey felt the seas had calmed somewhat enough to make a decisive attempt. He was about to employ a simple, time-tested—yet ingenious—United States Life-Saving Service rescue method. From its anchored position three hundred yards behind the wreck, the surfboat weighed their anchor (or raised it and stowed in the boat in order to get underway again). Keeper Dailey then directed the crew to go to the windward side but close to the wreck and drop anchor again. Being on the windward side of the wreck meant that the wind was coming from that direction and would have been pushing their surfboat toward the wreck had it not been anchored. Therefore, if the surfboat slowly let out a little bit of the anchor line, thereby giving it slack, the surfboat would slowly, gradually, and safely be under control as it approached the wreck. That is exactly what happened in that palpably tense scene. Now the anchor line would maintain a controlled distance between the surfboat and the wreck; however, it would not control the direction in which it might arc or swing. To counter this, Keeper Dailey, now within close range, tied a line to his boat hook and threw it toward the wreck, aiming at the rigging. Direct hit into the shrouds! As the *Annual Report* laconically states, "The fateful moment had arrived."[8]

SOME NAUTICAL TERMINOLOGY

Shrouds: So often shown in Hollywood movies simply as "ladders" to
climb up to sails, shrouds are actually supports of those tall masts, like
guy wires. And, yes, they were also used to climb up to the sails.

Boat hook: The hook at the end of a long pole of many feet had an almost
endless list of uses: grabbing lines overhead, retrieving items onboard
or overboard, sending items to sailors aloft, etc.

This allowed the rescue boat to safely get so close that the shipwreck survivors could jump into it. First Mate A. A. Thompson
slowly descended the rigging toward his promised salvation. But an
understandable obstacle to this success occurred. "As he came within
reach, the keeper, standing in the stern of the boat, seized him, but
the man, terrified at the frightful rush and roar of waters beneath him,
and doubtless unmanned by cold and hunger, and the many hours of
horror he had undergone, broke from the keeper's hold and clambered
up the rigging again."[9]

Trained to deal with panic as well as rescue, since it happened often,
Keeper Dailey calmly and cheerily encouraged the sailors to trust the
lifesavers, who knew what they were doing, and that it was safe. Thus
bolstered, the first mate tried again. But again, at the critical moment,
his fear seized him, and he tried to retreat. Forewarned and prepared,
Keeper Dailey simply jerked him onboard the surfboat. Dailey had to
do the same for the next survivor, the schooner's captain. The remaining
three sailors jumped into the rescue boat on their own. The lifesavers
had gone out; they had retrieved all the survivors. Half of the job was
done. Now, they had to get back to shore and safety.

The Fourth Likely End

Believe it or not, more complications occurred next. The strong wind
had changed directions, thus preventing the surfboat from returning

along the same course they had taken out. It wasn't, however, simply a matter of direction—this was in the heart of the treacherous Diamond Shoals. This meant that the surfboat could not go directly to its station but, rather, go a considerable distance out of its way around the other side of the shoals. This put them on a course to attempt a landing on the beach by the Cape Hatteras Lighthouse, many miles from their Creeds Hill Life-Saving Station. As the surfboat approached, it was recorded that the lighthouse keepers were watching them, considered how they may help, and had decided that, if they ever were to make a landing, it would not be until the morning.

Again, if only the lifesavers been lesser men—but these stalwart souls did not know how to give up. Through pure perseverance, dauntless resolution, and adrenaline they pressed on and landed near the lighthouse at around 2:00 a.m. Somehow the lighthouse keepers became aware and immediately assisted the survivors to the lighthouse quarters where they quickly prepared a hot meal for them, their first food since early the day before. Although the lifesavers themselves had their last meal twenty-two-hours earlier, they did not want to impose on the hospitality of the lighthouse keepers or interfere with the sailor's recovery, so they started for "home" on foot. Their station was five miles away! Through the night, through the storm, fighting sheer exhaustion. "These poor, plain men, dwellers upon the lonely sands of Hatteras"—part of the famous quote from the *Ephraim Williams*, ironically used here, and paraphrasing the rest—had taken their lives in their hands and, at the most imminent risk, had crossed the most tumultuous sea, they drudged on through the desolate sands "nothing more dismal could well be imagined than this Sahara,"[10] to get back to their quarters to be safe, sound, warm, and fed. They had gone out. And they had come back. They were lifesavers.

The Actual End

For the year 1881, the *Annual Report of the Operations of the United States Life-Saving Service* listed four occasions of issuing Awards of

Medals. The first was for Captain Charles Gnewuch for multiple rescues over a period from 1874 to 1880. The second was to the Life-Saving crew from Station No. 12 of the Fourth District rescuing sailors of the schooner *George Taulane*. The third was for Captain Charles P. Smith for saving three hundred passengers on his steamer *Seawanaku* by quickly beaching the ship ablaze in fire. The fourth was for the already nationally famous lady lighthouse keeper, Ida Lewis.

That morning, when the surfmen launched their boat into their destiny, they knew that if a ship wrecked in their part of the Graveyard of the Atlantic their "book" told them they had to go out, but it said nothing about coming back. What they did not know during their valiant struggle, "So Others May Live," was that they would succeed.

But they did get recognition and praise from the supervisor ending the official wreck report. He felt that metallic awards were not necessary, but that

> Such deeds attest themselves; and there are few scenes in human life more deeply affecting than the spectacle of this crew of men making their wills upon the beach, and leaving their small store of effects in charge of a comrade for the benefit of their families before entering upon a struggle of deadly peril for the lives of four unhappy creatures, who, in their dying misery, must have thought themselves abandoned forever by men, if not beyond all human aid. To have done this—to have quietly resigned the certainties for the chances of existence in such a case and under such circumstances—was more than noble.[11]

They were not lesser men. They were the *real-life* surfmen of the United States Life-Saving Service who eventually, and sadly, became part of America's forgotten heroes.

That morning, they only knew they were there to save lives. This they knew every day.

That morning, when they launched their surfboat into destiny, they didn't know that it would be a monumental success—*against all odds*!

ACKNOWLEDGMENTS

Nothing great and worthwhile is ever accomplished alone, and neither is this "labor of love," on my part. My number one cheerleader and coach is my wife, Linda Molloy. She participated for endless hours in every single step of this process; she read every word more than once and often just calmed me down.

I owe so much to Greta Schmitz, the acquiring editor for Globe Pequot. From my initial proposal, for many weeks until final submission, she consistently guided, advised, encouraged, and helped me produce this correctly.

To my other editors, doing the "working part for me," I thank and deeply appreciate my production editor, Felicity Tucker, and my copyeditor, Jacqueline Plante Wilson, who was incredibly detailed, accurate, and patient.

I never expected the enormously positive results or the reactions from my readers to volume 1, which has inspired this sequel. It has meant a great deal to me, and I am thankful.

This all started with encouragement and direct help to send in the initial proposal for volume 1. That came from my friends, colleagues, and Globe Pequot authors Bruce Roberts and Cheryl Shelton-Roberts. Thank you.

APPENDIX A: GLOSSARY OF HELPFUL NAUTICAL TERMS

This is not an exhaustive list but rather terms used in this text plus some general basics. For a complete list see: https://www.nauticed.org /sailingterms.

bilge—the lowest point of a ship's inner hull, its "basement," below the lowest deck and the hull. Collects leaks and drainage and must be pumped with bilge pumps constantly. All wooden vessels leak!

bow—back or rear of the vessel

breakwater—a structure constructed on a coast to protect an anchorage from the effects of weather.

"parted chains"—small platforms, built on either side of the hull of a ship, used to provide a wide purchase for the shrouds, and to assist in the practice of depth sounding.

ensign—the principal identifying flag or banner flown by a ship to indicate her nationality.

gale—from the Beaufort Scale table: a wind from thirty-two to sixty-three miles per hour (about fifty-one to 102 kilometers per hour)

to heave to, hove to—stopping a sailing vessel by backing some of the sails and lashing the helm to leeward, turning 180 degrees directly into the wind.

hurricane—from the Beaufort Scale table: a tropical cyclone with winds of seventy-four miles (119 kilometers) per hour or greater. Almost invariably accompanied by rain, thunder, and lightning and sometimes moves into temperate latitudes. Their biggest threat to ships is violent surf and rain. Their biggest threat to land is flooding.

jib—a triangular staysail at the front of a ship. The foot will be attached to the bow or to a bowsprit.

larboard—facing the front, the left side of the vessel. From the archaic "laying board" (to get from vessel to dock). Later changed to "port" due to similarity in sounds of "starboard" and "larboard." Port was the side the vessel docked to the port of entry.

mast—the tall straight timbers rising *vertically* to carry the sails. Each has a name depending on its location or function; for example, the main mast (often blurred by sailors as "mainmast"), fore mast (first), and mizzen (last).

pay off—a sailing vessel's head pays off when it falls further away from the direction of the wind and therefore drops to leeward. It is a term used particularly in relation to tacking.

port—*see* larboard.

rigging—the system of ropes, cables, and chains that support and control a sailing vessel's masts and sails. Two types: (1) standing rigging is the fixed rigging that supports masts including shrouds and stays; (2) running rigging is rigging that adjusts the position of the vessel's sails and spars including halyards, braces, sheets, etc. Simple definition: all the ropes, chains, and pulleys above the decks!

rope versus line—when the item is unused it is coiled or wound on something for storage and is called "rope." When it is employed for use on a ship, it forms a functioning line and is thus referred to as a "line." Each of the hundreds of lines on a ship has a specific name, such as "sheet," "clew," and "halyard," on which sail, on which mast, and on which side: port or starboard. Thus, the first job a new sailor had was "to learn the ropes."

schooner—a type of sailing vessel characterized by the use of fore-and-aft sails on two or more masts with the forward mast being no taller than the rear masts. Mainly used as the workhorse cargo vessel. The word "schooner" was probably first used in Gloucester, Massachusetts, coined from the Scottish *scon*, meaning "to send over water, to skip stones."

starboard—facing the front, the right side of the vessel. From the archaic "steering board side."

stern—the back, rear, or "aft" (after) part of the vessel.

storm—wind having a speed of sixty-four to seventy-two miles per hour (103 to 117 kilometers per hour).

stove—is to break, crush, bash, or severely dent, etcetera.

weighing anchor—literally means raising the anchor of the vessel from the sea floor and hoisting it up to be stowed onboard; nautical term indicating the final preparation of a sea vessel for getting underway.

yard—the large *horizontal* timbers carrying the sails and attached to the masts, again, each with special name based on location, side of vessel or function. Often confused in movies as "yard arm," which is only the final tip of the yard.

PRONUNCIATIONS

Bodie—pronounced as "body"

Chicamacomico—pronounced chick-uh-mah-COMIC-coh

Corolla—pronounced kuh-RAH-lah (kuh-ROLL-*uh* is the car)

Hatteras—natives pronounce as hat-TRISS

Ocracoke—okra coke (vegetable + soft drink)

APPENDIX B: LOCATIONS OF THE TWENTY-NINE NORTH CAROLINA UNITED STATES LIFE-SAVING SERVICE STATIONS

Compiled by the US Coast Guard History Program
(*A note about spelling. Many of these names are possessives and were originally spelled with the proper apostrophe. However, at some point that was dropped. Here are the latest spellings. They are listed alphabetically rather than geographically.*)

Station Big Kinnakeet, North Carolina
USLSS Station No. 21, Sixth District
Coast Guard Station No. 182
Location: On beach, 3¾ miles north by east of Cape Hatteras Light; 35–20' 00"N 75–30' 20"W
Date of Conveyance: 1899
Station Built: 1878
Fate: Abandoned in 1932

Station Bodie Island, North Carolina
USLSS Station No. 16, Sixth District
Coast Guard Station No. 175
Location: On Bodie Island, North Carolina, 1⅛ miles north by east of Bodie Island Light; 35–47' 30"N × 75–32' 00"W in 1878; 35–49' 40"N × 75–33' 20"W in 1915
Date of Conveyance: 1878

Station Built: 1878

Fate: Transferred from US Coast Guard to NPS, US Department of Interior in 1953

Station Bogue Inlet, North Carolina

Coast Guard Station No. 192

Location: Inner shore of Bogue Banks, half mile east of inlet; 34–39' 00"N × 77–05' 40"W

Date of Conveyance: 1903

Station Built: 1904

Fate: Still in operation

Station Caffeys Inlet, North Carolina

USLSS Station No. 10, Sixth District

Coast Guard Station No. 170

Location: Abreast of Currituck South, and 9⅝ miles south by east of Currituck Beach Light; 36–13' 40"N × 75–46' 20"W

Date of Conveyance: 1875

Station Built: 1874

Fate: Turned over to the General Services Administration (GSA) in 1964

Station Cape Fear, North Carolina

USLSS Station No. 25, Sixth District

Coast Guard Station No. 193

Location: On Smith's Island, Cape Fear; 33–50' 40"N × 77–57' 30"W

Date of Conveyance: 1881

Station Built: 1881

Fate: Station was discontinued in 1941.

Station Cape Hatteras, North Carolina

Coast Guard Station No. 183

Location: At Cape Hatteras, North Carolina, 1⅜ miles south of Cape Hatteras Light; 35–14' 20"N × 75–31' 20"W

Date of Conveyance: 1882

Station Built: 1882

Fate: Still in operation as the USCG MLB Station Hatteras Inlet

The 1939 replacement was turned over to the Cape Hatteras National Seashore as a Ranger Station.

Station Cape Lookout, North Carolina

USLSS Station No. 24, Sixth District

Coast Guard Station No. 190

Location: At Cape Lookout, North Carolina, 1⅜ miles southwest by west of Cape Lookout Light; 34–36' 30"N × 76–32' 20"W

Date of Conveyance: 1886

Station Built: 1887

Fate: Station was conveyed to the State of North Carolina in 1957. Station of same name is still in operation.

Station Chicamacomico, North Carolina

USLSS Station No. 18, Sixth District

Coast Guard Station No. 179

Location: On beach, 13⅝ miles south southeast of Bodie Island Light; 35–36' 40"N × 74-27' 50"W in 1915

Date of Conveyance: 1873

Station Built: 1874

Fate: Discontinued in 1954. Currently a museum.

Station Core Bank, North Carolina

Coast Guard Station No. 189

Location: On Core Bank, opposite Hunting Quarters, about halfway between Ocracoke Inlet and Cape Lookout; 34–51' 30"N × 76–18' 30"W

Date of Conveyance 1894

Station Built: Unknown

Fate: Turned over to the GSA in 1965

Station Creed's Hill, North Carolina

USLSS Station No. 22, Sixth District

Coast Guard Station No. 184

Location: On beach, abreast of Sandy Bay, and 5½ miles west-south-west of Cape Hatteras Light; 35–14' 30"N × 75–35' 15"W

Date of Conveyance: 1878

Station Built: 1878

Fate: Abandoned in 1947 (as of this writing, being restored as private residence)

Station Currituck Inlet, North Carolina

Also known as Old Currituck Inlet

USLSS Station No. 7, Sixth District

Coast Guard Station No. 168

Location: At Whale Head Hill, ⅜ mile southeast of Currituck Beach Light; 36–27' 30"N × 75–50' 40"W

Date of Conveyance: 1878

Station Built: 1874

Fate: Abandoned in 1950

Station Durant, North Carolina

Formerly Hatteras, also known as Durants

USLSS Station No. 23, Sixth District

Coast Guard Station No. 185

Location: On beach abreast of Sandy Bay, about 3½ miles east of Hatteras Inlet; 35° 12' 35" N × 75° 41' 10" W

Date of Conveyance: 1878

Station Built: 1879 (?)

Fate: Abandoned in 1939 (totally destroyed by hurricane Isabel; tower is part of rental condominium unit)

Station Fort Macon, North Carolina

Coast Guard Station No. 191

Location: Near east end of Bogue Banks, ¾ mile west of Beaufort Inlet Channel; 34–42' 00"N × 76–40' 50"W

Date of Conveyance: 1903

Station Built: 1904

Fate: Discontinued in 1963 and reestablished as a Coast Guard Group office

Station Gull Shoal, North Carolina

Coast Guard Station No. 180

Location: 11¾ miles south of New Inlet; 35–29' 50"N × 75–28' 40"W

Date of Conveyance: 1893

Station Built: 1878

Fate: Abandoned in 1940

Remarks: Keeper Rasmus S. Midgett was awarded a Gold Lifesaving
Medal for his rescue on August 18, 1899, while he was a member of
the Gull Shoal Life-Saving Station's crew

Station Hatteras Inlet, North Carolina

Coast Guard Station No. 186

Original Location: On beach, near east end of Ocracoke Island, 1⅛
miles west-southwest of Hatteras Inlet and 11½ miles east-northeast
of Ocracoke lighthouse

Date of Conveyance: 1882

Station Built: Original in 1883; second station built in 1917

Fate: still in operation.

Station Kill Devil Hills, North Carolina

USLSS Station No. 13, Sixth District

Coast Guard Station No. 173

Location: On beach, 1 mile east by south of Kill Devil Hills, and 12½
miles north-northwest of Bodie Island Light; 36–00' 10" N × 75–39'
40"W

Date of Conveyance: 1878

Station Built: 1878

Fate: Turned over to the GSA in 1964; moved to Currituck and reno-
vated beautifully as Twiddy & Co. office

Remarks: The crew from this station assisted Wilbur and Orville
Wright in their historic first heavier-than-air flight on December 17,
1903

About the name: there are numerous explanations, but none confirmed. Briefly, here is my theory.

Early rum was always referred to as "kill devil." Early distilling was notoriously poor and created a bad taste. So, spice was added. Originally, the term "spice" meant *only* hot pepper. Rum was made from molasses and had to be cooked. That could be done with a stove, a fire, a pan . . . or a kiln. Therefore, if someone referred to "Kiln-deviled" rum, that could easily be misunderstood. The place on the North Carolina Outer Banks? My next guess is that barrels of it washed ashore there from shipwrecks at some point!

Station Kitty Hawk, North Carolina

USLSS Station No. 12, Sixth District

Coast Guard Station No. 172

Location: On beach, east of Kitty Hawk, N.C., and 16¼ miles north-northwest of Bodie Island Light; 36–00' 10"N × 75–39' 40"W

Date of Conveyance: 1878

Station Built: 1878

Fate: Turned over to the GSA in 1964, became part of the present Black Pelican Restaurant

Remarks: The telegraph office near here is where the famous Wright brothers telegram was sent

Station Little Kinnakeet, North Carolina

USLSS Station No. 20, Sixth District

Coast Guard Station No. 181

Location: On beach, 8⅞ miles north by east of Cape Hatteras light; 35–25' 00"N × 75–29' 10"W in 1915.

Date of Conveyance: 1873

Station Built: 1873

Fate: Turned over to the GSA 1970; now owned by the National Park Service, Cape Hatteras National Seashore, and beautifully restored *but* not open to public due to finances

Station Nags Head, North Carolina

USLSS Station No. 14, Sixth District

Coast Guard Station No. 174

Location: On beach, 1⅛ miles south of Nags Head, N.C., and 7¼ miles north-northwest of Bodie Island Light; 35–56' 00"N × 75–36' 40"W in 1915

Date of Conveyance: 1874

Station Built: 1874

Fate: Turned over to the GSA in 1957; unceremoniously destroyed by real estate developers for a vacation beach house

Station New Inlet, North Carolina

Location: About 3 miles south of New Inlet; 35–37' 38"N × 75–28' 15"W

Date of Conveyance: 1881

Station Built: 1883 (?)

Fate: Discontinued in 1916

Remarks: A hurricane created the Inlet, and the station was built, but a later hurricane filled in the inlet and the station was unnecessary

Station Oak Island, North Carolina

Coast Guard Station No. 194

Original Location: Near east end of Oak Island, two miles west-north-west of Bald Head Light, and 4⅜ miles northwest by west of Cape Fear Light; 33° 53' 20" N × 78° 01' 20" W

Date of Conveyance: 1888

Station Built: 1899

Fate: Still in operation

Station Ocracoke, North Carolina

Coast Guard Station No. 187

Original Location: At Ocracoke, North Carolina, on northwest tip of Ocracoke Island, ½ mile north of Ocracoke Light; 35–06' 55"N × 75–59' 20"W

Date of Conveyance: 1904

Station Built: First station was built in 1904; second station was built during World War II

Fate: Still in operation as Small Seasonal Station (not this building); the 1904 was beautifully restored and used as the Outer Banks Campus of the North Carolina Center for the Advancement of Teaching (NCCAT)

Station Oregon Inlet, North Carolina

USLSS Station No. 16, Sixth District

Coast Guard Station No. 176

Location: 1½ miles south of Oregon Inlet, and 3⅝ miles southeast by south of Bodie Island Light; 35–47' 30"N × 75–32' 10"W

Date of Conveyance: 1874

Station Built: 1874

Fate: Still in operation

Remarks: A confusing story of names! The current USCG MLB Station is in operation; the Outer Banks Coast Guard History Preservation nonprofit is trying to rescue the existing but abandoned 1898 Oregon Inlet Station as of this writing.

Station Paul Gamiel Hill, North Carolina

USLSS Station No. 11, Sixth District

Coast Guard Station No. 171

Location: 5 miles north of Kitty Hawk; 36–08' 00"N × 75–43' 50"W

Date of Conveyance: 1878

Station Built: Unknown

Fate: Abandoned in 1949

Station Pea Island, North Carolina

USLSS Station No. 17, Sixth District

Coast Guard Station No. 177

Location: On beach, 6⅞ miles south southeast of Oregon Inlet and 9 miles southeast by south of Bodie Island Light; 35° 43' 15" N × 75° 29' 30" W (circa 1939)

Date of Conveyance: July 25, 1878

Station Built: 1878; rebuilt 1896 and 1931

Fate: Decommissioned in 1947; 1931 station a commercial building in Salvo, Hatteras Island; 1931 Cookhouse moved to Manteo, North Carolina as museum

Station Portsmouth, North Carolina

Coast Guard Station No. 188

Location: At Portsmouth, North Carolina, on northeast end of Portsmouth Island, 4¼ miles southwest by west of Ocracoke Light; 35–04' 00"N × 76–03' 05"W

Date of Conveyance: 1893

Station Built: 1894

Fate: Turned over to the War Assets Administration in 1946; restorations began in 2023.

Station Poyners Hill, North Carolina

USLSS Station No. 9, Sixth District

Coast Guard Station No. 169

Location: On beach, 5½ miles south southeast of Currituck Beach Light; 36–17' 10"N × 75–48' 00"W

Date of Conveyance: 1883

Station Built: 1878

Fate: Turned over to the GSA in 1956; no longer exists

Station Wash Woods, North Carolina

Coast Guard Station No. 166

Location: On beach, 7⅜ miles north by west of Currituck Beach Light; 36–32' 00"N × 75–52' 10"W

Date of Conveyance: 1914

Station Built: 1878

Fate: Abandoned in 1951; beautifully restored by Twiddy Realty as beach vacation rental; you have to have a 4×4 drive to get to it!

ENDNOTES

Chapter 1

1 "History," The Humane Society of the Commonwealth of Massachusetts, 2011, https://web.archive.org/web/20110714044634/http://www.masslifesavingawards.com/history/.

2 Bruce Roberts and Cheryl Shelton-Roberts, *American Lighthouses: A Comprehensive Guide to Exploring Our National Coastal Treasures* (Essex, CT: Globe Pequot Press, 2020).

3 "Port History," New York Shipping Association, www.sanynj.org/port-history/.

4 *The Erie Canal: A Brief History*, New York State Canal Corporation (2001).

5 James D. Charlet, *Shipwrecks of the Outer Banks: Dramatic Rescues and Fantastic Wrecks in the Graveyard of the Atlantic*, vol. 1 (Essex, CT: Globe Pequot Press, 2020), chaps. 19 and 20, respectively.

6 *Revised Regulations for the Government of the Life-Saving Service of the United States and the Laws upon Which They Are Based* (Washington, DC: Government Printing Office, 1884), sections 13–23.

7 Ibid., sections 24–26.

8 Ibid., sections 27–39.

9 Ibid., sections 40–46.

10 Ibid., sections 47–77.

11 Ibid., sections, 78–144.

12 Ibid., sections 145–79.

13 Charlet, *Shipwrecks of the Outer Banks*, vol. 1, chap. 1, 7–11.

14 *Revised Regulations*, Regulation No. 168; complete details are provided in Charlet, *Shipwrecks of the Outer Banks*, volume 1, chap. 1.

15 *Revised Regulations*, 20.

16 Charlet, *Shipwrecks of the Outer Banks*, vol. 1, chapter 1, 5–17.

17 *Revised Regulations*, 88.

18 *Revised Regulations*, figure 14.

19 *Revised Regulations*, No. 208.

20 Ibid., No. 88; with original spelling and grammar used.

21 Cheryl Shelton-Roberts and Bruce Roberts in their *North Carolina Lighthouses: The Stories behind the Beacons from Cape Fear to Currituck Beach* (Chapel Hill: University of North Carolina Press, 2019).

22 Ralph Shanks, *The US Life-Saving Service, Heroes, Rescues, and Architecture of the Early Coast Guard* (Novato, CA: Costano Books, 1996), 39.

23 Shanks, *The US Life-Saving Service*, 1.

Chapter 2

1 For the full story, see James D. Charlet, *Shipwrecks of the Outer Banks: Dramatic Rescues and Fantastic Wrecks in the Graveyard of the Atlantic*, vol. 1 (Essex, CT: Globe Pequot Press, 2020), chap. 13

2 "Lost to the Perils of the Sea," Cape Hatteras National Seashore, last updated March 19, 2018, online article https://www.nps.gov/caha /learn/historyculture/shipwrecks.htm.

3 Ben Dixon MacNeill, *The Hatterasman* (Winston-Salem, NC: J. F. Blaire, 1958), 1.

4 Ibid.

5 Ibid.

6 David Stick, *Graveyard of the Atlantic: Shipwrecks of the North Carolina Coast* (Chapel Hill: University of North Carolina Press, 1952), 1.

7 Leonard S. Tawes, *Coasting Captain, Journals of Captain Leonard S. Tawes, Relating His Career in Atlantic Coastwise Sailing Craft from 1868 to 1922* (Newport News, VA: The Mariners Museum, 1967); all spelling, grammar, and punctuation is maintained from the original.

8 Ibid., 92.

9 Ibid., 107.

10 Ibid., 148.

11 Ibid., 170.

12 Ibid., 323.

13 Ibid., 242.

14 Carolina Designs, Graveyard of the Atlantic, What's in a Name? Kip Tabb, December 15, 2018, https://blog.carolinadesigns.com/outer-banks-history/graveyard-of-the-atlantic/.

15 Stick, *Graveyard of the Atlantic,* 187.

16 David Stick, "Shipwrecks," NCPedia, 2006, https://www.ncpedia.org/shipwrecks.

Chapter 3

1 "Lighthouse Keepers," National Park Service, last updated October 20, 2023, https://www.nps.gov/calo/learn/historyculture/lh-keeper.htm.

2 *Regulations for the Government of the Life-Saving Service of the United States and the Laws Upon Which They Are Based* (Washington, DC: Government Printing Office, 1873).

Chapter 4

1 "Articles for Engagement of Surfmen," *Regulations for the Government of the Life-Saving Service of the United States and the Laws Upon Which They Are Based* (*1873*), Form 2, 40; original spelling, grammar, and punctuation maintained.

2 George I. Hagar, "The United States Life-Saving Service. Its Origin, Progress, And Present Condition," *Frank Leslie's Popular Monthly,* February 5, 1878, 170.

3 "Role of the Surfman," *Scientific American*, article excerpt, December 29, 1906, 485–86.

4 *Scribner's Monthly* 19, no. 3 (1880): 321; emphasis added.

5 James Otis, *The Life Savers: A Story of the United States Life-Saving Service* (New York: The Knickerbocker Press, 1899), 6.

6 "Role of the Surfman."

7 For more information, see https://www.gocoastguard.com/why-join.

Chapter 5

1 James D. Charlet, *Shipwrecks of the Outer Banks: Dramatic Rescues and Fantastic Wrecks in the Graveyard of the Atlantic*, vol. 1 (Essex, CT: Globe Pequot Press, 2020), chap. 1.

2 Ralph Shanks, *The US Life-Saving Service, Heroes, Rescues, and Architecture of the Early Coast Guard* (Novato, CA: Costano Books, 1996), 217.

3 Charlet, *Shipwrecks of the Outer Banks.*

Chapter 6

1 *Annual Report of the Operations of the United States Life-Saving Service for the Fiscal Year Ending June 30, 1913,* 58.

2 Ibid., 59.

3 Ibid.

4 *Instructions to Mariners in Case of Shipwreck: With Information Concerning the Life-Saving Stations upon the Coasts of the United States,* United States Department of the Treasury and Life-Saving Service (Washington, DC: Government Printing Office, 1888), 7–8; emphasis in the original.

5 The phrase has been popularly used for many years. Its origin is difficult to trace but is seen in 1905 in the *Review of Reviewers* by William T. Snead, reviewing "Lifeboat Men," illus. Felix Baker.

6 James D. Charlet, *Shipwrecks of the Outer Banks: Dramatic Rescues and Fantastic Wrecks in the Graveyard of the Atlantic*, vol. 1 (Essex, CT: Globe Pequot Press, 2020), chap. 3.

7 *Annual Report 1913,* 59.

8 Ibid., 60.

9 Ibid.

10 Ibid.

11 Ibid., 61.

12 *New York Times,* November 2, 1912.

13 *Annual Report 1913,* 123.

Chapter 7

1 *Annual Report of the Operations of the United States Life-Saving Service for the Fiscal Year Ending June 30, 1908*, 35.

2 *New York Times*, March 24, 1862.

3 *New York Times*, April 7, 1864.

4 "Towboat History," GlobalSecurity.org, https://www.globalsecurity.org/military/systems/ship/towboat-hist.htm.

5 *Annual Report 1908*, 35.

6 Ibid., 36.

7 Ibid.

8 Ibid.

9 Ibid., 37.

10 Ibid.

11 Ibid.

12 *Instructions to Mariners in Case of Shipwreck: With Information Concerning the Life-Saving Stations upon the Coasts of the United States,* United States Department of the Treasury and Life-Saving Service (Washington, DC: Government Printing Office, 1888).

13 *Annual Report 1908*, 37.

14 Ibid.

15 Ibid.

Chapter 8

1 Ralph Shanks, *The US Life-Saving Service, Heroes, Rescues, and Architecture of the Early Coast Guard* (Novato, CA: Costano Books, 1996), conclusion of chap. 1.

2 Ralph Shanks, *The U.S. Life-Saving Service, Heroes, Rescues, and Architecture of the Early Coast Guard* (Novato, CA: Costano Books, 1996), 1.

3 From commodityonline, https://www.commodityonline.com/market-place/reports/cotton-seed-oil-cake/174#:~:text=Cottonseed%20cake%20or%20cottonseed%20meal,%2C%20cake%2C%20flakes%20or%20pellets.

4 *Annual Report of the Operations of the United States Life-Saving Service for the Fiscal Year Ending June 30, 1891* (Washington, DC: Government Printing Office, 1893), document no. 1599, 40.

5 See *Instructions to Mariners in Case of Shipwreck: With Information Concerning the Life-Saving Stations upon the Coasts of the United States,* United States Department of the Treasury and Life-Saving Service (Washington, DC: Government Printing Office, 1888), chap. 1, section "Soundings."

6 See James D. Charlet, *Shipwrecks of the Outer Banks: Dramatic Rescues and Fantastic Wrecks in the Graveyard of the Atlantic*, vol. 1 (Essex, CT: Globe Pequot Press, 2020), chap. 23, 205 for details.

7 *Annual Report 1891*, 40.

8 Ibid., 40.

9 See William R. Wells II, "Semper Paratus: The Meaning," e-article, 2006, https://media.defense.gov/2017/Jul/01/2001772265/-1/-1/0/SEM PERPARATUSTHEMEANING.PDF, for extensive background.

10 *Annual Report 1891*, 40.

11 Ibid.

12 Ibid., 41.

13 Ibid.

14 See appendix A of this volume.

15 *Annual Report 1891*, 42.

16 For the complete text, see appendix B.

17 *Annual Report 1891*, 42–43.

Chapter 10

1 *Annual Report of the Operations of the United States Life-Saving Service for the Fiscal Year Ending June 30, 1883*, 207.

2 David Stick, *Graveyard of the Atlantic: Shipwrecks of the North Carolina Coast* (Chapel Hill: University of North Carolina Press, 1953), 112.

3 Ibid.

4 *Annual Report 1883*, 207.

5 Ibid., 207.

Chapter 11

1 *Annual Report of the Operations of the United States Life-Saving Services for the Fiscal Year Ending June 30, 1900*, 38–39; emphasis added.

2 Clement Clarke Moore, "A Visit from St. Nicholas," published for the first time on December 23, 1823.

3 *Annual Report 1900*, 39.

4 Ibid, 39.

5 Madame Martha J. Coston, "Night Signals" [Coston Flares], Signal Corps Association, http://www.civilwarsignals.org/pages/signal/signal pages/flare/coston.html.

6 *Annual Report 1900*, 39.

7 "Instructions To Mariners In Case Of Shipwreck: With Information Concerning The Life-saving Stations Upon the Coasts of the United States"; actual period capitalization.

8 *Annual Report 1900*, 40.

9 *New York Times*, December 24, 1899.

10 Ibid.

11 *Annual Report 1900*, 41.

12 Ibid.

13 Ibid., 42.

14 Ibid.

Chapter 12

1 James D. Charlet, *Shipwrecks of the Outer Banks: Dramatic Rescues and Fantastic Wrecks in the Graveyard of the Atlantic*, vol. 1 (Essex, CT: Globe Pequot Press, 2020), chap. 16.

2 US Department of Homeland Security, United States Coast Guard (COMDTINST M1650.25D, May 2008), chap. 4.

3 The Steamboat Inspection Service was a United States agency created in 1871 to safeguard lives and property at sea. It merged with the Bureau of Navigation in 1932 to form the Bureau of Navigation and Steamboat Inspection, which in 1936 was reorganized into the Bureau

of Marine Inspection and Navigation. The Bureau of Marine Inspection and Navigation's responsibilities were transferred temporarily to the United States Coast Guard in 1942. The Bureau was abolished in 1946, when its functions were transferred permanently to the Coast Guard.

4 *"ADRIFT ON GANGPLANK.* Castaway Saved. After Three Days—Twelve May Have Perished," *New York Times,* January 18, 1906.

5 Ibid.

6 Ibid.

7 Ibid.

8 Ibid.

9 "WAS SOLE SURVIVOR—Karl Sommers Near Death—Rescued From Raft by Steamer—Sch Stevenson's Crew All Lose Lives—Boston Vessel Strikes on Shoals," *The Boston Daily Globe,* January 26, 1906.

10 Ibid.

11 Editors of Encyclopaedia Britannica, "yellow journalism," *Encyclopaedia Britannica,* June 26, 2024, https://www.britannica.com/topic/yellow-journalism.

12 *Virginia Pilot,* December 18, 1903.

13 *The Boston Daily Globe,* January 26, 1906.

14 Ibid.

Chapter 13

1 Editors of Encyclopaedia Britannica, "schooner," *Encyclopaedia Britannica,* October 16, 2023, https://www.britannica.com/technology/schooner. This article was most recently revised and updated by Jeff Wallenfeldt, manager, Geography and History.

2 Department of Commerce, Bureau of Navigation, *Annual List of Merchant Vessels of the United States, with official Numbers and Signal Letters and, Lists of Vessels Belonging to the United States Government with distinguishing signals,* 1871, 7.

3 *Annual Report of the Operations of the United States Life-Saving Service for the Fiscal Year Ending June 30, 1886,* 117.

4 Ibid.

5 Ibid.

6 *Annual Report 1886*, p. 117.

Chapter 14

1 Excerpts from "History of Cape Verde," Cape Verdean Museum, https://capeverdeanmuseum.org/history#:~:text=The%20history%20 of%20Cape%20Verde,during%20the%20Spanish%2DPortuguese%20 Inquisition.

2 Graham McBride, "Sailing Ship Rigs," Maritime Museum of the Atlantic, n.d. https://maritimemuseum.novascotia.ca/research /sailing-ship-rigs.

3 Sonny Williamson, *Shipwrecks of Ocracoke Island* (Marshallberg, NC: Grandma Publications, 2000).

4 National Park Service, "Wreck of the *Vera Cruz VII*," https://www .nps.gov/calo/learn/historyculture/veracruzvii.htm.

5 Ibid.

6 *Annual Report of the Operations of the United States Life-Saving Service for the Fiscal Year Ending June 30, 1903*, 155.

7 "Wreck of the Vera Cruz VII," National Park Service, Cape Lookout National Seashore, last updated October 20, 2023, https://www.nps .gov/calo/learn/historyculture/veracruzvii.htm.

8 *Annual Report 1903*, 155.

9 Ibid.

10 "Wreck of the Vera Cruz VII."

11 "Boutwell, USRC George S. (1873, Revenue Cutter)," from the C. Patrick Labadie collection at Edward J. Dowling Collection, University of Detroit. http://www.nemoha.org/2899779/data.

12 All quotes in this section from United States Congressional Serial Set, vol. 4676, *Report of Commissioner-General of Immigration, Bertram N. Stump, Inspector*, 64–65.

13 All of the following quotes in this section are Stump's words from the report listed in note 12.

14 Sonny Williamson and Philip Howard, "Shipwrecks of Ocracoke Island," *Ocracoke Island Journal,* Thursday, January 25, 2018.

15 "Wreck of the *Vera Cruz VII.*"

Chapter 15

1 James H. Tuten, "Timber," *South Carolina Encyclopedia*, last updated August 25, 2022, http://www.scencyclopedia.org/sce/entries/timber/.

2 U.S. Bureau of Statistics, CPI Inflation Calculator, www.bls.gov /data/inflation_calculator.htm.

3 Hiteshk, "What Is a Pilot Boat?" *Marine Insight*, September 26, 2012, https://www.marineinsight.com/types-of-ships/what-is-a-pilot-boat/.

4 Dennis L. Noble, "A Legacy: The United States Life-Saving Service," https://uslife-savingservice.org/wp-content/uploads/A-History -of-the-USLSS-Denis-Noble.pdf.

Chapter 16

1 "Diamond Shoals," OuterBanks.com (Visitor's Guide), n.d. https:// www.outerbanks.com/diamond-shoals.html.

2 *Annual Report of the Operations of the United States Life–Saving Service for the Fiscal Year Ending June 30, 1910.*

3 Ibid.

4 Philip Howard, "Bett's Dream and the Wreck of the Banana Boat," *Village Craftsman*, November 15, 2015.

5 Philip Howard, "Steamship Brewster and Bananas," *Ocracoke Island Journal,* January 26, 2018.

6 Ibid.

Chapter 17

1 Bill Sharpe, "The Catastrophe that Shook America and Led to Establishment of All-Year Beach Control by Our Coast Guard," *The State*, November 3, 1951.

2 The full, dreadful detailed stories are in James D. Charlet, *Ship-wrecks of the Outer Banks: Dramatic Rescues and Fantastic Wrecks in the Graveyard of the Atlantic*, vol. 1 (Essex, CT: Globe Pequot Press, 2020), chaps. 19 and 20.

3 Sharpe, "Catastrophe that Shook America."

4 Dennis R. Means, "A Heavy Sea Running: The Formation of the U.S. Life-Saving Service, 1846–1878," *Prologue Magazine* 19, no. 4 (1987): n.p.

5 Dennis L. Noble, *That Others Might Live: The US Life-Saving Service, 1878–1915* (Annapolis, MD: US Naval Institute, 1994).

6 Dr. Dennis Noble, "A Legacy: The United States Life-Saving Service," 3, https://uslife-savingservice.org/wp-content/uploads /A-History-of-the-USLSS-Denis-Noble.pdf.

7 Sumner Increase Kimball, *Regulations for the Government of the Life-Saving Service of the United States*, www.media.defense.gov/2019 /Jul/12/2002156401/-1/-1/0/1873-USLSS-REGS.PDF.

8 *Regulations for the Government of the Life-Saving Service, 1884*, Form 1803.

9 "The Book Says You Have To Go Out; It Don't Say Nothing About Coming Back," part IV, Ocean City Life-Saving Station Museum, 2020.

10 United States Coast Guard, U.S. Department of Homeland Security, "About USCG," https://www.uscg.mil/About/.

Chapter 18

1 "Timber Piles," Timber Piling Council, 2021, https://www.timber pilingcouncil.com/new-page.

2 *Annual Report of the Operations of the United States Life-Saving Service for the Fiscal Year Ending June 30, 1909*, 46–51.

3 Ibid., 48.

4 Ibid., 47–48.

5 Ibid.

6 Ibid., 48–49.

7 Ibid., 49.

8 Ibid., 50.

9 Ibid.

10 Ibid., 51.

Chapter 19

1 Hon Graham A. Barden of North Carolina in the House of Representatives, Saturday, June 19, 1948, *Congressional Record: Proceedings and Debates of the United States Congress*, 94, part 12, p. A4252.

2 *Annual Report of the Operations of the United States Life-Saving Service for the Fiscal Year Ending June 30, 1908*, 46–51.

3 James D. Charlet, *Shipwrecks of the Outer Banks: Dramatic Rescues and Fantastic Wrecks in the Graveyard of the Atlantic*, vol. 1 (Essex, CT: Globe Pequot Press, 2020), 87.

4 *The Regulations of the Life-Saving Service of 1899*, Article VI, "Action at Wrecks," section 252, 58, http://www.uscg.mil/history/faqs/LSS motto.asp.

5 *Annual Report of the Operations of the United States Life-Saving Service for the Fiscal Year Ending June 30, 1909*.

6 Ibid., 45.

7 Ibid., 45.

8 Ibid., 46

9 Ibid., 48.

10 Ibid.

Chapter 20

1 "Phosphate Rock," Minerals Database, Minerals Education Coalition, n.d., https://mineralseducationcoalition.org/minerals-database/phosphate-rock/.

2 *Annual Report of the Operations of the United States Life-Saving Services for the Fiscal Year Ending June 30, 1883*, 177.

3 Ibid.

4 Ibid.

5 Ibid., 178.

6 Ibid.

7 Ibid.

Chapter 21

1 James D. Charlet, *Shipwrecks of the Outer Banks: Dramatic Rescues and Fantastic Wrecks in the Graveyard of the Atlantic*, vol. 1 (Essex, CT: Globe Pequot Press, 2020), chap. 9.

2 *Annual Report of the Operations of the United States Life-Saving Service for the Fiscal Year Ending June 30, 1885*, 167.

3 Ibid.

4 "Beaufort Wind Scale," National Weather Service, n.d., https://www.weather.gov/mfl/beaufort.

5 *Annual Report 1885*, 167.

6 Ibid.

7 "How to Sail Safely through a Storm," *North Sails* (blog), September 2016, https://www.northsails.com/sailing/en/2016/09/how-to-sail-safely-through-a-storm.

8 *Annual Report 1885*, 167.

9 "Five Fathom Bank Lightship: Delaware Bay," Delaware Bay Lighthouse Keepers and Friends Association, last updated August 27, 2018, https://www.delawarebaylightkeeper-friend.org/five_fathom.htm.

10 *Annual Report 1885*, 167.

11 *New York Times*, December 28, 1884.

12 *Annual Report 1885*, 168.

13 Ibid.

14 Ibid.

15 Ibid.

Chapter 22

1 *Annual Report of the Operations of the United States Life-Saving Service for the Fiscal Year Ending June 30, 1908*, 38.

2 See ibid., 27.

3 Ibid., 39.

4 Ibid.

5 Ibid.

6 Ibid.

7 Ibid.

8 Ibid., 41.

9 Ibid.

10 Ibid., 27.

Chapter 23

1 Both of these names are frequently misspelled. The latter is understandable; the former is singular—shoal.

2 "Delaware Breakwater," *Wikipedia*, last updated August 6, 2023, https://en.wikipedia.org/wiki/Delaware_Breakwater.

3 *Annual Report of the Operations of the United States Life-Saving Service for the Fiscal Year Ending June 30, 1891*, 37.

4 Ibid., 37–38.

5 Information from *Sea Chest*, a student publication of the Cape Hatters Secondary High School.

6 *Annual Report 1891*, 38.

7 Ibid., 39.

8 Ibid.

9 "The Lank's Survivors," *Delaware Gazette and State Journal*, January 29, 1891, 3; all spelling and punctuation have been left as-is.

Chapter 24

1 All remaining quotes are from the *Annual Report of the Operations of the United States Life-Saving Service for the Fiscal Year Ending June 30, 1890*: for the Sixth District, 25.

2 Ibid., 479.

3 *Annual Report of the Operations of the United States Life-Saving Service for the Fiscal Year Ending June 30, 1908*, 39.

4 *Annual Report 1890*, 25.

5 Ibid., 26–29.

6 Ibid., 26.

7 Ibid.

8 Ibid., 27.

9 Ibid.

10 The wreck was first spotted on the 24th and unsuccessfully responded to on the 25th. On the 26th, three attempts all failed; the storm was still too strong on the 27th to try again. Finally, on the 28th, lifesavers were able to reach and rescue the sole survivor! "The Lank's Survivors," *Delaware Gazette and State Journal*, January 29, 1981, 3; all spelling and punctuation have been left as-is.

11 *Annual Report 1890*, 28–29.

Chapter 25

1 *Annual Report of the Operations of the United States Life-Saving Service for the Fiscal Year Ending June 30, 1890*, 30.

2 Ibid.

3 Ibid., 31.

4 Ibid.

5 Ibid.

6 Kip Tabb, "A Shipwreck Mystery at Nags Head," Carolina Designs, January 24, 2019, https://blog.carolinadesigns.com/2019/01/24/a-ship wreck-mystery-at-nags-head/.

Chapter 26

1 Austin J. Coolidge and John B. Mansfield, *A History and Description of New England, General and Local* (Boston, MA: Austin J. Coolridge, 1859), 364–67.

2 Chapter 1, "Historic and Archaeological Resources," https://www.wiscasset.org/uploads/files/1_history_10-06.pdf.

3 Mimi Bigelow Steadman, "Wiscasset: Many Reasons to Stop and Browse," MaineBoats.com, https://maineboats.com/print/issue-155/wiscasset.

4 *Annual Report of the Operations of the United States Life-Saving Service for the Fiscal Year Ending June 30, 1890*, 32.

5 James D. Charlet, *Shipwrecks of the Outer Banks: Dramatic Rescues and Fantastic Wrecks in the Graveyard of the Atlantic* (Essex, CT: Globe Pequot), 14.

6 James D. Charlet, *Shipwrecks of the Outer Banks: Dramatic Rescues and Fantastic Wrecks in the Graveyard of the Atlantic*, vol. 1 (Essex, CT: Globe Pequot Press, 2020), chap. 5.

7 *Annual Report 1890*, 32.

8 Ibid., 189.

9 Ibid., 479.

10 Ibid., 33.

11 Ibid., 34.

12 Ibid., 35; in its original printed configuration and punctuation.

Chapter 27

1 Pete Lesher, "A Load of Guano: Baltimore and the Fertilizer Trade in the Nineteenth Century," *Northern Mariner* 18, nos. 3–4 (2008): 121–28.

2 Tim Wenger, "This Map Shows How Many European Countries Can Fit Into the Continental US," Matador Network, April 30, 2018, https://matadornetwork.com/read/map-shows-many-european-countries-can-fit-continental-us/.

3 *Annual Report of the Operations of the United States Life-Saving Service for the Fiscal Year Ending June 30, 1881*, 54–58.

4 James D. Charlet, *Shipwrecks of the Outer Banks: Dramatic Rescues and Fantastic Wrecks in the Graveyard of the Atlantic*, vol. 1 (Essex, CT: Globe Pequot Press, 2020), chap. 11.

5 *Annual Report 1881*.

6 Ibid., 56.

7 Ibid.

8 Ibid., 57.

9 Ibid.

10 Ibid.

11 Ibid., 58.

INDEX

A

A. B. Goodman, 246–57
Ada F. Whitney, 128–35
Angela, 102–5
Annie E. Blackman, 222, 231, 241
Aragon, 97
Ario Pardee, 198–205
Ariosto, 108–15
Articles of Engagement for Surfmen, 38, 167
Asher J. Hudson, 92
Austin, Keeper Daniel B., 195–97

B

Barkentine, 137
Battler, 85
beach apparatus drill, 9–10, 49, 114
Big Kinnakeet Station, 124, 135, 153, 211
Bodie Island Life-Saving Station, 239, 250
Bodie Island Lighthouse, 232
Brewster, 151–59
Brig, 137

C

Caffeys Inlet Life-Saving Station, 104–5, 176, 192, 195–97
Cape Hatteras Diamond Shoals, 24, 110, 116, 118–19, 124–26, 151, 181, 187
Cape Hatteras Life-Saving Station, 41, 153, 158, 181, 187–88, 210–11, 250
Cape Hatteras Lighthouse, 25, 27, 152, 250, 256
Cape Hatteras, NC, 22–28, 187

Cape Henry Life-Saving Station, 85, 224
Cape Point, NC, 21, 24, 157
Carroll A. Deering, 116, 126
Catherine, Captain J. W., 202
C. Grinnell, 63
Chantauguan, 92
Charles S. Hirsch, 98, 171–78
Chicamacomico Cookhouse, 14
Chicamacomico Life-Saving Station, 56, 213, 215, 216
Corbell, Keeper Malachi, 195
Cragside, 69–77
Creeds Hill Life-Saving Station, 153, 158, 186, 188, 210, 250, 256
Currituck Beach, 163, 203

D

Delhi, 90
Diamond Shoals, 41, 153, 158, 181, 187–88, 210–11, 250
Diamond Shoals Light, 153
Diamond Shoals Lightships, 27, 152, 154, 250

E

Ephraim Williams, 102, 252, 256
E. S. Newman, 102
Etheridge, Keeper Patrick H., 55–59, 181–83, 185–90, 209–10
Europa, 118, 120, 122–23

F

Fernandez, Julio M., 136–38, 144–45
Five-Fathom Bank, 201
Francis E. Waters, 147, 221–22, 230–36, 237, 241
Frank O. Dame, 223

G

Garnett, Robert Lee, 225–29
Gillchrist, Captain W. K., 207–8
Grace, Robert C., 225, 229
Gulf Stream, 22–25, 28
Gull Shoal Life-Saving Stations, 56, 60–61, 213–16, 234, 266

H

Harris, Keeper Thomas, 100, 175–77
Hatteras Inlet, 28, 71, 74–76, 86, 124, 148–50, 153–57, 264, 266
Hatteras Island, x, 108, 135, 146, 149–50, 153, 213–14
Henry P. Simmons, 221–29, 231, 237, 241
Hercules, 92
Hester A. Seward, 146–50, 231
Honiton, 95
Houses of Refuge, 5, 7–8, 44
Howard, Keeper James, 71–77, 110, 113–14, 148–49
Hunter, Captain Frank Wall, 172–74
Huron, 6, 102, 163–65

J

John Maxwell, 52–60
Joseph Baymore, 88

K

Katahdin, 61, 67–68
Kill Devil Hills Life-Saving Station, 84, 89, 96–98, 232–34, 266
Kimball, Sumner I., 6–7, 87, 162–70, 243
Kitty Hawk, 122, 164
Kitty Hawk Station, 80–101, 103, 171, 175, 267

L

Labrador Current, 23, 25
Leonora, 206–12

Linton, Elizabeth "Bett," 155–57
Lizzie S. Haynes, 221–22, 231, 237–43
Luola Murchison, 83, 86
Lyle gun, 5, 10–12, 16, 34, 49, 56, 66, 75, 97, 103, 114, 133, 176–77, 192, 195–96, 203, 216–17, 227–28, 240–42

M

Mary Ann, 90
Mary Bradford, 85
Massachusetts Humane Society, 3, 5, 8
Metropolis, 6, 102, 163–66
Montrose W. Houck, 100

N

Nags Head, 147, 163, 235–36
Nag's Head Station, 98, 163, 180–81, 232, 234, 268
Nathaniel Lank, 213–20
Nuova Ottavia, 102

O

Ocracoke Beach, NC, 76
Ocracoke Life-Saving Station, 28, 71–76, 109–15, 124, 268
Ocracoke, NC, 28, 69–77, 110, 115, 138, 143, 149, 152–55
Oran, 135
Oregon Inlet Life-Saving Station, 28, 239–43, 269
Outer Banks, NC, ix, x, 2, 13–16, 20–21, 28, 48, 102, 108, 118, 126, 132, 136, 147, 149, 192, 194

P

Paine, Keeper Benjamin, 216, 241
Paul Gamiels Hill Life-Saving Station, 95–100, 103–5, 171, 175, 197

Portsmouth Life-Saving Station, 136–45, 270

Priscilla, 102

Pugh, Keeper David M., Gull Shoal, 215–17

R

Robert H. Stevenson, 116–26, 185

S

Saxon, 61–68

schooner, 130–31

Seward, G. F., 231

Seward, T. J., 147, 230–31

Sipple, Captain N. J., 214, 218–19

Smith, Captain Henry A., 198–204

Steward, Captain, 249

Strathairly, 102

Sumner, Karl, 119–20, 122

T

Tall, Captain L. S., 231

Terrell, Keeper Ferdinand G., 139, 142

Thomas J. Martin, 192–97

Tiger, 20

U

United States Life-Saving Service, 2–19

US Coast Guard, 7, 17–19, 50

US Revenue Cutter Service, 7, 17–19, 50

V

Vera Cruz VII, 136–45

Vermont, 62

Victoria J. Peed, 84–85

W

Wash Woods Life-Saving Station, 198, 203–4, 226–29, 270

Welaka, 223–24

Wescott, Keeper Josiah H., Chicamacomico, 216

Wiscasset, Maine, 238

Wm. B. Davidson, 99

Wormell, Willis B., 117

ABOUT THE AUTHOR

James D. Charlet is a freelance writer and an authority on the US Life-Saving Service on North Carolina's iconic Outer Banks who contributes to local and national media with articles on Outer Banks and nautical history. Charlet taught North Carolina history for twenty-four years and authored a state-adopted textbook on the subject. He has worked with the Wright Brothers National Memorial, the Cape Hatteras Lighthouse, the Fort Raleigh National Historic Site, was the lead interpreter at Roanoke Island Festival Park (celebrating the Roanoke Voyages), and—most importantly—has been involved with the Chicamacomico Life-Saving Station Historic Site and Museum for twenty-one years and was the site manager of the historic site for ten years, retiring from there in 2015.

Charlet is a regular contributor to *Island Free Press* and *My Outer Banks Home* and has a feature article in the 2019 *Outer Banks Magazine* and the cover story of the *Outer Banks Magazine* 2023. In 2024, he was part of a travel feature on the Discovery Channel, and has been filmed and recorded on Spectrum Channel, WRAL-TV Raleigh, and WUNC Public Radio. In his spare time, James leads tours, educational programs, speaking engagements, and live presentations as "Keeper James." His most prestigious presentation venues include featured speaker at *Our State* magazine's "Best of Our State" at the Pinehurst Resort in January of 2023; Old Baldy Lighthouse, Bald Head Island; Ocracoke Festival and "Day at the Docks," Hatteras Village; Anniversary of the RMS *Titanic* sinking speaker at the National Park Service Hatteras Weather Bureau; and invited to speak at the Cape Hatteras Lighthouse for the summer of 2023 and 2024. Two of his presentations were videoed and are now on the National Park Service, Cape Hatteras National Seashore website.

"I'm working on volume 3 and have notes for volumes 4 and 5—there is just *too* much of this great heroic history to stop now!"